Foreword

In the United States of America, tax money is used to imprison and seize the property of low-level drug offenders (gutting the 4th Amendment in the process), while certain units of the U.S. government simultaneously foster the global trade in narcotics to finance covert operations. Women and children are bought and sold like chattel by global criminal networks which use them for sex or harvest their body organs for resale. Weapons-grade nuclear materials are stolen and sold to the highest bidder (including terrorist organizations). Recent U.S. presidents have routinely circumvented the Constitution, accepted dirty money, abused their public office, and rubbed elbows with some of the world's most heinous organized criminals. Criminality in the upper echelons of government is apparently the norm, as Suharto in Indonesia, Mobutu in Zaire, Hussein in Iraq, and Ferdinand and Imelda Marcos in the Philippines are just a few examples of "kleptocratic" rulers who amassed billions of dollars looting national treasuries. Next to pediatric oncology, organized crime is the most depressing of subjects.

Organized crime, in its most significant forms, involves loose associations and networks of powerful political and economic elites who *organize* crime. In one of my very first graduate classes, I remember Professor Jenkins asking our small group to define "corruption." I've never forgotten it, because the point he made goes to the very heart of the way organized crime *should be* perceived. That is, bankers, police officers, politicians, and businessmen are not *corrupted* by organized criminals. That's letting the bankers, police officers, politicians, and businessmen off too easy. Corruption is a word that literally means "something that was once good has gone bad." Saying that so-called upperworld players are corrupted implies that they were good to begin with and that the real culprits are in a different class. Not true. If we

i

look at organized crime at the level where the most important decisions are made, where the distribution of resources is governed, then we see that political and economic elites are the most important players in the informal patron-client networks which comprise organized crime. To wit, one cannot corrupt something or someone that was no good to begin with, or was predisposed to be a criminal.

While the active role played by societal elites in the coordination of criminal enterprises has been noted time and again, my perception is that somehow the message is not sinking in (or perhaps it's just that those in the position to do something about the problem lack the "political will" to do so– or to be more pessimistic, perhaps those in a position to do something about organized crime like things just the way they are). Government and law enforcement officials focus on "street level" crimes which gain the headlines, and when they do pay attention to organized criminality, they address the problem as if focusing on *organizations* of criminals will somehow suspend criminal activity. Even in academic circles the study of organized crime seems to pivot on the study of criminal *organizations* with precise boundaries that structure themselves according to the demands and constraints of variables internal and external to the *organization*. Although such an approach is not entirely inappropriate, the problem with viewing organized crime in terms of criminal organizations is that this conceptualization explicitly frames the participation of upperworld players as peripheral or external to the process– politicians and bankers are not seen as organized criminals, but as *associates* of organized criminals, external to the actual criminal group. I see this as a serious mistake, one which I hope the present work addresses.

Part I of this book attempts to demystify organized crime, to describe its principal attributes, and to paint an overview of the problem as it exists today on a global scale. While organized crime is not easily defined or classified, one may conclude that it is a phenomenon which transcends issues related to ethnicity, is generally far more informal in its structure and processes than a formal legal organization, and is coordinated to some extent by political and economic elites from around the globe.

ii

Part I concludes with an overview of the impact of organized crime and a description of prominent transnational criminal enterprises. Part II examines organized crime in the United States. The unique history provided is one intended to highlight the way in which the phenomenon has evolved from the localized vice enterprises of colonial America to the coordinating influences of machine politics in the 19th century and on to the complex criminal networks that exist today. In Part III, theoretical perspectives are examined. My goal here is to prod readers to envision organized crime not in terms of *organizations* of criminals, but rather as informal relationships among a wide variety of both "underworld and "upperworld" societal participants.

In my undergraduate organized crime classes, I usually begin by asking my students the first thing that pops into their heads when I say "organized crime." They almost invariably respond with "Mafia." I say "banks." I guess the bright side is that law enforcers and academics will never starve for lack of work or research topics.

Preface:
On the History of Organized Crime

The history of organized crime emerges through an understanding of urban underworlds. In these areas the business of crime was planned, contacts were made, many crimes carried out, and the methodologies for the integration of organized criminals into civil society were established.[1] Recognizing the existence of such underworlds is only a first step, however. Like all other quasi-institutions, urban underworlds changed in response to outside pressures, such as population growth, ever more rapid urbanization and suburbanization, and industrialization. These quantitative and qualitative changes in urban structures and economies accounted for different patterns of organized crime in the nineteenth and twentieth centuries. Modern capitalism created lucrative new enterprises for criminals. Economist and historian David Landes captured some of the essential changes.

> Mass production and urbanization stimulated, indeed required, wider facilities for distribution, a larger credit structure, an expansion of the educational system, the assumption of new functions by government. At the same time, the increase in the standard of living due to higher productivity created new wants and made possible new satisfactions, which led to a spectacular flowering of those businesses that cater to human pleasure and leisure: entertainment, travel, hotels, restaurants, and so on.[2]

Urban organized criminals who were specialists in vice, violence, and corruption penetrated segments of licit pleasure businesses while also controlling illicit ones. The pleasurable commodities and leisure businesses are heavily regulated by the state. This control created a climate for criminal conspiracies that thrived on the systematic avoidance of regulation. The variety of criminal conspiracies in the economic sector that were devoted to pleasure (some exceptionally unhealthy) and leisure enterprises (i.e., narcotics syndicates, bootleg syndicates, linen and good suppliers to hotels and restaurants who monopolize through violence, sports entrepreneurs connected to gambling syndicates with interests in prostitution and pornography, and vending machine operators that terrorized their way into choice locations such as saloons and movie theaters) represent some of the most significant arenas for organized criminal expansion within the past two centuries.

Perhaps the apotheosis of this particular development was revealed in the early 1970s when a sports conglomerate came under scrutiny. Details about the firm and its subsidiaries were provided by Congressman Sam Steiger of Arizona and Nevada's Attorney General Lee Johnson. According to the two men, the company had a greater hold upon American professional sports than any other entity and was also joined to organized crime in a variety of ways. In 1970, Congressman Steiger noted that it "controls or owns completely over 450 separate corporate entities in at least 23 states, the District of Columbia, Canada, Puerto Rico, and England."[3] The business had developed from "a concessionaire for the Detroit Tigers in 1927 to a present day structure holding concession rights for seven major league baseball clubs, eight professional football teams, four hockey teams, plus concessions at fifty horse and dog tracks throughout the United States."[4] The company also operated as the concessionaires at approximately three hundred theaters, and at bowling alleys, drive-in theaters, airport restaurants, and air-catering services. In addition, they owned outright a professional basketball team and had obtained an interest in a National Hockey League club.

The Nevada attorney general's investigators noted that it was a financial "laundromat" for organized crime, providing phony loans to racketeers: "Organized crime . . . is faced with one major consistent problem, that is how to invest its 'bad' or 'black' money in legitimate enterprises. . . . It [is] necessary for these men to hide their interest behind 'loans' ostensibly made to them, which they in turn invest."[5] The investigators uncovered loans and other business arrangements between the firm and organized crime figures from Detroit, Cleveland, St. Louis, Chicago, Wheeling (West Virginia), Las Vegas, Los Angeles, and New York.

Organized crime has thus been a method of integrating segments of the urban poor into the political economy of urban capitalism. Naturally, the modes and timing of integration differed according to the population size and ethnicity of the urban poor, the structure of law enforcement, and the political economy of cities. Since the Gilded Age (1890s), organized crime in the United States moved into tertiary industries and the control of significant unions and has infiltrated as well other aspects of modern economic life mentioned by Professor Landes. Organized criminal syndicates became deeply enmeshed in both distribution facilities and credit structures. In addition, organized criminals who for decades have worked closely with political officials overwhelmed the government's new functions, particularly those associated with the regulation of the construction industry and protection of the environment.[6]

Some of this discussion parallels what organized crime consultant Ralph Salerno noted in 1967.[7] He found that organized criminals over time reduced free competition, restrained trade, and established illegal monopolies. They operated in auto dealerships, factoring, restaurants and wholesale food distributorships, garment manufacturing, juke boxes and vending machines, nightclubs, trade associations, trucking, and waste disposal. Salerno also stated that profits from these endeavors were mixed with those from purely illicit activities to form the sums necessary for a final stage of infiltration–"big business." Some affected areas that Salerno listed were banking, construction, credit card companies, insurance, mortgages, real estate, and financial securities.

Interestingly enough, Salerno also posited three stages of corruption that accompanied the progression of organized crime into big business. In the first stage, organized criminals corrupt the criminal justice system. In the next stage the corruption occurs among "licensing agency officials and others employed in supervisory or regulatory agencies." The final stage is marked by organized criminals working directly with the highest political officials in the nation.

One example among many can be found in FBI documents generated by an attorney who was a confidential informant in 1963. The attorney posing as a corrupt lawyer worked with organized criminals in schemes dealing with the International Brotherhood of Teamsters' pension funds. The source also dealt with some of the most important Congressional politicians whose sideline included "kickbacks" on pension fund loans for mortgages to third parties. Among the politicians on the take was Rhode Island's Congressman Ferdinand St. Germaine and Speaker of the House John W. McCormack.[8] The latter was certainly no surprise to the FBI for it also had unimpeachable information that the Speaker had taken over $75,000 several years earlier as an inducement to help cover up the 1956 kidnaping and murder of a Dominican Republic dissident in New York.[9] In fact, on this issue numerous politicians were paid off.

While the historical manifestations of organized crime must be understood within the broader developments of American politics and economics, it is also the case that immigration has played a vitally important role.

The power of ethnic criminal organizations are always contingent upon a large population base whose patterns of social and geographic mobility reflect a strong adherence to working-class life styes and *petty bourgeois* capitalism. Italian Americans in New York predominated in the construction trades, worked as waterfront laborers, labored as garbage men, and came to control the unions representing these trades. And given that these unions were devoid of any transforming ideology, and that violence is a mainstay of working class culture, it did not take much to zip to the top of these organizations. In addition, the vast bulk of this population came from areas in which personal violence was endemic for public authority, which represented the interests of a tiny elite, and was incompetent.[10] Civil society was embodied by a rigid and conservative Church and absentee landowners. Living in agro-villages, working as landless laborers, the population turned resolutely inward trusting few outside the boundaries of kith and kin. Italian-Americans stayed in place, culturally and geographically, for a longer period of time than other European immigrant groups that journeyed to the U. S. around the same time.[11] Their zeal for security was reflected through the prism of past experience in which family and place took center stage and combined with a generalized suspicion of the outside and outsiders.[12]

Nothing lasts forever. Italian-American neighborhoods in New York City have substantially declined– suburbanization and other forms of mobility have taken root. The patterns of working class life have irrevocably changed. It is thus no wonder that numerous observers are of the opinion that New York's La Cosa Nostra generation of the 1980s was the last Italian-American one to exert extraordinary criminal control.[13] It was inevitable that the criminals who control New York's streets and political capital would represent other ethnic populations.[14]

One illustration of this transformation became evident in the 1970s. For many years the most dynamic center of New York's heroin trade was in Northeast Manhattan running on an east-west axis along 116th street and a north-south one along Pleasant Avenue. Few without criminal business chose to linger around that intersection. The neighborhood that sat at the epicenter of heroin importation and wholesaling was known as East Harlem or Italian Harlem. It had housed the largest Italian-American population in New York City according to the WPA Guide to New York published in 1939. At that time there were about 150,000 persons in this one square mile area making it "the most densely populated section of Manhattan and the largest colony of Italian-Americans in the country."[15]

East Harlem drug traffickers were well known by the 1940s. The leading organized criminals then, and for many years to come, were Michael Coppola, Salvatore Santoro, Frank Livorsi, Joseph Gagliano, Joseph Vento, John Schillaci, John Ormento, and Dominick Petrelli. They and their associates managed a number of organized crime enterprises including the traffic in heroin. For decades organized crime and heroin trafficking continued on in basically the same hands and out of the same locations. It was passed down from father to son, from uncle to nephew in all the old familiar places.

Although the rhythm of life had seemed immutable, by the mid-1960s East Harlem began to experience accelerating and dramatic population changes . In little more than a decade Italian East Harlem had just about disappeared. The resident population became almost completely African-American and Hispanic. The very few remaining Italian-American residents stayed for economic and religious reasons.[16]

The center of East Harlem's Catholicism was the Church of Our Lady of Mount Carmel in which the Madonna of 115th Street reigned. As Robert Anthony Orsi wrote in his fine study "Faith and Community in Italian Harlem," the Madonna's church had become the village church for the area replacing the "scores of hometown saints that had once scattered the devotional energies" of the residents.[17] In April 1986, the church's front door was bolted shut, through there was still an entrance through the rectory on 116th Street. On the day of its close, there were but "two worshipers . . . in the church, both black" while "parked near the front door was a sedan with a cardboard decal reading EL BARRIO TAXI SERVICE."

Don Liddick is familiar with all these historical issues and many more dealing with the sociology and criminology of organized crime. His work should be required reading for all interested in the phenomena of organized crime.

–Alan A. Block

associations and actors, but it also is incorrectly identified as a criminal *organization*. In fact, the real mafia is not a formal organization operating in the United States or anywhere else, but is merely a way of doing things that is or was unique to the western part of the island of Sicily.

Myth: *Although they are criminals, organized crooks operate under a code of "honor" which is in many ways more respectable than common political and business practices in so-called "legitimate" society.*

The idea that there is "honor among thieves" seems to apply to *organized* thieves as well. The fantasy that organized criminals adhere to a code of honor derives from several widely accepted myths, including Cosa Nostra's (the name applied to Italian organized crime groups) prohibition against dealing drugs and the fanciful notion that organized criminals only kill other organized criminals. Of course the distribution of illicit drugs has been and continues to be one of the biggest income producers for organized criminals (including Cosa Nostra members), while the countless innocent murder victims of loansharks, labor racketeers, and extortionists would certainly disagree with the notion that organized criminals only kill their own kind. Nevertheless, there does exist a real foundation for this notion of honor which is said to bind organized crooks.

For the *mafioso* in western Sicily, honor was a very real and very important concept in their every day lives. Pino Arlachi explains:

> The mafia was a form of behavior and a kind of power, not a formal organization. To behave as a *mafioso* was to behave honorably.[12]

However, while being "honorable" is something that literally means possessing or earning respect, the attainment of respect among the *mafioso* did not and does not adhere to contemporary notions of integrity or correct behavior.

> Honor was connected less with justice than with domination and physical strength.[13]

and

> In a system whose basis was the struggle for supremacy, the most unequivocal way of asserting one's own pre-eminence was to take another man's life. In the mafia scale of values, where conflicts of honor played such a central role, it was in the highest degree honorable to take and kill a fearsome adversary... Any man of honor had to commit at least one act of murderous violence.[14]

What made this social situation worse was the fact that no man could be the object of even the slightest insult and not respond violently if he wished to keep his honor. To be insulted and not respond would be disastrous for a man in western Sicily or Calabria, for he would immediately lose all social standing. Adultery, broken engagements, and threats to one's family had to be met with murderous violence, or all honor would be lost. With the mafia "mind-set," to be honorable meant being recklessly violent.[15] While a criminal *organization* called "the Mafia" was not transplanted from Sicily to the United States,[16] this distorted notion of honor did cross the Atlantic with some Italian-American organized criminals.

Through the years and with the help of popular books and films like *The Godfather*, the mafia conception of honor came to be modified and accepted by the general public as reasonable, while organized crooks cited their actions as "honorable" so as to rationalize their murderous criminality. The thinking goes something like: Organized criminals are really no worse than corrupt politicians, and at least street-level crooks aren't pretentious about what they do; or they are only providing goods and services demanded by the public; or they only act violently in order to defend their business interests and their families– just what any other man would do– and so on. The point is that this notion of honor is really nothing more than a smoke-screen, a massive rationalization for both the average frustrated citizen who sometimes wishes he/she could avenge every insult and the organized criminal who often does.

Myth: *Organized crime in the United States is synonymous with a criminal*

9

organization called Cosa Nostra. The Cosa Nostra is a rigidly structured and hierarchical organization that spans the United States.

Today, nearly all scholars agree that organized crime is comprised of a wide variety of ethnically homogenous *and* heterogeneous criminal organizations, *as well as* countless less formal associations and networks of individuals from all sectors of society. Nevertheless, the myth that organized crime in America is embodied as a vast and singular organization of Italian criminals has dominated both the government's and the general public's thinking on the subject for many years. The genesis and development of this myth, commonly called the alien-conspiracy theory of organized crime, has been examined by a number of important organized crime scholars, and is a subject worthy of discussion.[17]

Gangs of Italian criminals operated in American cities throughout the nation as early as the late 1800's– anti-immigrant sentiments and sensational journalists fueled the sinister idea that a wide-scale ethnic conspiracy existed at that time. Later, throughout the 1930's and 1940's, the idea that a *national* crime organization was operating an underworld empire began to develop. While crime fighter Thomas Dewey verbalized the idea of a national crime organization in economic terms, it was Harry J. Anslinger of the Federal Bureau of Narcotics who revived the ethnic theme. Anslinger, who had some early experiences with Black Hand extortionists in the pre-Prohibition days, gave credence to the talk of a pervasive Mafia organization as he observed the prevalence of Italian names in his narcotics files. The notion of a national crime cartel was further bolstered when, in 1939, Richard Dixie Davis, a former associate of notorious gangster Dutch Schultz, wrote a series of articles for *Collier's* out of which the legendary Purge Day of 1931 was born. As the story goes, under the direction of Lucky Luciano, a group of younger Italians, in one fell swoop, assassinated as many as one hundred Mustache Pete's (old-style mafia leaders) across the nation. Out of this purge was born a national criminal organization overseen by the Commission, which was a board of directors comprised of the most important Italian criminals. While historical research reveals that as many as only four persons were actually murdered during the great purge, the alleged national implications of the event is what popular journalists and public officials seemed to grasp. Less than a year after the publication of Davis' sensational articles, Brooklyn District Attorney William O'Dwyer obtained testimony from persons (most notably Abe Kid Twist Reles) who alleged that they were part of a murder ring hired by a national crime syndicate, apparently confirming the notion of a giant criminal conspiracy.[18]

It was in this context that freshman Democratic Senator Estes Kefauver of Tennessee sought to establish a crime commission to investigate interstate gambling and racketeering. That the creation of the Special Senate Committee to Investigate Organized Crime in the United States chaired by Estes Kefauver was motivated by politics is undeniable– Kefauver himself went on to gain the Democratic Vice-presidential nomination in 1956. Although the Kefauver Committee failed to obtain or recommend any legislative remedies for the organized crime problem, it did manage, with the guidance of sensationalists and extensive television coverage, to revive the sinister notion of the Mafia. After receiving testimony from law enforcement officials and criminals for twelve months in cities across the Country– the crooks never heard of the Mafia, while agents from the FBN were convinced it was real– the Committee concluded:

> There is a sinister criminal organization known as the Mafia operating throughout the country with ties in other nations... The Mafia is a direct descendant of a criminal organization of the same name originating in the island of Sicily.[19]

Not long after Kefauver dramatized the idea of Italian-American organized crime, a gathering of sixty-five Italians at the home of Joseph Barbara in Appalachin New York on November 19, 1957 was interpreted by the law enforcement community as undisputed proof that a national organization called the Mafia existed. The belief that organized crime in America consisted of an Italian-run super-organization was perpetuated in 1963 when criminal-turned-informant Joseph Valachi testified before the Senate Permanent Subcommittee on Investigations of the Senate Committee (the McClellan Committee), attesting to the existence of a nationwide criminal organization called Cosa Nostra. Although his statements before the Committee and to federal investigators were full of inconsistencies and no supporting evidence could be found,[20] it was Valachi's testimony that revealed the new name for the Mafia (Cosa Nostra, translated as "this thing of ours") and formed the basis for the conclusions of President Johnson's Task Force on Organized Crime in 1967, which stated:

> Organized crime... involves thousands of criminals working within structures as complex as those of any large corporation, subject to laws more rigidly enforced than those of legitimate governments. Its actions are not impulsive, but rather the result of intricate conspiracies.[21]

Two years later, in his now famous book *Theft of the Nation*, Donald Cressey stated unequivocally: "I believe that the Cosa Nostra organization is so extensive, so powerful, and so central that precise description and control of it would be all but a tiny part of all organized crime."[22] The conclusions of Johnson's Task Force in 1967 formed the basis for the governmental response to the organized crime phenomenon. Both the Omnibus Crime Control and Safe Streets Act of 1968 and the Organized Crime Control Act of 1970 were direct offshoots of the 1967 Committee, and provided for solutions in line with aggressive law enforcement techniques including the widespread use of electronic surveillance and witness immunity. The multitude of successful Italian organized crime prosecutions through the 1990's has been offered as further substantiation that a huge nationwide ethnic conspiracy on the part of Italian-Americans does indeed exist.[23]

While the existence of Italian-American crime organizations and a "Commission" overseeing some of their affairs is grounded in fact, there is absolutely no evidence that suggests organized crime groups function much like legal corporations, or that a governing "Commission" exercises authority over different groups on a *national* scale. In fact, the force of law, the dynamics of the marketplace, and empirical reality all indicate the exact opposite. Nevertheless, attempts by historians and social scientists to demystify common misconceptions about organized crime have generally failed, while the general public, much of the law enforcement community, and the federal government continue to embrace what may well be nothing more than the romantic fancy of popular writers. The most egregious mistake seems to be equating all of organized crime with Cosa Nostra. Scholars now agree that organized crime in America is not comprised exclusively or even primarily of Italian-American criminals. Although Italian-American groups have perhaps been the most dominant at one time or another, organized criminality is not bounded by ethnicity or race. Likewise, most researchers agree that organized crime is not a formal corporate-like super-organization national in scope, but instead is comprised of countless less formal organizations and networks that frequently operate in relatively confined geographic areas.[24]

Based on erroneous assumptions, fostered by political considerations, and perpetuated by sensational journalists and the mass media, the popular understanding of organized crime has become what Dwight Smith has called a mystique– an understanding not founded on economic and social realities, but rather the irresponsible conjecture of persons motivated by politics who are willing to exploit deep-rooted anti-immigrant/racial sentiments.[25]

Myth: *Criminal organizations are structurally very similar to legal corporations, and operate like a bureaucracy. Like any formal legal organization, organized crime groups are characterized by a hierarchical authority structure, a rational division of labor, formal rules and procedures that govern employee behavior, and rigid organizational boundaries.*

Whether to justify the acquisition of resources or simply because the idea is somehow more sinister and romantic, the preconceived notion that organized crime is really a super-efficient bureaucratic (a contradiction in terms, if ever there was one) corporate-like organization was nurtured by law enforcers like Thomas Dewey and

Harry Anslinger since the earlier part of the twentieth century. The idea of organized crime's corporate/bureaucratic structure has also been advanced in a number of high-profile governmental hearings, most notably the Kefauver hearings in 1951 and the McClellan Committee hearings in the late 1950's and early 1960's. In addition, numerous criminal informants from Abe Reles to Joe Valachi to Jimmy Frattiano have testified in trials and before government committees attesting to the rigid bureaucratic structure of organized crime. Finally, the bureaucracy myth was elevated to the level of accepted fact in President Johnson's Task Force Report on Organized Crime in 1967.[26]

The proliferation of the bureaucracy myth is tied to the central question asked by those who study organized crime: Just how organized is it? While the government would say, "extremely well-organized," the empirical evidence suggests that the answer is "not very." Before examining scholarly research and observation, though, it is first necessary to reconstruct the development of the particularly egregious myth that organized crime is like a corporation or bureaucracy.

The principal sources from which the government has constructed its misconception of organized crime are organized crooks who flipped (guys who agreed to give testimony in exchange for some sort of lenient treatment or protection). Genovese crime "family" soldier turned government informant Joe Valachi is perhaps the most influential source of information that has been used to construct the alien-conspiracy/bureaucracy myth, yet a thorough examination of his testimony before the McClellan Committee strongly suggests that he was coached by his FBI interrogators.[27] Not only is much of Valachi's testimony inconsistent, but his position as a low-level member of the Cosa Nostra makes it illogical that he would even be privy to information related to the structure of this alleged national criminal organization.[28] Although much of his testimony was based on hearsay, Valachi's statements in 1963 nevertheless formed the basis for the most important conclusions made in President Johnson's Task Force on Organized Crime four years later.[29]

Other informants have been similarly dubious. Jimmy Fratianno, the self-proclaimed mafia boss of Los Angeles, contradicted himself on three separate occasions concerning the number of bosses who sat on the Cosa Nostra's "governing board."[30] A comparison of Fratianno's biography, *The Last Mafioso*, with his testimony at various mob trials demonstrate that entire segments of his revelations are factually impossible.[31] Even when informants were in a position to provide valuable information, their stories always seemed to be subjected to some twist or exaggeration. A very lucid example of this tendency towards hyperbole is provided by Alan Block, who concludes that the evidence related by a well-placed informant (Abe "Kid Twist" Reles) to the authors of a now famous book, *Murder, Inc.*, was interpreted incorrectly so as to conform with the preconceived notion of the "Bureaucratic Super-Organization." Block writes:

> What Turkus and Feder described and concluded was simply not what Reles related. For instance, when Reles talked about cooperation in the Brooklyn underworld, Turkus and Feder called it organization. When Reles talked about favors being done by one racketeer for another, Turkus and Feder wrote about orders and a smooth chain of command. When Reles talked about the geographic mobility of various criminals, Turkus and Feder held it was proof of the national scope of the cartel..... And finally, when Reles talked about the shifting, changing, bickering, competitive, murderous world of organized crime, Turkus and Feder surmised that this untidiness was only the inevitable and necessary fallout of the consolidation of organized crime. Everything, no matter how counter-factual, led to the big conspiracy, The Organization.[32]

The notion that organized crime is best described as a singular and highly bureaucratic corporation of Italian criminals is based largely on the hearsay testimony of low-level crooks who would have said anything to save their necks. Evidence contrary to the alien conspiracy/bureaucratic position has been simply ignored or assimilated into the existing orthodoxy.[33] For example, in recent years the proliferation of non-Italian organized crime groups has forced alien-conspiracy/bureaucracy theorists to re-think their position. However, rather than acknowledging a serious flaw in the "official" version, government officials have adopted what Gary Potter calls the "pluralist revision." Potter observes that

> conspiracy/bureaucracy theorists have been ...steadfast.... to the fundamental assertions of the alien conspiracy model in accounting for non-Italian groups. New groups are defined as ethnically, racially, or culturally homogenous. All have "alien" origins, are described in terms of some kind of culturally delineated "family" structure that resembles a rational corporate bureaucracy, and are rabidly expansionist in organization size and market share.[34]

So while the players may be changing, the corporate/bureaucratic structure of criminal organizations remains. And as always, the ethnic component remains central to the governmental conceptualization.

Of course, the reality is far different. Rather than relying on the oral histories of questionable characters and filling in the blanks as needed, a number of academics have not only examined valuable source documents, but have actually observed criminal groups. Research has shown that organized crime is not a single vast corporate-like organization (or even a number of bureaucratic organizations), but consists of thousands of less formal groups which at times would not even qualify as *organizations*. Because they operate in a hostile environment where intervention by law enforcers is a constant threat, illegal enterprises tend to be highly adaptive, informal in their structure, and often brief in duration. For example, in an examination of New York City's cocaine industry in the 1910's, Block found that

> ...it was fragmented, kaleidoscopic, and sprawling. It was organized and coordinated not by any particular organization, but by criminal entrepreneurs who formed, re-formed, split and came together again as opportunity arose and when they were able.[35]

Mark Haller has studied organized crime in a variety of settings, and arrives at a similar conclusion. As opposed to the bureaucracy "model" which stresses hierarchy and centralized control, Haller suggests a "partnership model," where organized

An Empirical, Theoretical, and Historical Overview of Organized Crime

AN EMPIRICAL, THEORETICAL, AND HISTORICAL OVERVIEW OF ORGANIZED CRIME

Donald R. Liddick

Criminology Studies
Volume 6

The Edwin Mellen Press
Lewiston•Queenston•Lampeter

Library of Congress Cataloging-in-Publication Data

Liddick, Don.
  An empirical, theoretical, and historical overview of organized
crime / Donald R. Liddick.
     p. cm. -- (Criminology studies ; v. 6)
  Includes bibliographical references and index.
  ISBN 0-7734-7965-1
  1. Organized crime. 2. Organized crime--United States--History.
I. Title. II. Series.
HV6441.L57 1999
364.1' 06--dc21   99-15792
                                            CIP

| This is volume 6 in the continuing series |
| Criminology Studies |
| Volume 6 ISBN 0-7734-7965-1 |
| CrS ISBN 0-7734-8583-X |

A CIP catalog record for this book is available from the British Library.

Cover design by Edward Myers.

Copyright © 1999 Donald R. Liddick

All rights reserved. For information contact

The Edwin Mellen Press	The Edwin Mellen Press
Box 450	Box 67
Lewiston, New York	Queenston, Ontario
USA 14092-0450	CANADA L0S 1L0

The Edwin Mellen Press, Ltd.
Lampeter, Ceredigion, Wales
UNITED KINGDOM SA48 8LT

Printed in the United States of America

This book is dedicated to Daniel S. Liddick

(You're right Pap– it's a business).

Table of Contents

Notes

1.These ideas were first presented in my paper titled "Some Thoughts on the State of Comparative Research in the Study of Organized Crime" presented at the 1977 annual meeting of the Society for the Study of Social Problems. The paper was later incorporated into Block and Chambliss, Chapter 6.

2.David Landes, The Unbound Prometheus: Technological Change and Industrial Development in Western Europe from 1750 to the Present (Cambridge: Cambridge University Press, 1969), 9.

3.New York State Senate Select Committee on Crime, Papers: Digest of Testimony of Congressman Steiger, 4 March 1970.

4.New York State Senate Select Committee on Crime, Papers: Nevada Attorney General Lee Johnson, "Report, Sportservice Corporation," n.d., 2.

5.Ibid., 3.

6.On these topics see New York State Task Force, Corruption and Racketeering in the New York City Construction Industry: An Interim Report (Ithaca, NY: ILR Press, 1988); Andrew Szasz, "Corporations, Organized Crime, and the Disposal of Hazardous Waste: An Examination of the Making of a Criminogenic Regulatory Structure," Criminology, Vol. 24, February 1986; and U.S. Senate, PSI, Profile of Organized Crime: Mid-Atlantic Region (Washington, DC: Government Printing Office, 1983), 230-252, 402-468.

7.My copy of Salerno's paper, "The Classic Pattern of Organized Crime," was in the New York State Senate Select Committee on Crime Papers.

8.On St. Germaine see "Airtel" from SAC, New York (137-9495) to Director, FBI, Attention, Assistant Director A. Rosen, "Subject, Criminal Informant, NY 3936-C, April 17, 1963.

9.FBI, report by Special Agent Heinrich Von Eckardt at Santa Domingo, Dominican Republic, with the following dates, April 25, 1963, April 29, 1963, and May 5, 1963. The file number is not filled in.

10.See, Anton Blok, The Mafia of a Sicilian Village, 1860-1960: A Study of Violent Peasant Entrepreneurs (New York: Harper & Row, 1974); and Pino Arlacchi, Mafia Business: the Mafia Ethic and the Spirit of Capitalism (London: Verso, 1986); and Tribunale di Palermo, Ufficio Istruzione Dei Process Penali, "Mandato Dicattura,"

Palermo, Sicily, September 29, 1984; and Alan A. Block and Bruce Bullington, "Thinking About Violence and Change in the Sicilian Mafia," Violence, Aggression and Terrorism, 1987.

11.See, Thomas Kessner, The Golden Door: Italian and Jewish Immigrant Mobility in New York City (New York: Oxford University Press, 1977); and the brilliant memoir by Marianna De Marco Torgovnick, Crossing Ocean Parkway (Chicago: University of Chicago Press, 1994).

12.See, Jane Catherine Schneider, "Of Vigilance and Virgins: Honor, Shame and Access to Resources in Mediterranean Societies," Ethnology, Vol. 10, 1971; and Danilo Dolci, Sicilian Lives (New York: Pantheon, 1981).

13.See, James B. Jacobs with Christopher Panarella and Jay Worthington, Busting the Mob: United States v. Cosa Nostra (New York: New York University Press, 1994).

14.One of the boldest predictions of this transformation has been argued by Bruce J. Nicholl. He contends that "long before 1980, the ground was prepared for a blossoming of Chinese Organized Crime activity in the United States." In the ensuing years, entire Chinese criminal organizations were transferred to the U.S. "The result," he stated, "has been the virtual displacement of Traditional Organized Crime by the Chinese on the east coast of the United states and the establishment of the control of criminal activities on the west coast by Chinese Organized Crime groups and gangs." How the ground was prepared is not exactly clear though it would appear to be the result of the growth of the Chinese population on both the east and west coasts. The criminological transformation is driven by large-scale Chinese immigration within which Chinese criminals have seen their opportunity and seized it. Bruce J. Nicholl, "Integration of International Organized Crime Activity," (unpublished paper presented at the National Strategy Information Center conference, "The Gray Area Phenomenon and Transnational Criminal Activity,) Washington, D.C., December 4, 1992), p. 10.

15.Works Progress Administration, Guide to New York (New York, 1939), p. 269.

16.The Drug Enforcement Administration compiled a detailed report in December 1976 on drug traffickers active along Pleasant Avenue particularly a violent and unstable group called the Purple Gang. The DEA identified 20 individuals who were the original members of the Purple Gang brought up in the Pleasant Avenue/East Harlem neighborhood. By that time five had been murdered, two were in prison for murder, another on drug charges, another for assault, and two more were on parole for drug offenses and assault. One other Purple was a suspect in a murder investigation. That left only eight still hanging around and they were under intensive DEA surveillance. Only two of the gang members still on the street remained in

Manhattan, and just one of them in the old neighborhood. Four had moved to Yonkers north of The Bronx, one to The Bronx, one to lavish quarters in Yorktown Heights quite a bit to the north, and another to Lodi, New Jersey.

In addition to the original 20 gangsters, the DEA identified 108 associates of the Purple Gang. Most of them were also from the Pleasant Avenue/East Harlem neighborhood, and most of them had also relocated. The locations of 102 heroin racketeers (including the few living original Purples) were pinpointed by the end of 1976. Forty-seven percent were in The Bronx; about 16 percent in Yonkers and nearby towns; around 5 percent had crossed the Hudson River and lived in towns such as Nyack, Nanuet, and Pearl River; and another 5 percent in New York State villages north of Westchester County. All told, 73 percent went north. Of the remainder, about 9 percent moved to the borough of Queens or to Long Island, and 10 percent lived in nearby New Jersey towns. That left only 7 of the heroin racketeers still in Manhattan, not quite 7 percent and only 4 of them in the old neighborhood. See, Drug Enforcement Administration, Department of Justice, Unified Intelligence Division, "The Purple Gang," File Number GF:C1-76-4167, December 7, 1976.

17.Robert Anthony Orsi, The Madonna of 115th Street: Faith and Community in Italian Harlem (New Haven: Yale University Press).

Acknowledgments

Aside from my own occasional musings and some ideas about how to conceptualize organized crime, this book is largely a compilation based on the work of many others– academics, law enforcement and government investigators, journalists, and national and international security specialists. The persons responsible for the journals *Transnational Organized Crime* and *Trends in Organized Crime*, as well as the folks at the Ridgway Center at the University of Pittsburgh are worthy of special recognition for their work at the "cutting edge" of this field.

Thank-you to Professor Alan Block, my mentor and the gentleman who was kind enough to grace this volume with his insightful preface. Thanks also to Gary Potter, Frank Hagan, and Jay Albanese for taking the time to read my work and provide valuable feedback.

Thanks to Dan Mudry, Tanya Conde and Pat McKula in the UPG computer center. You guys consistently responded to my queries with expediency and thereby prevented me from abusing my computer. Much thanks.

Finally, a special thanks to my son Edward, who is responsible for this book's cover art, and who accompanied me on our strange adventure Easter weekend 1999. We made it Eddie!

Chapter 1

Organized Crime: Perception and Reality

In order to acquire a full understanding of organized crime, it is perhaps first necessary to define what it is *not*. Few social phenomena have been mis-perceived to the degree that organized crime has. To the lay-person, organized crime is synonymous with the "Mafia," a secret and ultra-powerful criminal organization comprised of Italian gangsters. To the law enforcement community and the U. S. Government, it is a number of well organized, conspiratorial, ethnically homogenous criminal groups which seek to subvert the American way of life. The truth is less romantic than these misconceptions, yet far more sinister and frightening. Rather than ethnic minority street-level criminals who provide illegal goods and services, organized crime is best viewed as countless informal networks of "underworld" and "upperworld" societal participants. Unfortunately, the common perception of organized crime is that politicians, law enforcement officials, and "legitimate" business-people are mere *associates* of the *real* crooks.

Organized Crime and Public Perception

Perhaps the most disturbing thing about organized crime, and one of the conditions which ensures its perpetuation, is the ongoing love affair the people of the United States share with common hoods. Americans have adored gangsters throughout the 20th century, idolizing the John Dillingers and John Gottis of the world while everyday heroes all around us are apparently too mundane or boring for the attention-deficit American psyche. When John Gotti (the boss of New York City's Gambino crime "family") was being tried on racketeering charges on three separate occasions from 1986 to 1991,[1] New Yorkers assembled outside the courtroom to demonstrate their support, carrying signs, frolicking, and back-slapping the "Dapper Don." Like Al Capone before him, the impeccably dressed Gotti became a media darling as he continuously managed to get himself acquitted, all to the delight of mainstream America. Of course the truth is that Gotti murdered people and ordered people to be murdered, among other criminal endeavors. Jimmy Hoffa was another of America's beloved organized criminals. To many union members, Hoffa was nothing less than a working-class hero, apparently due to his humble beginnings (a dock worker) and the fact that he literally fought his way to the top. The truth is less romantic, as the benefits Hoffa earned for the union membership were soon lost to the mobsters who controlled him.[2] Still, many Teamsters revere Hoffa to this day (a fact illustrated by his son's prominence in the union in the late 1990's).

What could lead so many people to embrace common criminals? Perhaps the answer lies with conditions inherent in many societies, four inter-related social realities: 1) organized crime is *functional* in that it fills a societal gap or need; 2) economic stratification and class envy fosters acceptance of criminal elements; 3) citizens have become increasingly distrustful of government and economic elites; and 4) machismo, or the "mafia" mind-set, is attractive to many people because at some level it fulfills a psychological need. A discussion of these elements follows.

Public ambivalence toward organized crime may exist in large part because criminal enterprises are in many ways *functional*. Quite a few people demand the goods and services organized criminals provide (gambling, drugs, sex, etc.), and see nothing wrong with the purchase of those products and services. Illegal lotteries still prevalent in many cities are a case in point. Ivan Light has observed that because mainstream financial institutions have generally failed to provide adequate financial services in poor neighborhoods, blacks responded to the "service vacuum" by inventing the numbers game, which framed an "alternative institutional system for the savings-investment cycle in the slum."[3] In the 1960's, the numbers industry was so important to New York City blacks that James R. Lawson, then president of the

Harlem Council for Economic Development, put black control of the numbers market on a par with new housing, diversified business and light industry, and a rent strike as necessary components of an economically revitalized Harlem.[4] In the 1970's Harold Lasswell and Jeremiah McKenna found that numbers gambling extracted more money from the community of Bedford-Stuyvesant than residents paid in federal income tax, and that numbers bankers were the single largest provider of ghetto jobs.[5] So while mainstream America sees "organized crime," disenfranchised folk with limited opportunities see jobs and a vehicle to a better life. In this light the provision of illicit goods and services may be viewed as a functional non-governmental response to unemployment and poverty in impoverished ghetto communities.

A wide range of economic strata with real wealth concentrated among relatively few persons is probably an unavoidable consequence of a capitalist economic system. While conditions such as these will naturally breed envy, the situation in America is viewed as inherently unfair, illustrated by the widespread acceptance of the progressive income tax. In a country where people are taught to desire the "good life" but where the vast majority spend their lives working to merely pay bills and at best build a modest inheritance for their children, it is not surprising that some come to respect organized crooks for having the "balls" to cut some corners and attain what most cannot. While the majority of right-thinking citizens reject such methods for themselves, they nevertheless manage to rationalize that such methods are not entirely inappropriate since political and economic elites apparently "cut corners" with even greater frequency. If fact, one could argue that public acceptance of organized crime is directly related to the increased awareness that the most significant acts of criminality are committed by political and economic elites.

The average "Joe" was no doubt well aware of corruption at the municipal level as early as the 19th century, but wholesale distrust of the United States Government is a legacy of the post-Vietnam/post-Watergate era. While the United States witnessed only two major crises involving corruption at the federal level between

1860 and 1920, every White House Administration since Nixon's has been plagued with scandals (although this is probably due to better reporting as opposed to any moral superiority on the part of earlier Administrations!) Understandably, a 1992 study found that almost 70% of the public believes that government is untrustworthy, the highest percentage since the question was first asked in 1964.[6] Worse, ordinary citizens with limited incomes watch as political and economic elites not only break the law, but go unpunished with regularity. The public's attitude is exemplified best by an excerpt from one of the most popular films in American history: when Michael Corleone (a crime boss) explains to his fiancé that he is just like any senator or president, she responds that senators and presidents don't have men killed. His response is the correct one– that his fiancé is naive. Like the Corleone crime "family" depicted in *The Godfather*, organized crooks like John Gotti are viewed with less hostility than organized crooks like Richard Nixon, Ivan Boesky, or Webster Hubbell– at least "traditional" organized criminals are not pretentious about their criminality.

Recognizing public dissatisfaction with government, organized criminals have at times shrewdly set themselves up as champions of the common man. For example, Al Capone distributed food to Chicago's indigent and supplied alcohol to people who resented being told what was good for them. In many inner-city communities numbers gamblers solicit funds for hard-luck cases as they go about their daily rounds, and some have even become prominent philanthropists in black neighborhoods, making contributions to churches, athletic programs, and the needy.[7] Likewise, South American drug lords like Pablo Escobar have re-invested cocaine money by building schools, hospitals, and other public works.[8] Once again, organized crime can be viewed as fulfilling a societal need that neither government nor the private sector has adequately addressed.[9]

Another factor that endears so many people to organized criminals is the belief that in some ways, criminal entrepreneurship is actually *honorable*. While feelings such as these are massive rationalizations and completely false, this warped construction of reality is nevertheless accepted. Whether one calls it machismo or the "mafia" ethic, the idea that a true man never allows himself or his family to be disrespected without some kind of counter-response lies at the heart of every red-blooded American male. Most grown-up adults recognize that a certain amount of disrespect must be tolerated in order to get along in the real world, but one suspects that American citizens (and not just men) think it would be personally rewarding if one could be like John Wayne as he was in his films, or Don Corleone in *The Godfather* (fictional characters who put up with absolutely no disrespect and avenged any insult or threat). This is what makes organized crime so fascinating and attractive for many ordinary people: organized criminals rise above the dull and sometimes oppressive realities of contemporary life. Of course, the reality is that organized criminals merely use this high-minded solicitation of "honor" as an excuse to indiscriminately kill people.

Myth and Reality

Myths surrounding organized crime are created and perpetuated for a number of reasons. The U.S. Government and the law enforcement community perpetuate the myth that organized crime is best characterized as a conspiracy on the part of domestic minority ethnic groups or foreign criminal organizations because this suggests that the problem is not indigenous to the United States, and therefore sweeping changes in our political and economic structures are not necessary as a solution. The media/entertainment industry cultivates sensational and romantic myths about organized crime because its sells newspapers, books, air-time, and movie tickets. The general public embraces organized crime for a number of reasons, including the fact that certain myths associated with the phenomenon address unmet needs related to self-esteem and honor.

Whatever the reasons, understanding the true nature of organized crime is hindered by numerous blatant and outrageous falsehoods. Before moving on to a discussion of the attributes of organized crime (chapter 2), it is therefore necessary to first explore some of the more common misperceptions.

Myth: *The "Mafia" is a secret and ultra-powerful organization of Italian criminals that originated in Sicily and now operates throughout the United States and in other regions of the world.*

As opposed to a highly bureaucratic and rigidly structured organization founded on the island of Sicily and transplanted whole into the United States, *mafia*, in fact, was a system of patron-client relations that bridged legitimate and illegitimate segments of Sicilian society. Arising out of moral, social, economic, and geographic conditions unique to Western Sicily, *mafioso* emerged in the early nineteenth century in response to the abolishment of the feudal system and the subsequent need for power brokers to mediate and enforce contracts and other relationships (a function which the weak central Italian government could not provide). Recruited from the ranks of the peasant class, *mafioso*, through violence and threats of violence, entrenched themselves in a patronage system where they entered the service of both the landed gentry and the peasants, providing certain functions within the sub-cultural system. As patrons of landowners the *mafioso* arranged for adequate rents and the continued suppression of the peasants, and as patrons to the peasants they promised work and the continuation of contracts. "Mafia," then, is best viewed as a *system* or *method* characterized by patronage, where political middlemen exploited factors inherent to the rural, agrarian, and kin-based culture and political economy of western Sicily– the mafioso brokered the flow of resources among the societal participants.[10]

In recent years the term "mafia" has been applied to virtually any criminal organization, network, or informal association that falls within the realm of organized criminality. There is the "Dixie Mafia," the "Russian Mafia," the "Black Mafia," and so on– Dwight Smith has observed that the common misuse of the term has come to imbue the word "mafia" with all the meaning of an infant's gurgle.[11] As it turns out, not only is the term "mafia" indiscriminately used to label a wide range of criminal criminals are seen as merely pooling resources, sometimes for a single "job." Haller argues that fluid and informal arrangements such as these are highly functional because it leaves the criminal enterprises less vulnerable to law enforcement intervention. That organized crooks do not typically arrange themselves in long-lasting rigidly structured organizations also makes sense due to observed personality traits. Haller observed:

> Criminal entrepreneurs generally have had neither the skills nor the personalities for the detailed, bureaucratic oversight of large organizations. They are instead, hustlers and dealers, for whom partnership arrangements are ideally suited. They enjoy the give and take of personal negotiations, risk-taking, and moving from deal to deal.[36]

Haller also offers an alternative explanation regarding the structure and functioning of Cosa Nostra. As opposed to exercising strict authority over organizational members as is common in formal legal organizations, Haller argues that the relationship between Cosa Nostra bosses and their subordinates is similar to the Chamber of Commerce or Rotary Club. Like the Chamber of Commerce or Rotary Club for legal businessmen, Cosa Nostra groups would be seen, not as an organization that operates illegal (or legal) businesses, but as an association that businessmen join partly to further their business careers.[37] Haller's observation indicates that organized crime is not a bureaucratic and corporate-like super-organization, but is comprised of various associations of individuals who network with one another to further countless individual criminal enterprises.

Other research findings are similar. Observations of criminal enterprises in the cities of Detroit, Seattle, Reading, Philadelphia, New York, and Chicago all reveal that organized crime is not under the central control of a single bureaucratic organization, but is instead characterized by countless informal and fluid criminal associations, either in the form of temporary partnerships or networks of patron-client relationships.[38] For instance, Francis A.J. Ianni and Elizabeth Reuss-Ianni conducted three years of field research with a New York City Cosa Nostra "family" and concluded that the group was nothing like a formal bureaucratic organization, but was instead best characterized as

> ...traditional social systems, organized by action and by cultural values which have nothing to do with modern bureaucratic virtues. Like all social systems, they have no structure apart from their functioning; nor do they have structure independent of their current personnel.[39]

The Iannis' research suggested that the domination of Italian-American organized criminals has been the result of complex patterns of intermarriage and shared business activities which tie Italian-American crime families together. Their study revealed that highly organized syndicates do exist at the local level, not held together by membership in a national organization as suggested by alien conspiracy/bureaucracy theorists, but (in the case of Cosa Nostra groups) those cultural values which are based on the southern Italian system of family and kinship.[40]

Myth: *Criminal organizations tend to be large, long-lasting criminal enterprises which maintain monopoly control over illegal markets on a nationwide scale.*

Numerous empirical studies of organized crime indicate that criminal enterprises tend to be relatively small, short-lived, and limited in scope geographically.[41] Even when regional monopolies in illicit markets have been observed, the centralized control exhibited was limited in range and ephemeral. Likewise, criminal enterprises are generally far less formal in structure than their legal counterparts. The reason that organized crime is far less organized than has been suggested by the government and some scholars is due to legal and economic realities which naturally constrain illegal enterprises.

The consequences of product illegality have been explored extensively by economist Peter Reuter. Reuter suggests that because criminal entrepreneurs provide goods and services which happen to be illegal, the size and scope of illegal firms are constrained. Using principles of industrial organization and marketplace dynamics, Reuter observed that the cost of getting a product or service to the customer involves primarily compensation to those individuals involved in the distribution of the illegal product or service. The size and scope of firms is determined by whether the business chooses to integrate transactions within the firm or the marketplace– a decision which is based on the ease of monitoring performance and the flow of information. It follows that conditions influencing variables such as the flow of information will have direct consequences for the nature of a given illegal market.[42]

Reuter suggested that there are three factors which have direct consequences for entrepreneurs conducting business in an illegal market: 1) the need to restrict knowledge of participation in the enterprise, 2) the lack of external credit markets, and 3) the lack of court enforceable contracts. As a result of these conditions, the assets of an illegal enterprise are subject to seizure at any time, while all participants risk arrest and imprisonment.[43] Obviously, the immediate repercussion of product illegality is the need to control the flow of information about participation in the illegal enterprise. Employees of the firm pose a major threat to the enterprise because they are in a position to provide information which may lead to arrest or the seizure of assets, or even the takeover of the operation by other criminals. The illegal businessman therefore structures his relationships so that the firm is segmented, lowering the number of employees with whom he comes into contact. Organized criminals may also seek to intimidate employees, or alternately, to provide incentives for loyal performance. In either case, the costs of production are increased due to the necessary boost in wages or commissions. Lower ranking employees are at higher risk, and as more employees are grouped together, the risks increase. As risks increase, the entrepreneur finds it necessary to compensate employees at higher rates to ensure loyalty. Out of necessity, then, illegal businessmen must keep work groups small so that production costs and the flow of information are limited. Smaller work groups increase administrative costs, and prevent enterprises from taking advantage of economies of scale, where larger units of production decrease overall costs.[44]

Reuter also observed that illegal enterprises tend to be unintegrated. Vertical integration refers to the internalization of a function previously performed by those to whom a firm sold its services, or providing an input previously purchased from an independent firm. The illegal status of a given business apparently reduces the incentive for integrating a function. In general, enterprises and the relationships among functionaries in illegal markets are unstable. Employees tend to be disproportionately unreliable and must be closely monitored, which is expensive. Illegal entrepreneurs therefore recognize that it is more profitable to allow certain workers to operate on a *commission* basis. Since the incentives for entering into employment relationships are reduced, Reuter concludes that illegal enterprises tend to be vertically unintegrated and relatively small.[45]

Another factor inhibiting the scope of an illegal operation is the availability of capital external to the organization. Illegal enterprises do not have recourse to external credit markets– for criminal ventures with a modest cash flow and the necessity of maintaining a cash reserve, this presents a serious restraint on growth. Illegal businesses cannot present audited books, and lenders are not assured of access to collateral. Since illegal businesses do not exist independent of the principle entrepreneur, loans are extremely risky because the death or incarceration of the customer negates the possibility of repayment. Equity financing is also unlikely since the required amount of written records necessary to ensure the proper disbursement of profits among partners is not realistic for illegal firms. Similarly, because owners of illegal businesses are unable to generate goodwill (relationships with customers and other intangibles which amount to the value of a firm beyond its net assets) it is difficult to establish market value for ownership of an illegal enterprise.[46]

A study of the gambling market in New York City in the 1970's conducted by Reuter and Jonathan Rubinstein (1982) revealed that the markets were indeed populated by numerous small, often ephemeral enterprises whose relationships were closer to competition than collusion.[47] Based on their observations, the researchers also concluded that the geographic scope of illegal enterprises tend to be localized,

20

with branches in no more than one metropolitan area. The research suggested that the most significant reason for this is the difficulty in monitoring the performance of distant agents. In addition, transportation and communication networks pose greater risks as the geographic spread of the illicit operation increases. As illegal businesses grow and become more prominent, law enforcement agencies are likely to take a greater interest. Even if those agencies can be neutralized through payoffs, this still increases the overhead costs of conducting business. For similar reasons, illegal enterprises are not likely to diversify their product lines– a greater range of products or services would increase the likelihood of exposure to law enforcement pressure. Finally, because the product or service offered by the illegal entrepreneur is proscribed by law, a major avenue for national retailing and production is unavailable: Illegal businesses cannot advertise their products as legal businesses do.[48]

In sum, it is the position of economist Peter Reuter that illegal enterprises lack the endurance of legal firms. Illegal entrepreneurs are disadvantaged. Unlike legal businesses, they are unable to tap economies of scale, develop goodwill, obtain external finance, or advertise, due primarily to law enforcement pressure and the lack of contracts backed by the weight of law. Economic factors arising from a proscribed status such as increasing "cost curves" structure illegal markets so that they are populated by numerous fragmented, localized, fleeting, and undiversified firms. Reuter concluded that because many small firms in a given market is not indicative of centralized or monopolistic control, illegal markets are generally quite competitive.[49]

Myth: *Ethnicity is the key element in understanding the structure, functioning, and membership guidelines of criminal organizations.*

The ethnic background of organized criminals has been and remains the central issue among government officials, journalists, and many academicians in their attempts to account for the organized crime phenomenon. While for many years the

Italian-American "Mafia" or Cosa Nostra was the sole focus of attention, in recent years many additional criminal organizations defined by exclusive ethnic memberships have been widely recognized. For example, President Reagan's Commission on Organized Crime in the mid-1980's observed the existence of Russian, Nigerian, Canadian, Korean, Vietnamese, and other ethnic criminal groups operating in the U.S. (an entire hearing was devoted to the subject of Asian organized crime).[50] Nevertheless, alien-conspiracy/bureaucracy theorists have stood fast in their conviction that organized crime is perpetuated by groups defined by their ethnic homogeneity. As Gary Potter observes, "the long-term fear is that a new, non-Italian ethnic hegemony may emerge."[51] So the official view remains grounded in racism– it is the "evil foreigner" or ethnic minority who is the real organized crime threat.

While many criminal groups are defined by a common ethnicity (trust in criminal endeavors is a valuable asset, and a common language and culture can foster this), the truth is that much of organized crime involves ethnically diverse individuals who cooperate as needs and opportunities arise. Numerous historical observations are illustrative of this point. For example, numbers gambling enterprises employ managers and collectors of bets from a variety of racial backgrounds. Black neighborhoods in Chicago have been populated by numbers organizations that were licensed for a fee by Italian-Americans, managed by Japanese-American bankers, and staffed by African-American runners and collectors.[52] In a study of the New York City numbers market, police documents revealed that Italian-Americans, Jewish-Americans, Hispanic-Americans, and African-Americans prominently filled the ranks of numbers enterprises. The author of that study noted, however, that if the ethnic backgrounds of New York City police officers had been included in the analysis (a sensible pursuit since the NYPD played such an active role in the organization of the numbers industry), the frequency distributions would have looked quite different, and included more than a few whites.[53]

Other research confirms that organized criminal associations often cross racial boundaries.[54]   Several prominent examples are Philadelphia's K&A gang (Irish-Jewish-Italian), Chicago's "Outfit" (Italian-Irish-Jewish-Greek-Welch), and the infamous Jewish gangster Meyer Lansky's long-term association with Cuban, Italian, and Corsican hoods.[55] Stephen Fox, who has authored a sweeping history of organized crime in 20th century America (*Blood and Power*), observed that some of the most important bootleggers during the Prohibition era were not only Italian and Jewish-Americans as is commonly believed, but also Irish criminals such as Dan Carroll, Joe Kennedy, and Owney Madden, and WASP's like Roy Olmstead in Seattle and the Shelton brothers in East St. Louis.[56]

But it's not enough to merely note that a wide range of ethnically diverse characters occupy the ranks of organized crime, or that criminal associations often cross racial divisions. The most important point to recognize is that the significance of ethnic background has been vastly overstated by those who continue to embrace the alien conspiracy/bureaucracy orthodoxy.[57] Gary Potter has noted that:

> The argument has always been the same: forces outside of
> mainstream American culture are at work which seek to pervert an
> otherwise morally sound, industrious, and democratic people.[58]

One suspects that the myth is not merely a misinterpretation, but is shrewdly perpetuated by a government which not only knows what is palatable to the American people, but is also aware that blaming immigrant cultures is simpler than recognizing the economic and political realities which truly lie at the core of the organized crime problem. Yes, some criminal groups are shaped by a common ethnicity, and cultural factors related to race and heritage are certainly important in understanding the nature of organized crime. Nevertheless, empirical evidence suggests that the structure and functioning of criminal organizations and associations transcends issues of ethnicity, while a more useful understanding of the phenomenon is dependent on being cognizant of the central role played by so-called "legitimate" societal members in the organization of crime.

Despite the empirical reality, popular notions of organized crime remain ethnicity-centered. Aside from the government's alien-conspiracy/bureaucracy orientation, there is another prominent organized crime theory which focuses on the issue of ethnicity. Deeply rooted in the blocked opportunity tradition of sociological thought (discussed in chapter 6), the theory of ethnic succession interprets organized crime as an American way of life, where differential opportunities for economic gain predispose the lower classes, often minority ethnic groups, to engage in criminal behavior. Called a "stepladder of social ascent" by Daniel Bell, the process of economically disadvantaged ethnic groups acquiring money, power, and an improved social position through organized criminality is the essence of this perspective. According to Bell, as one ethnic group achieved respectability and entrance into the legitimate business world through illegal means, a new group of disadvantaged ethnics would emerge to fill the vacancy in the illegal market sector.[59] While Bell acknowledged that in the South and on the West Coast organized crime was comprised of many different groups, some of them predominantly native white Protestants, the urban north witnessed a "distinct ethnic sequence in the modes of obtaining illicit wealth."[60] Francis Ianni and Elizabeth Reuss-Ianni explain:

> The Irish came first and early Irish gangsters started the climb up the ladder. As they came to control the political machinery of the large cities, the Irish won wealth, power, and respectability through consequent control of construction, trucking, public utilities, and the waterfront. The Irish were succeeded in organized crime by Jews and the names of Arnold Rothstein, Louis "Lepke" Buchalter, and Jacob Shapiro dominated gambling and labor racketeering for a decade. The Italians came last and did not get a commanding leg-up on the ladder until the late 1930's.[61]

Francis Ianni further developed the ethnic succession position through three years of field research with an Italian-American organized crime family in New York City.

Ianni's research demonstrated that the recent domination of Italian-American criminals has been the result of complex patterns of intermarriage and shared business activities which tie American crime families together. With Ianni's perspective, organized crime is seen as a function of a common culture, as opposed to having a national membership. In the case of Italian-American dominance, real and fictive kinship ties have created "localized clan-like syndicates" in cities throughout the nation.[62] In line with the theory of ethnic succession, Ianni also observed that the kinship model which had tied Italian-American crime families together was fading as a result of three generations of acculturation. Additional research indicates that while more and more third generation Italian-Americans are pursuing legitimate business and professional careers, new waves of economically disadvantaged ethnic groups like African-Americans and Hispanic-Americans are controlling illicit activities.[63]

Although the increasing prevalence of Asian-American, African-American, and Latin-American organized criminal groups would seem to substantiate the ethnic succession framework, some challenges to this position have surfaced. Predominant among critics of the ethnic succession thesis is Peter Lupsha, who asserts that organized crime is not based on either a "narrow or limited status or mobility ladder for early twentieth century immigrants, or frustration or anger at the thwarting of mobility desires of immigrants by the dominant culture." Rather, the entrance into organized criminal activities is seen as "a self choice based on individual skills and a personal rationalization which perverts traditional American values and culture."[64] Lupsha suggests that the path to upward mobility was not so narrow as ethnic succession theorists propose, evidenced by the large number of Italian, Jewish, and Irish immigrants who prospered through legitimate channels. Also, the movement of Italian organized criminals out of illicit business activities may not be as widespread as Francis Ianni and others have suggested. For example, both Gus Tyler[65] and Lupsha[66] have observed the continued dominance of Italian criminal groups, who may simply be licensing and franchising new ethnic groups in the higher risk/lower profit sectors of the illegal marketplace. In any event, the principal limitation of the ethnic succession position is that it explains events (perhaps inaccurately) that have occurred in just one region (the Northeast) of one country (USA).

Conclusion

Common myths and romantic notions about the "mafia" have been perpetuated by the media and the government, and have been embraced by the general public. While the public facilitates the continuation of organized crime by demanding illegal goods and services and rationalizing away brutal realities, the law enforcement and academic communities have also been hampered by the blind acceptance of an orthodoxy based on ahistorical conclusions and false conceptualizations. The purpose of this first chapter has been to address the misperceptions associated with organized crime and to introduce the phenomenon in terms of social and economic realities.

Organized crime in America is an *American* social phenomenon, created and perpetuated by political, economic, and cultural variables indigenous to the United States. Organized crime is *not* the embodiment of an evil alien conspiracy, nor is it a singular bureaucratic super-organization controlling illegal activities throughout the nation. Although sophisticated and far-reaching criminal organizations do exist, legal and economic realities ordain that most criminal associations are relatively informal and limited in scope. While it is true that Italians, the Irish, and Jews have at one time or another exhibited predominance in certain illicit spheres, illegal entrepreneurship transcends the participation of any one ethnic group. Moreover, organized crime is a phenomenon that is global in proportions, and one that is best exemplified as informal networks of patron-client relationships in which the most important players are typically political and economic elites.

Having stated all that, there is little else that is known for sure about organized crime. Particularly disturbing is the fact that after decades of scientific endeavor, formulators of organized crime theory are still, in many ways, chasing their own tails. Nowhere is the lack of consensus greater, the research more desultory, than in those attempts to define the phenomenon.

Endnotes

[1]Michael D. Lyman and Gary W. Potter (1997). Organized Crime. Upper Saddle River, NJ: Prentice Hall, Inc.

[2]Dan E. Moldea (1978). The Hoffa Wars. New York: Shapolsky.

[3]Ivan Light (1977). "Numbers Gambling Among Blacks: A Financial Institution," American Sociological Review, Vol. 42, December: 892-904.

[4]Don Liddick (1999). The Mob's Daily Number: Organized Crime and the Numbers Gambling Industry. Lanham, MD: University Press of America.

[5]Harold Lasswell and Jeremiah McKenna (1972). The Impact of Organized Crime on an Inner City Community. New York: The Policy Sciences Center.

[6]David R. Simon (1996). Elite Deviance, 5th edition. Needham Heights, Mass.: Allyn and Bacon.

[7]Ivan Light (1977). "The Ethnic Vice Industry," American Sociological Review, Vol. 42, June: 464-479.

[8]Rensselaer W. Lee III (1989). The White Labyrinth. New Brunswick, NJ: Transaction.

[9]Peter Lupsha (1996). "Transnational Organized Crime versus the Nation-State," Transnational Organized Crime, Vol. 2, No. 1, pp. 21-48.

[10]Jay Albanese (1985). Organized Crime in America. Cincinnati: Anderson Publishing Company; Joseph Albini (1971). The American Mafia: Genesis of a Legend. New York: Appleton-Century Crofts; Pino Arlachi (1987). Mafia Business: The Mafia Ethic and the Spirit of Capitalism. New York: Verso; Anton Blok (1974). The Mafia of a Sicilian Village, 1860-1960. New York: Harper and Row; Henner Hess (1973). Mafia and Mafioso: The Structure of Power. Lexington, MA: D.C. Heath.

[11]Dwight C. Smith (1975). The Mafia Mystique. New York: Basic books.

[12]Arlachi, 87:4.

[13]Arlachi, 87:13.

[14]Arlachi, 87:18.

28

[15]Arlachi, 1987.

[16]Albini, 1971.

[17]For a more detailed examination of the myths surrounding Cosa Nostra, serious students must look at Albini (1971), Smith (1975), and Albanese (1985). Also see William Howard Moore (1974). The Kefauver Committee and the Politics of Crime. Columbia: University of Missouri Press; Humbert Nelli (1976). The Business of Crime: Italians and Syndicate Crime in the United States. New York: Oxford University Press; Alan Block (1983). East Side-West Side: Organizing Crime in New York, 1930-1950. New Brunswick, NJ: Transaction; Alan Block (1991). The Business of Crime. Boulder: Westview Press; Alan Block (1994). Space, Time, and Organized Crime. New Brunswick, NJ: Transaction.

[18]Block, 1983; Moore, 1974.

[19]Moore, 1974.

[20]Block, 1983; Nelli, 1976.

[21]President's Commission on Law Enforcement and the Administration of Justice. Task Force Report: Organized Crime. Washington D.C.: U.S. Government Printing Office. 1967.

[22]Donald R. Cressey (1969). Theft of the Nation: The Structure and Operations of Organized Crime in America. New York: Harper and Row. p. 109.

[23]Block, 1991.

[24]Francis A. J. Ianni (1972). A Family Business: Kinship and Social Control in Organized Crime. New York: Russell Sage Foundation; Albini, 1971; Block, 1983; Nelli, 1976.

[25]Smith, 1975.

[26]Task Force Report, 1967.

[27]Personal interview, Alan Block, Spring 1994.

[28]Smith, 1975; Block, 1991.

[29]Albanese, 1985.

[30]Ibid.

[31]Gary Potter (1994). Criminal Organizations: Vice Racketeering, and Politics in an American City. Prospect Heights, IL.: Waveland Press, Inc.

[32]Block, 91:13.

[33]Potter, 1994.

[34]Potter, 94:8-9.

[35]Alan A. Block (1979). "The Snowman Cometh: Coke in Progressive New York," Criminology, 17:75-99.

[36]Mark H. Haller (1990). "Illegal Enterprise: A Theoretical and Historical Interpretation," Criminology, 28:222.

[37]Haller, 90:226.

[38]Potter, 1994.

[39]Ianni, 72:20.

[40]Ianni, 1972.

[41]Peter Reuter (1983). Disorganized Crime: The Economics of the Visible Hand. Cambridge, Mass.: MIT Press; Peter Reuter (1985). The Organization of Illegal Markets: An Economic Analysis. Washington D.C.: U.S. Government Printing Office; Block, 1979; Potter, 1994; Haller, 1990.

[42]Reuter, 1983, 1985.

[43]Reuter, 1985.

[44]Ibid.

[45]Ibid.

[46]Ibid.

[47]Peter Reuter and Jonathan Rubinstein. Illegal Gambling in New York: A Case Study in the Operation, Structure, and Regulation of an Illegal Market. Washington D.C.: U.S. Government Printing Office. 1982.

[48]Ibid.

[49]Ibid.

[50]President's Commission on Organized Crime (1985). Organized Crime of Asian Origin. Washington D.C.: U.S. Government Printing Office; President's Commission on Organized Crime (1986). The Impact. Washington D.C.: U.S. Government Printing Office.

[51]Potter, 94:9.

[52]Task Force Report, 1967.

[53]Don Liddick (1997). "Race, Ethnic-Succession, and Organized Crime: The Ethnic Composition of the Numbers Gambling Industry in New York City," Criminal Organizations, Vol. 10, No. 4, pp. 13-18.

30

[54]Howard Abadinsky (1990). <u>Organized Crime</u>. Chicago: Nelson-Hall; Block, 1979; Liddick, 1997; Haller 1990; the reports of the Pennsylvania Crime Commission (1970-1993).

[55]Potter, 1994.

[56] Stephen Fox (1989). <u>Blood and Power</u>. New York: William Morrow.

[57]Jay Albanese calls this the "ethnicity trap."

[58]Potter, 1994.

[59]Daniel Bell (1976). "Crime as an American Way of Life," in <u>The Crime Society</u>, ed. Francis A.J. Ianni and Elizabeth Reuss-Ianni. New York: New American Library.

[60]Ibid.

[61] Francis A.J. Ianni and Elizabeth Reuss-Ianni (1976). <u>The Crime Society</u>. New York: New American Library.

[62]Ianni, 1972.

[63]Francis A.J. Ianni (1974). <u>Black Mafia: Ethnic Succession in Organized Crime</u>. New York: Simon and Schuster; Ianni, 1972; President's Commission, 1985.

[64]Peter Lupsha (1981). "Individual Choice, Material Culture, and Organized Crime," <u>Criminology</u>, 19:3-24.

[65]Gus Tyler (1976). "Socio-dynamics of Organized Crime," in <u>The Crime Society</u>, Francis Ianni (ed.) New York: New American Library.

[66]Lupsha, 1981.

Chapter 2

Defining and Classifying Organized Crime

A single precise definition of organized crime does not exist. In fact, Jay Albanese has observed that there are about as many definitions of organized crime as there are authors.[1] A survey of the literature reveals that the plethora of definitions are often ambiguous and sometimes diametrically opposed, while many "official" accounts of organized crime are merely descriptions of criminal activities, lacking the level of generalization necessary to constitute a definition.[2] Despite the lack of consensus, an overview of some of the more prominent definitions may be helpful.

The definition of organized crime proposed by sociologist Donald Cressey and adopted by the FBI states:

> An organized crime is any crime committed by a person occupying, in an established division of labor, a position designed for the commission of crime, providing that such division of labor also includes at least one position for a corrupter, one position for a corruptee, and one position for an enforcer.[3]

The Federal Bureau of Alcohol, Tobacco, and Firearms suggests the following definition:

> Organized crime refers to those self-perpetuating, structured, and disciplined associations of individuals, or groups, combined together for the purpose of maintaining monetary or commercial gain or profits, wholly or in part by illegal means, while protecting their activities through a pattern of graft and corruption.[4]

One of the more recent "official" definitions of organized crime was presented by President Reagan's Commission on Organized Crime in 1986:

> Organized crime is the collective result of the commitment, knowledge, and action of three components: the criminal groups, each of which has at its core persons tied by racial, linguistic, ethnic, or other bonds; the protectors, persons who protect the group's interests; and specialist support, persons who knowingly render services on an ad hoc basis to enhance the group's interests. The criminal group is a continuing, structured collectivity of persons who utilize criminality, violence, and a willingness to corrupt in order to gain and maintain profit and power. The characteristics of the criminal group, which must be evidenced concurrently are: continuity, structure, criminality, violence, membership based on a common denominator, a willingness to corrupt, and a power/profit goal.[5]

Public officials generally tend to think of organized crime as a formal bureaucratic organization structured to achieve a specific set of goals. However, many academics reject the government's conception altogether. In fact, other definitions reflect a variety of perspectives and conceptual models. One of the better definitions of organized crime was posited by a founder of the scientific study of crime in America, Edwin Sutherland:

> Organization results from the interaction of criminals, where criminal organizations may be either formal associations with a recognized leadership and a division of labor, or an informal similarity and reciprocity of interests and attitudes.[6]

Another prominent organized crime researcher, Francis A.J. Ianni, sees organized crime as a system of relationships among individuals who are bound together through real or imagined kinship ties. Ianni says organized crime is:

> An integral part of the American social system that brings together a public that demands certain goods and services that are defined as

illegal, an organization of individuals who supply those goods and services, and corrupt public officials who protect such individuals for their own profit.[7]

Joseph Albini also views organized crime as a complex system of relationships as opposed to a standardized model of bureaucracy. He defines organized crime as:

> Any criminal activity involving two or more persons, specialized or non-specialized, encompassing some form of social structure, with some form of leadership, utilizing certain modes of operation, in which the ultimate purpose of the organization is found in the enterprises of the particular group.[8]

Subscribing to a patron-client view of organized crime, Alan Block suggests the following definition:

> Formulated through patron-client cliques and coalitions, organized crime is a system composed of underworld and upperworld individuals in complicated relations of reciprocity.[9]

In the definition proposed by Block, organized crime is no longer perceived as a distinct entity which exerts a corrupting influence on upperworld government and business institutions. Instead, organized crime functionaries are recognized as being "in symbiosis with the legal and political bureaucracies of the state."[10] Still other academics have abandoned the term "organized crime" and all of the misconceptions associated with that term in favor of the phrase "illegal enterprise," defined as:

> the extension of legitimate market activities into areas normally proscribed, for the pursuit of profit and in response to latent illicit demand.[11]

Obviously the course of research has not been guided by any one conception of the phenomenon. In an effort to consolidate the variety of perspectives and descriptions proposed by public officials and academicians, Jay Albanese conducted an analysis of organized crime definitions, based upon a compilation by Frank Hagan. In looking at the different definitions, Albanese concluded that the most frequently cited organized crime attributes, from most cited to least cited, are: 1) organized, continuous hierarchy, 2) rational profit through crime, 3) use of force or threat, 4) corruption of public officials, 5) public demand for services, 6) monopoly control of illegal markets, 7) restricted membership, 8) non-ideological, 9) specialization of work tasks, 10) codes of secrecy, and 11) extensive planning. A composite definition, based on the researchers examined by Hagan, might read:

> Organized crime is a continuing criminal enterprise that rationally works to profit from illicit activities that are in great public demand. Its continuing existence is maintained through the use of force, threats, and the corruption of public officials.[12]

In any case, since there is a serious lack of consensus regarding a definition of organized crime, a useful way to arrive at an understanding is to explore those individual attributes of organized crime most frequently cited in the academic literature. Therefore, the following discussion focuses on the notions that organized crime is characterized by: 1) continuing hierarchies, 2) rational profit through crime, 3) the use of violence or threats, and 4) the corruption of public officials.

The Attributes of Organized Crime

1. Organized crime consists of a continuous, organized hierarchy.

Although this is the most frequently cited attribute, research indicates that few organized criminal enterprises are continuous, or last for very long. Likewise, there is quite a bit of evidence which demonstrates a lack of hierarchy in criminal groups. A hierarchical structure is descriptive of an organization where the members are ranked one above another based on differences in authority. Typically there is one or a few persons at the top of a hierarchy and increasing numbers as authority decreases, therefore the structure of the group is essentially pyramidal in shape.

However, a description of the relationships among organized criminals would rarely look so neat. As observed by Joseph Albini, power relationships in organized crime are complex and changeable, and are virtually impossible to chart.[13] Even Donald Cressey, the most important contributor to the hierarchical model, noted the limitations in such a conceptualization. Cressey stated that the intelligence provided by informants and used to develop "organizational charts" of Cosa Nostra families relied upon by government officials was lacking in three vital elements:

> First, there is no description of the positions and social bonds making up the organizational units necessary to actual street-level operation of illicit enterprises... Second, the hierarchical structure as described by informers is the structure of membership roles, not of the relationships between members and indispensable outsiders such as street-level workers, attorneys, accountants, tax experts, and corrupt public officials. Third, the structure described refers only to "official organization... Cosa Nostra informants have not described... the many unofficial positions any organization must contain.[14]

Quite significantly, Cressey also observed that the organizational positions in Cosa Nostra were more like "processes" than they were like the "things" he made them out to be in the 1967 Task Force Report on Organized Crime. If criminal organizations were charted, Cressey said that they would not look like the neat hierarchical pyramids displayed on posters at governmental hearings, but more like roadmaps, with the lines that connect the various positions going off in all directions.[15]

2. Organized criminals are motivated by profit, and their methods are criminal.

That what motivates organized criminals is the acquisition of wealth and power is self-evident. However, the issue of criminality is one that needs to be explored more closely. Although it may seem obvious that there cannot be organized crime without some sort of *crime*, in reality there is often a very fine line between legal and illegal business behaviors. For example, loan-sharking or usury is a crime where "underworld" money-lenders charge exorbitant interest rates. Yet this same practice is *legally* pursued by "easy credit" finance companies, banks which provide credit cards to consumers with a poor credit history, and check-cashing concerns which lend money at rates technically prohibited by law. The point is that the distinction between legal and illegal business behaviors is often quite blurry. Illegal entrepreneurs do business with legitimate businessmen, while often simultaneously owning or managing their own legal enterprise.[16] Legal retailers purchase stolen goods, legal businessmen acquire loans at illegal interest rates, bankers involve themselves in questionable investments and the illegal movement of funds, and politicians knowingly engage in exchange relationships with illegal entrepreneurs. Perhaps understandably, organized criminals perceive little difference between their actions and the behavior of "legitimate" business people.[17]

Obviously, a simple black-white dichotomy of "good guys" and "bad guys" is not adequate in describing the range of legal and illegal business behaviors. John Landesco realized this in the 1920's when he observed that organized crime in Chicago at that time was a "mirror of the legitimate business world."[18] Dwight Smith followed up on this notion in 1975 when he suggested that all economic activity can be ranked on a continuum which he called the "spectrum of legitimacy." Smith's point was that the boundaries between legal and illegal business behaviors are often very vague and sometimes non-existent.[19]

3. Organized criminals commonly use violence or threats to attain their goals.

That organized criminals use violence in their illegal business activities is axiomatic. Countless historical observations of organized crime in the United States reveal the brutal methods illegal entrepreneurs use to limit competition, control personnel, and silence would-be informers. Nevertheless, there is some empirical research which suggests the amount of violence attributed to organized crooks may be exaggerated. For example, in their study of the vending machine business (an industry traditionally controlled by organized criminals), Reuter, Rubinstein, and

Wynn discovered that:

> The growth of the amusement business and its technological transformation has given rise to market forces which simply prevent old-time muscle tactics and coercion from being effective.[20]

Peter Reuter arrived at a similar conclusion in his investigation of the loan-shark business. Reuter discovered that violence was seldom used by money-lenders in New York City, where the illegal businessmen relied on their *reputation* for violence to ensure the timely collection of debts.[21] In the event of non-payment, loan-sharks evidently have found that it is better for business not to kill the customer, and that taking over the debtor's enterprise is more lucrative. The bottom line seems to be that while violence often does serve a function within the criminal underworld, the consequences of violence for criminal groups are often detrimental. Even in those instances where competition is successfully limited or wealth is otherwise acquired, the prevalence of violent behavior generally undermines organizational goals and stability, often due to increased publicity and subsequent demands for a law enforcement response.

There are a number of factors that determine whether or not organized crooks will choose to utilize violence, the most important of which is the particular kind of illegal activity being pursued. The utilization of violence and its consequences is dependent on the structure of a given illegal market and the structure of criminal firms within that market. The nature of the product or service, the technology required to provide the illegal good or service, the degree of external pressure exerted on the criminal firm from various spheres, and factors which restrict entry into the given illegal market are all variables which affect the structure of illegal enterprises, the relationships among those enterprises, and the role of violence in governing those illegal relationships. For example, numbers gambling, bookmaking, and the illegal gambling industry in general exhibit relatively few acts of violence.[22] The reasons for this are several. For one, the nature of gambling requires that providers of gambling services have on hand a large capital reserve to protect against possible losses.[23] Such a constraint tends to limit entry into the market, which at least partially diminishes the need to use violence for the purpose of eliminating competition. For similar reasons, the monitoring and control of lower-level personnel in illegal gambling enterprises rarely involves violence, because retailers to the market are highly dependent on their superiors and the capital reserve of their superiors. In addition, violence can only be used to further illicit goals if there is a ready focus for that violence– in the bookmaking industry, for example, most wagers are accepted by telephone,[24] which makes it difficult to identify competitors let alone coerce them. Finally, violence rarely plays a role in the actual provision of illegal gambling services, since clientele are willing and demanding consumers.[25]

On the other hand, the distribution of illegal drugs is exemplified by a high incidence of violent behavior. Entry into the market is not restricted, since a relatively small initial investment may be quickly transformed into enough capital to become a major retailer. Likewise, a potentially large profit-margin (greater than most other forms of illegal entrepreneurship) ensures that the industry is characterized by intense competition, and violence. Violence is also used more readily in the illegal drug industry as a means of controlling inferior personnel. Unlike gambling retailers, middle and lower level drug retailers are not so dependent on their superiors. In fact, the relationship may be a one-transaction deal, since the profits can be so great that a dealer might choose to "retire" after a single endeavor. Because the profits are so great and the possibility of cheating is high (especially in those relationships where the product is distributed on consignment), violence is often resorted to as a means of exercising influence and maintaining control. Finally, because drug customers are willing, violence does not generally play a role in the delivery of the product to the consumer (although the greater cash transactions involved do precipitate some "rip-offs").[26]

The role of violence in the realm of industrial racketeering is somewhat different than with the provision of illegal goods and services. In the world of labor/management relations, the service provided by criminal entrepreneurs is violence itself. Whether by assuming influential positions in trade unions, setting up legitimate businesses in the service sector of certain industries, or establishing and controlling employer associations, organized criminals restrain trade through extortion.[27] The degree to which criminals use violence and threats of violence in this arena is considerable, since the attainment of organizational goals is in fact dependent on the propensity to utilize violent methods. However, violence may become dysfunctional for the attainment of illicit goals when a certain line is crossed, as in the murder of a prominent union official.[28]

The inability to control the behavior of organizational functionaries is an important factor in determining whether violence will be utilized by organized criminals. Typically, lower level organized criminals are uneducated and unreliable. Criminal entrepreneurs do not have access or recourse to resources available to legal employers– recruiting competent personnel, training and monitoring those personnel, and punishing recalcitrant employees is often beyond the means of the illegal employer. In short, controlling the behavior of employees is often difficult in the illegal business world. Violence is sometimes resorted to for that reason, but once again, this tends to undermine the stability of operations.[29]

The manifestation of violence itself may be viewed alternately as a breakdown of a given criminal order, or as evidence of an inexorable movement towards centralization through violence. If the history of organized crime in America was characterized by a period of intense violence followed by a sustained period of little violence, then one might conclude that a successful centralization of organized criminal activities had taken place. However, this is clearly not the case, as violent behavior among illegal entrepreneurs has waxed and waned over the course of years, typifying the uneven and changeable nature of criminal associations.

4. A key feature of organized crime is the corruption of public officials. In fact, were it not for this component, organized crime would not exist in any significant form.

On its face this statement is certainly accurate. However, there is a significant point that needs to be made concerning how the vast majority of laymen, law enforcers, and academics conceptualize (incorrectly) the nature of "corruption." In the realm of organized crime, corruption refers to the process whereby otherwise law abiding citizens, businessmen, and public officials are seduced into wrongdoing by evil organized criminals. So the participation of public officials and legitimate businessmen in organized crime is seen as being passive– their function is peripheral to the activities of the *real* organized criminals. According to governmental models,[30] crooked bankers, district attorneys, lawyers, and police captains are not members of organized crime, but are merely "protectors," "associates," or "specialized support" for the core members of ethnically defined criminal organizations.

Over the last three decades, many scholars have advanced the idea that organized crime involves primarily the distribution of illegal goods and services to willing and demanding consumers. The problem lies in concentrating blame on just the illegal entrepreneurs, particularly as organized crime is a social network that includes not only vice entrepreneurs and labor racketeers, but also politicians, law enforcement officials, court officials, business persons, and consumers. All of these players engage in complex and changeable networks of patron-client relationships that may be viewed as the "social world" of organized crime. From this perspective, legitimate businesses are not *infiltrated* and public officials are not *corrupted*. Instead, they are viewed as existing in a state of symbiosis with those law breakers that traditionally have been perceived as organized criminals.[31]

"Corruption" is a word that literally means something that was once good has gone bad. But "traditional" organized criminals like vice entrepreneurs have never "corrupted" the police. From the very beginning of police departments one of their primary roles in large cities was to regulate vice, a process that involved extracting profits from the illicit industries. If we say that police officers were corrupted by vice entrepreneurs, this implies that the suppliers of vice did something *to* the police. In reality, the opposite is true. It was the police who did something *to* the criminals who provided vice services. This is a subtle but significant point, one that transcends mere semantics.

The point is, developing a criminology of organized crime is dependent on recognizing that public officials, power brokers, illegal entrepreneurs, and otherwise "legitimate" business people are equal participants in countless exchange relationships where there are no organizational boundaries. From this perspective, the *active* role played by those persons who have traditionally been perceived as mere "associates" of organized criminals becomes highlighted. Mayors, drug dealers, bookmakers, pimps, district attorneys, "Cosa Nostra" bosses, madams, police officers, lawyers, numbers bankers, corporate executives, and national politicians are all full and participating members of the various patron-client cliques, networks, factions, coalitions, and informal groups which comprise organized crime.

Because this conceptualization is a departure from the orthodox view of organized crime, several historical examples are in order. The Knapp Commission Report on police corruption in New York City, the Pennsylvania Crime Commission's profile of Chester, Pennsylvania, and John Gardiner's classic study of vice and corruption in Reading, Pennsylvania are quite illustrative.

The Knapp Commission

Many academic studies support the idea that the true organizers of crime are the police and other important public officials. One of the best examples of this is provided by the Knapp Commission, a five member board that was comprised of citizens appointed by the mayor of New York City. The Knapp Commission investigated the nature of corruption in the New York City Police Department, held public hearings, and submitted a report to Mayor John V. Lindsay on December 26, 1972. The Commission discovered a wide range of illegal practices including kickbacks to police from tow-truck operators and various extortion schemes that targeted both legal and illegal businessmen. However, the most egregious and best organized illegality involved the management of the illicit gambling industry by the police. The Commission and its staff found that police collected tribute from gamblers on a regular basis, that the methods employed by police in collecting these funds were highly systematic, and that the form of corruption itself had remained unchanged despite periodic scandals and police shake-ups. The Commission further concluded that police "corruption" in association with illegal gambling was so pervasive that virtually all illicit gambling operations were free of police intervention, except for token arrests. In 1971, a Harlem numbers operator testified at a Commission hearing, stating: "You can't work numbers in Harlem unless you pay. If you don't pay, you go to jail... You go to jail on a frame if you don't pay."[32]

The Knapp investigators found that the payoff system was very systematic. Plainclothes police officers collected bi-weekly or monthly payoffs on the first and fifteenth of each month. Payments were collected by bagmen at locations distant from the precinct in question and the illegal gambling operation. The proceeds were then distributed among virtually all of the plainclothes officers in the given division, with patrolmen receiving an equal share. Supervisory personnel and the bagmen generally received a share and a half. Division plainclothesmen met once a month to divide up monies and discuss matters concerning "the pad," such as raising or lowering the required payoffs and recruiting new officers into the scheme. Newly assigned officers had to wait two months before they could get on the pad while fellow officers determined if they were "trustworthy." Officers usually recovered the two months worth of lost revenue by collecting "severance pay" when transferred from the unit. The pattern of collection and distribution appeared to be quite standardized, and included all eight police divisions examined by the Commission.[33]

Chester, PA

Perhaps one of the best examples of the inseparable collusion between municipal officials and the providers of vice is the small city of Chester, Pennsylvania. A report published by the Pennsylvania Crime Commission reveals that in that city there was no observable difference between the crooks in city hall and the crooks on the street.

Chester is a small economically depressed community just south of Philadelphia with a large African-American population. Numbers gambling was and is one of the more significant rackets in the city. In the 1970's, the most significant numbers boss in Chester was Frank Miller, an African-American who managed to maintain some degree of independence from the nearby Angelo Bruno "family." Investigations by both the Pennsylvania Crime Commission and the FBI revealed that Miller's operation was well-protected by Chester city officials, including Robert Kinlaw, a Chester police inspector who was simultaneously employed in the Miller enterprise as a collector of bets, and the mayor and chief patron of Chester's organized crime apparatus, John Nacrelli.[34] Nacrelli served as mayor in Chester from 1968 until 1979, when he was convicted for taking payments from Miller to protect his gambling operation. Before his conviction, Nacrelli exercised complete control over political affairs and the government of Chester. He served as a patron to the major gambling operators by controlling the Chester police department and directing them to eliminate competitors. He also directed patronage matters in several Chester city departments and dominated the Chester Republican Executive Committee. Upon his release from federal prison after only two years, the former mayor went to work for a Cosa Nostra connected video poker machine distributor ostensibly as a "sales representative," a position which involved intimidating a rival competitor to remove machines from local taverns. (The competitor's car was fire bombed. At a meeting with Nacrelli several hours after the incident, the lucky competitor was told to get out of town, whereupon competition in the video poker business ceased in Chester). Since 1982, Nacrelli has been described as Chester's chief power broker:

> Nacrelli's activities since 1982 can be described as the blending of political "consulting" activities and business "representation" activities. To this day, the one person to see in Chester, if one intends to do business there, is Nacrelli.[35]

Even after his arrest and conviction as mayor of the city, Nacrelli retained a controlling interest over patronage matters and the affairs of the Chester City Council and the Chester School District.[36] As informal power broker, John Nacrelli mediated patron-client exchanges in Chester as effectively as he did as mayor– all in this city where crime and government were no longer distinguishable.

John Gardiner's study of Reading, PA

Yet another prime example of the symbiotic patron-client relationships among public officials and street level vice vendors is John Gardiner's study of organized crime in Reading, Pennsylvania. From the 1940's to the early 1960's, Abraham Minker was the "largest independent syndicate leader in Pennsylvania."[37] Minker, a Russian immigrant born in 1898, began his criminal career as a bootlegger during Prohibition and ran a "conglomerate of illegal activities in Reading, the largest of which was a numbers gambling enterprise."[38] Although Minker was considered to be an independent operator, he paid 30% of his numbers gambling profits to the New York City Genovese "family" to operate without interference or competition. In addition to numbers gambling, Minker also controlled dice games and sports betting, extorted money from jukebox operators, and operated the largest "continuous process column" (a still) ever found in the United States.[39]

Minker maintained monopoly control of the rackets in Reading by regulating access to crucial services like lay-off banks and loanshark's capital, maintaining a reputation for violence, and fostering close ties with important city officials. In the early 1950's a city government bent on reform decimated the syndicate, but the return of a Democratic administration paved the way for Minker's reign as "vice czar" until his arrest and conviction in 1965 for extorting money from parking meter concerns which sought city contracts. Also convicted in the kickback scheme was Reading's mayor John Kubacki. Minker and Kubacki were brought down by police chief Charles Wade, who testified that he had agreed to purchase the job of chief from Minker for $10,000, and that he had been put on the syndicate's payroll while serving as top cop.[40] Campaign contributions usually ensured that city mayors, councilmen, district attorneys, and judges who were elected in Berks County were hand-picked by Minker. When Minker financed a losing candidate in a Democratic primary for mayor, he later backed the "reform" candidate (Kubacki) in the general election. Kubacki went on to become one of Reading's most corrupt mayors.[41]

Once again, the principal way that Minker established and maintained monopoly control of vice was through his relationships with Reading's public officials. Because he controlled the police force, it was not difficult to have competitors arrested and thereby eliminated. Again, patrons (the police— controlled by the mayor through appointments and promotions) provided important services for their client (Minker). However, the relationships here are a bit more complex, as Minker also provided services for public officials, serving as a kind of "broker" in a number of situations where elected officials desired to use their positions for entrepreneurial purposes. John Gardiner explains the exchange relationships among the various criminals:

> Just as the officials, being in control of the instruments of law enforcement, were able to facilitate Stern's (a pseudonym for Minker) gambling enterprises, so Stern, in control of a network of men operating outside the law, was able to facilitate the officials' corrupt enterprises. As will be seen later, many local officials were not satisfied with their legal salaries from the city and their illegal salaries from Stern and decided to demand payment from prostitutes, kickbacks from salesmen, etc. Stern, while seldom receiving any money from these transactions, became a broker: bringing politicians into contact with salesmen, merchants, and lawyers willing to offer bribes to get city business; setting up middlemen who could handle the money without jeopardizing the officials' reputations; and providing enforcers who could bring delinquents into line.[42]

In many instances then, Minker served as a patron to public officials in Reading. What Minker got out of it was allegiance from his clients— often simply because he had incriminating knowledge of their scams (just as the police had knowledge of his gambling enterprises which at times placed them in the superior role of patron). As can be seen, Minker and Reading's officials seemed to have an almost equal amount of power. The city administration had considerable leverage in that they had the weight of law behind them, while Minker enjoyed the position of power broker and controlled the entire illegal labor force.

Summing up: the changing nature of corruption.

Organized crime historians have noted time and again that public officials are the principal organizers of crime. Mark Haller has observed that the most important source of coordination among illegal enterprises in American cities has been oversight by local political organizations. According to Haller, the process of regularizing payoffs to politicians and the police has always resulted in some sort of coordination or regulation.[43] Block would agree, noting that law enforcers and politicians are not always limited to the passive role of accepting payments to ignore violations– they often assume the more active role of business manager or partner.[44] Documentation by the Pennsylvania and Chicago Crime Commissions, as well as individual studies of organized crime in Reading,[45] New York City,[46] Philadelphia,[47] Detroit,[48] and Seattle[49] all revealed that the most important illegal functionaries in the criminal networks examined were public officials. Based on these consistent findings, there can be little doubt that the *active* participation of the police and other public officials in organized crime can be found in virtually any area where there are significant illegal marketplaces.

The continued prevalence of official "corruption" is due to its functional nature– payoffs to the police and crooked politicians merely grease the wheels of illegal entrepreneurship. Like their legal counterparts, illegal business-people seek to limit competition. To the extent that payments by criminals are regularized, then, public officials have an interest in the success of the illegal business, and will attempt to suppress competition by arresting or harassing those entrepreneurs who do not make payments. Historically, applying pressure to non-favored illegal establishments has served a dual function. Not only is competition limited, but politicians and the police can present the illusion of serious law enforcement.[50] From another perspective, public officials may be viewed as *licensing* illegal franchises. Those entrepreneurs who do not pay the required fee for a license are not approved, and risk pressure from law enforcers.[51] Once again, it is the law enforcement community that exerts an organizing and centralizing influence on criminal industries.

Perhaps no historical observation is more revealing than the one John Landesco made of the funerals of organized criminals. Landesco observed that these ceremonies were not only a testament to the wealth and power of the deceased, but also a "revelation of the intimate relations between politics and crime."[52] In an examination of three gangster funerals in 1920's Chicago, Landesco found that the personal ties between criminal bosses and politicians that were concealed in life were disclosed upon death. Honorary and active pallbearers at the funerals of Big John Colosimo, Anthony D'Andrea, and Angelo Genna (underworld leaders in Chicago at the time) *included ten aldermen, twenty-five judges, two state senators, two state representatives, two U.S. Congressmen, and thousands of additional mourners including prominent citizens.*[53]

Historian Mark Haller has observed important changes in the nature of "corruption" since the early part of this century. In the age of machine politics, where municipal officials systematically used the power of their political parties in a purely entrepreneurial fashion, it was not uncommon for each ward within cities to have its own police court. Politicians selected police captains and city magistrates, so important criminal justice system functionaries owed their political patrons for their appointments. The result was local criminal justice systems that were mere "cogs in the political machine." As a result, some entrepreneurs successfully linked their political and economic interests over extended periods of time. Known as the "Lords of the Levee," Chicago aldermen Michael "Hinky Dink" Kenna and "Bathhouse" John Coughlin served on the Chicago city council for nearly fifty years, overseeing vice activities in the Loop (Chicago's entertainment district) until the early 1940's.[54] Since the 1960's, however, a number of factors have undercut the control of local politicians over the police and courts. These variables include civil service reform, police unionization, the centralization of police commands, the redrawing of police districts so that they no longer correspond with political wards, and the implementation of new laws which have empowered state and federal officials to intervene in local criminal situations.[55] The result is that now police often act independently of politicians in establishing patron-client ties with other illegal entrepreneurs.

Recent scandals in the New York City and Philadelphia police departments reflect the greater independence police enjoy in their manipulation of and participation in illegal businesses. In 1993, the release of the Mollen Commission report was yet another black eye for the NYPD. In that report, the investigative Commission concluded that some of the most important drug dealers in the city were New York City police officers. The Commission also found that the police operated in small fluid units similar to urban gangs– quite a departure from the bureaucratic and systematized payoff schedule reported by the Knapp Commission 20 years earlier.[56] The analogy to urban street gangs also applies to the recent activities of Philadelphia's 39th precinct. Officers there patrolled Philadelphia neighborhoods in small groups that robbed drug suspects of narcotics and money. To date, twelve officers have been charged in the scandal, resulting in the dismissal of nearly 300 drug cases and the remittance by the city of $3.5 million to settle related lawsuits.

Conclusion

As can be seen, the active participation of public officials in organized crime at the municipal level has been well documented. Worse, the complicity of national and international leaders in criminal networks is becoming more and more obvious (see chapters three and five). In sum, it would seem that an accurate conceptualization of the phenomenon is one where public officials, "legitimate" business-people, and "traditional" organized crooks are perceived as being equally embroiled in the changeable networks which comprise organized crime.

One final point concerning the attributes of organized crime must be made. Every one of the four attributes discussed– continuing hierarchy, profit motive/criminality, use of violence, and public corruption– have either been overstated or warped in some way. Many organized crime enterprises are quite short-lived, while criminal authority structures often fail to conform to notions of hierarchy. In many cases the use of violence has been overstated, while the blurred line between legitimate and illicit commerce is rarely addressed by policy-makers. The least cited of the four attributes most frequently mentioned by would-be definers of organized crime (referring to Hagan's/Albanese's compilation) is also a dimension which has been characterized incorrectly. In fact, one could argue that not only should the role of public officials in organized crime be reconceptualized, but also that public corruption should have been the most frequently cited attribute by those scholars who attempted to define the phenomenon.

Classifying Organized Crime

In Part I of this book, much energy has been devoted to describing what organized crime is not. In discussing the most frequently cited attributes of organized crime, some strides have even been made toward understanding what organized crime is. Still, the fact remains that very little is known about this phenomenon, and the need for further scholarly research is sorely needed. Aside from the glaring lack of an agreed upon definition, there also remains (among other things) the significant problem of classifying the different types of organized criminal activities. Joseph Albini has correctly observed that "efforts at producing a typology of organized crime have produced instead a confusion of terms, a lack of uniformity in classification, and in general, a semantic collage."[57] A "semantic collage" indeed– attempting to sort through the mire of terms such as "mafia," "organized crime," "illegal enterprise," "white-collar crime," "syndicated crime," "professional crime," and "racketeering" is at the very least problematic, and more likely an exercise in futility.

Like the multitude of organized crime definitions, viewing the problem from a variety of perspectives has resulted in a large number of diverse typologies. A notable example is the work of Thomas Schelling, a respected economist who proposed a typology describing underworld businesses, classified as black markets, racketeering, black market monopolies, cartels, cheating, organized criminal services, and corruption of police and politics.[58] Another classifier of organized crime is Joseph Albini, who divides organized crime into political-social organized crime, mercenary crime, in-group oriented crime, and syndicated crime.[59] In attempting to explain the organization of criminal working groups, Mary McIntosh suggested four types of organized criminality: the "picaresque" organization of bandits and thieves, the craft organization of routine urban thefts, the project organization of technically advanced large-scale frauds, and the business organization of racketeering/syndicated crime.[60] In attempting to explain the emergence of criminal groups, Peter Lupsha suggests a "stage-evolutionary model," where organized crime is seen as evolving from predatory, to parasitical, to symbiotic forms.[61]

In developing a typology of organized crime, it may be useful to see it as a sub-category of organized *criminality*, a broad "kingdom" of relatively coordinated criminal activities (as opposed to crimes committed by individuals) that include the following:

> **1) terrorism--** organized criminal activities with a political or ideological motivation involving acts of discriminate and indiscriminate violence for the purpose of affecting social or political change.

> **2) organized crime--** the provision of illegal goods and services, various forms of theft and fraud, and the restraint of trade in both licit and illicit market sectors, perpetuated by informal and changing networks of "upper-world" and "under-world" societal participants who are bound together in complex webs of patron-client relationships.

> **3) corporate crime--** various crimes committed by legal corporations, including but not limited to tax evasion, unlawful environmental pollution, restraint of trade, rebate scams, misrepresentation in advertising, price-fixing, various financial frauds including the unlawful manipulation of securities, the production and sale of unsafe products, bribery of regulatory officials, and the

laundering of illegally generated revenue.

4) governmental crime-- crimes committed by government officials, government agencies, and entire nation-states. These crimes include but are not limited to the acceptance of bribes and unlawful gratuities, collusion with corporations in various wrongdoings, violation of international treaties, war crimes, experimentation on unknowing citizens, and genocide.

Although this book is concerned primarily with organized crime as described above, it is impossible to discuss that form of organized criminality without recognizing the interplay between organized crime, terrorism, corporate crime, and governmental crime. In fact, classifying types of organized criminality is confounded to some extent because a continuum of types exists *within* categories, and because these types have elements which overlap into other categories. For example, within the organized crime category, misconduct by an elected government official and the distribution of narcotics by outlaw motorcycle gangs, while two very different kinds of criminal behavior, would both fall under some of the more common organized crime definitions.[62] The overlap between the broader types of organized criminality (terrorism/organized crime/corporate crime/governmental crime) is also quite evident when examining any number of present day large scale criminal networks. For example, to fund their activities terrorist groups often engage in organized crime-like activities, including "protection rackets" (organized extortion) and the distribution of narcotics.[63] Likewise, entire governmental units (the CIA, for example) have been known to facilitate and in some instances actively participate in the distribution of illicit drugs so as to finance covert operations/bolster political agendas.[64] This taxonomic dilemma is expressed well by Alan Block:

> I wonder which category to invoke when considering crimes such as loan-sharking committed in tandem by racketeers and bankers; or how to define criminality associated with the looting of pension and welfare funds, in which cabals of organized criminals, government and private lawyers, and accountants are prominent? Which term is

appropriate when analyzing financial schemes designed to evade
taxes and "launder" money for corporate executives, mobsters, drug
smugglers, politicians, attorneys, etc., carried out in offshore banks
and tax-haven countries such as The Bahamas, the Netherlands
Antilles, Panama, and the Cayman Islands. Clearly such situations
involve organized criminals doing white-collar-type crimes, and
white-collar criminals frequently acting like racketeers.[65]

The massive criminality engaged in by the Bank of Credit and Commerce
International (BCCI) included drug trafficking, arms smuggling, bank fraud, and
money laundering on a global scale. The cast of characters included prominent
politicians, bankers, corporate executives, terrorists, and more "traditional" organized
crooks from around the world. A full analysis of the criminality of BCCI reveals that
the scandal could properly be described as organized crime, corporate crime, or
governmental crime– the point being that there simply is no neat classification
scheme when it comes to describing organized criminality.

For the purposes of this volume, let us say that organized crime, as a sub-category
of organized criminality, involves those activities related to the management and
coordination of various illegal distribution systems, including *but not limited to* the
supply of illicit drugs, alcohol, and untaxed cigarettes, large scale thefts, the fencing
of stolen property, the smuggling of various goods, and the provision of illegal
gambling, sex, and money-lending services. The multiple and complex forms of
industrial/labor/business racketeering is also a component of organized crime.
However, because the role of criminal elements within the realm of industrial
racketeering manifests characteristics which clearly set this aspect of organized crime
apart from the provision of illicit goods and services, it may be useful to differentiate
between these behaviors. While industrial or business racketeering involves
primarily the act of extortion, the distribution of controlled substances and the supply
of services like gambling, usury, and prostitution entail the provision of these goods
and services *to willing and demanding consumers*. Block has categorized those
entities that provide illegal goods and services as "enterprise syndicates," and those

criminal groups which exert power through private violence and other types of illegal leverage as "power syndicates."[66] This distinction between organized criminals who provide demanded goods and services and organized criminals who essentially extort is important and useful.

Conclusion

One could explore the myths surrounding organized crime and dilemmas in defining and classifying the phenomenon almost endlessly. While there remains considerable disagreement on how to properly conceptualize the problem, scholars do seem to agree that significant forms of organized crime could not exist without the participation of public officials. Still, while scholars like William Chambliss and Joseph Albini have written of patron-client and symbiotic relationships in describing organized crime, there seems to be a stubbornness among government officials as well as academics in clinging to the notion that there is some kind of *boundary* between "traditional" crooks like Cosa Nostra bosses and those "upperworld" players who participate in the organization of crime. At the risk of sounding "trendy," this author would suggest that a "paradigm shift" is a necessary foundation for a unified scholarly effort in accounting for the nature and persistence of organized crime networks. In short, organized crime should be characterized in a manner such that elite members of the so-called "legitimate" business and political world are viewed as the principal organizers of crime.

Finally, since the primary purpose of this chapter was to define and classify, allow the author to offer his own definition of organized crime: the provision of illegal goods and services, various forms of theft and fraud, and the restraint of trade in both licit and illicit market sectors, perpetuated by informal and changing networks of "upperworld" and "underworld" societal participants who are bound together in complex webs of patron-client relationships. (Patron client relationships are discussed fully in chapters six and seven). For now, however, let us turn to a discussion of the impact of organized crime as a regional and global phenomenon.

54

Endnotes

[1]Jay Albanese (1985). <u>Organized Crime in America</u>. Cincinnati: Anderson Publishing Company.

[2]Ibid.

[3]Howard Abadinsky (1990). <u>Organized Crime</u>, 3rd ed. Chicago: Nelson-Hall.

[4]Howard Abadinsky (1985). <u>Organized Crime</u>, 2nd ed. Chicago: Nelson-Hall.

[5]President's Commission on Organized Crime (1986). <u>The Impact: Organized Crime Today</u>. Washington D.C.: U.S. Government Printing Office.

[6]Edwin H. Sutherland (1961). <u>White Collar Crime</u>. New York, New York: Holt, Rinehart, and Winston.

[7]Francis A. J. Ianni, 1972. <u>A Family Business: Kinship and Social Control in Organized Crime</u>. New York: Russell Sage Foundation.

[8]Joseph Albini (1971). <u>The American Mafia: Genesis of a Legend</u>. New York: Appleton-Century Crofts.

[9]Alan A. Block (1991). <u>Masters of Paradise</u>. New Brunswick, NJ: Transaction.

[10]William Chambliss (1988). "Vice, Corruption, Bureaucracy, and Power," in <u>Criminal Justice: Law and Politics</u>, ed. George F. Cole. Pacific Grove, CA: Brooks/Cole.

[11]Dwight Smith (1975). <u>The Mafia Mystique</u>. New York: Basic books.

[12]See Frank Hagan (1983). "The Organized Crime Continuum: A Further Specification of a New Conceptual Model," <u>Criminal Justice Review</u>, 8 [Spring], 52-57.

[13]Albanese, 1985.

[14]Albini, 1971.

[15]Donald R. Cressey (1972). <u>Criminal Organization: Its Elementary Forms</u>. New York: Harper and Row.

[16]Cressey, 1972.

[17]Mark Haller (1990). "Illegal Enterprise: A Theoretical and Historical Interpretation," <u>Criminology</u>, 28: 207-235.

[18]Ibid.

[19]John Landesco (1929). Organized Crime in Chicago. Chicago: University of Chicago Press.

[20]Smith, 1975.

[21]Peter Reuter, Jonathan Rubinstein, and Simon Wynn (1982). Racketeering in Legitimate Industries: Two Case Studies. Washington, D.C.: National Institute of Justice.

[22]Peter Reuter (1983). Disorganized Crime: The Economics of the Visible Hand. Cambridge, Mass.: MIT Press.

[23]Peter Reuter and Jonathan Rubinstein (1982). Illegal Gambling in New York: A Case Study in the Operation, Structure, and Regulation of an Illegal Market. Washington D.C.: U.S. Government Printing Office; Don Liddick (1995). Numbers Gambling in New York City, 1960-69: A Social and Political History. Unpublished PhD dissertation. The Pennsylvania State University.

[24]Don Liddick (1999). The Mob's Daily Number: Organized Crime and the Numbers Gambling Industry. Lanham, MD: University Press of America.

[25]Reuter, 1983.

[26]Liddick, 1995.

[27]Michael Lyman and Gary Potter (1997). Organized Crime. Upper Saddle River, NJ: Prentice Hall.

[28]Alan A. Block (1983). East-Side West-Side: Organizing Crime in New York, 1930-1950. New Brunswick, NJ: Transaction.

[29]James Neff (1989). Mobbed Up. New York: Dell.

[30]Peter Reuter (1985). The Organization of Illegal Markets: An Economic Analysis. Washington D.C.: U.S. Government Printing Office.

[31]President's Commission on Organized Crime, 1986.

[32]For a more complete rundown of this framework, see Alan A. Block and William Chambliss (1981). Organizing Crime. New York: Elsevier; Chambliss, 1988.

[33]The Knapp Commission Report on Police Corruption (1972). George Braziller: New York.

[34]Ibid.

[35]Pennsylvania Crime Commission (1980). A Decade of Organized Crime. St. David's, PA: Commonwealth of Pennsylvania.

[36]The Pennsylvania Crime Commission (1989). 1989 Report. Conshohocken, PA: Commonwealth of Pennsylvania.

56

[37]Ibid.

[38]The Pennsyvlania Crime Commission (1992). 1992 Report. Conshohocken: PA.: Commonwealth of Pennsylvania.

[39]Ibid. p. 12.

[40]Ibid.

[41]Ibid.

[42]John Gardiner and David J. Olson (1967). Task Force Report: Organized Crime. (Annotations and Consultants' Papers). "Appendix B: Wincanton– The Politics of Corruption." Washington D.C.: U.S. Government Printing Office.

[43]Gardiner and Olson, 67:66.

[44]Haller, 1990.

[45]Block, 1983.

[46]John A. Gardiner (1970). The Politics of Corruption: Organized Crime in an American City. Beverly Hill, CA: Russell Sage Foundation.

[47]Block, 1983; Liddick, 1995.

[48]Gary Potter and Philip Jenkins (1985). The City and the Syndicate: Organizing Crime in Philadelphia. Lexington, MA: Ginn Press.

[49]Albini, 1971.

[50]William Chambliss (1978). On the Take: From Petty Crooks to Presidents. Bloomington: Indiana University Press.

[51]Chambliss, 1988.

[52]Haller, 1990.

[53]John Landesco (1976). "The Funerals of Gangsters," in The Crime Society, Francis and Elizabeth Ianni, ed. New York: New American Library.

[54]Ibid.

[55]Haller, 1990.

[56]Ibid.

[57]The Mollen Commission Report on Police Corruption (1993). City of New York.

[58]Albini, 1971.

[59]Thomas C. Schelling (1967). "Economic Analysis of Organized Crime," appendix D in Task Force Report: Organized Crime. President's Commission on Law Enforcement and the Administration of Justice. Washington D.C.: U.S. Government Printing Office.

[60]Albini, 1971.

[61]Mary McIntosh (1975). The Organisation of Crime. New York: MacMillan.

[62]Peter Lupsha (1996). "Transnational Organized Crime versus the Nation-State," Transnational Organized Crime. Vol. 2, No. 1, pp. 21-48.

[63]Albanese, 1985.

[64]Brian Freemantle (1995). The Octopus: Europe in the Grip of Organized Crime. London: Orion; Alex P. Schmid (1996). "Links Between Transnational Organized Crime and Terrorist Crimes," Transnational Organized Crime, Vol. 2, No. 4, pp. 41-81.

[65]Alfred A. McCoy (1992). "Heroin as a Global Commodity: A History of Southeast Asia's Opium Trade," in War on Drugs, Alan Block and Alfred McCoy (ed.) Boulder: Westview Press.

[66]Block, 91:2-3.

[67]Block, 1983.

Chapter 3
The Impact of Organized Crime

William Chambliss has concluded that crime is "a cornerstone on which the political and economic relations of democratic-capitalist societies are constructed."[1] Social science research suggests that Chambliss' position is accurate. World events in the 1990's indicate that emerging democracies and unstable conflict-ridden regions are especially vulnerable to the proliferation of criminal networks. Still, observations from around the world indicate that organized crime thrives in a variety of economic and political situations, and in virtually any place where proscribed goods and services are demanded or where oversight of industry, government, and the administration of justice is inadequate.   Profits generated from criminal entrepreneurship and the nexus between "underworld and upperworld" criminals shape the course of national and international affairs,[2] and deeply affect the "social processes" of communities at the local level.[3]

The majority of this chapter will document the dimensions and impact of organized crime on a global scale. First, however, a discussion of organized crime's effect on local communities is important and necessary.

Organized Crime and Local Communities

At the local or regional level, the effects of organized crime have been fairly well documented.   While there is no genuine consensus (Anderson, for example, concluded that illegal gambling played an insignificant role in the economy of Philadelphia),[4] many researchers feel that illegal industries are very important to local economies and play a significant role in community decision-making.[5] In some instances, criminal industries have even been the source of local political change.[6]

Of course actually measuring the impact of organized crime on communities is difficult to do, explaining perhaps why there is a dearth of research in this area. One notable exception was a study conducted by Harold Lasswell and Jeremiah McKenna. These researchers used econometric models and a mathematical consulting firm to measure the impact that the distribution of illicit drugs and the provision of numbers gambling services had on the Brooklyn community of Bedford-Stuyvesant. They concluded that numbers gambling and drug trafficking greatly affected the "social process" of Bedford-Stuyvesant,[7] especially those "value categories" of power and wealth. For example, in their search for social indicators, the researchers found that numbers gambling extracted more money from the community of Bedford-Stuyvesant than residents paid in federal income tax, and that numbers bankers were the single largest provider of ghetto jobs.[8] The power process or decision-making process of the community was measured by examining the disposition of arrests over the study period. Of the 356 persons arrested in numbers gambling raids from 1961 to 1970, only six persons received a jail sentence. The vast majority of persons either had their cases dismissed or were acquitted.[9] The researchers went on to examine a broad number of social indicators related to other value categories, and concluded that the illegal enterprises examined had a significant impact on the entirety of the community's "social process."[10]

While research on the impact of organized crime tends to focus on urban communities, criminal networks are also quite prevalent in rural areas.[11] In rural America alcohol bootlegging, drug cultivation, prostitution, gambling, loansharking, and organized theft are quite common. Marijuana cultivation seems to be particularly important in sparsely populated counties, and is considered to be the economic mainstay in many rural farming communities.[12] In fact criminal enterprises are important to local communities throughout the world. In the Russian Far East, police say the cultivation of hemp has saved local economies from collapse.[13] Coca farmers in Bolivia and Peru and poppy growers in Afghanistan and Myanmar no doubt feel the same way.

The case can be made that organized crime is a "community social institution," and is in many ways functional. Providing highly demanded products and services like sex, gambling, and drugs provides jobs for the unemployed,[14] capital for re-investment in the community,[15] and a non-violent alternative to more predatory crimes like robbery and burglary. In fact, the legal market's failure to service significant consumer populations is largely responsible for the existence of vice enterprises.[16] Lyman and Potter explain the functional nature of organized crime in local communities:

> High demands for illicit services generate huge profits...some community members benefit directly in the form of campaign funds, investment opportunities, assistance in negotiations relative to public service, and so on. Organized Crime also occupies an important position in a community's socialization function. It not only socializes its participants but supports broader dimensions defining parameters of acceptable behavior, legally or illegally. Organized crime serves as a model for use of talents, including innovation, in specific social settings and as a means for adapting to exigencies within social, political, and economic environments.
> Organized crime frequently compliments functions of formal social control agencies... it provides protection against other forms of predatory crime. It sets limits on illegal behavior and controls disruptive aspects where the law often fails.
> Organized crime often provides a socially acceptable means for social participation to persons otherwise excluded from community functions. Existing as a massive social network, organized crime is interconnected with numerous segments of a community and provides opportunities for political, social, and economic participation. It services a complementary function to "upperworld" agencies with important forms of support. Finally, it often serves a cohesive function by strengthening social interaction patterns within some families and other social groupings within a community.[17]

In short, organized crime fills a social and economic void resulting from the failures of legitimate public and private institutions. One might even view criminal entrepreneurship as an alternative form of social welfare. Nevertheless, the urban decay characteristic of inner cities and the destitute living conditions in many rural communities suggest that organized crime is a poor substitute for the investment of private industry or public-sponsored revitalization.

Having discussed the effect of organized crime in local communities, let us now turn to an examination of its impact on a global scale.

The "Political-Criminal Nexus"

Organized crime in its many forms is at least partly responsible for over-priced goods, unsafe products, an unclean natural environment, the corruption of public officials at all levels of government, the exploitation of women and children for illicit sex, massive thefts, the evasion of income and excise taxes, the poisoning of men, women, and children with harmful drugs, the proliferation of arms trafficking and the subsequent exacerbation of regional conflicts, capital flight from developing nations, and the outright murder of brave and honest people who oppose all of this. The global economic crisis of the late 1990's is largely the result of large-scale transnational criminal networks. Large chunks of International Monetary Fund (IMF) bail-outs meant to bolster foundering economies are funneled directly into the offshore bank accounts of the criminal elite.[18] The problem is increasingly one of global proportions, and is confounded by the fact that the most significant criminals are high-ranking national and international politicians and businessmen.[19]

In a May 1996 report, Brian Sullivan of the Institute for National Strategic Studies characterized organized crime as an international problem and a growing national security threat for the U.S. In addition to international drug trafficking, Sullivan cited the smuggling of illegal immigrants, murder for hire, terrorism, corruption of public officials, currency and document counterfeiting, arms trafficking, and the pirating of intellectual properties as growing concerns.[20] Worse still, organized crime has reached the highest levels of American government: journalists, government investigators, and academics have linked organized crime and recent U.S. presidents, including the Nixon, Reagan, and Clinton administrations[21] (see chapter five of this volume).

Elsewhere, criminal entrepreneurs are destabilizing new democracies in Eastern Europe and the former Soviet Union, and undermining the sovereignty of weak nations in the Caribbean, Latin America, and West Africa.[22] A number of state failures in Africa including Liberia, Somalia, and most recently Zaire (now Congo) have resulted in the rise of "warlords" who often find themselves isolated and deprived of legitimate capital. Stephen Ellis, the Director of the Africa study center at Leiden University, warns that such conditions create incentives for unstable regimes to develop partnerships with arms traffickers and drug traffickers, or even to blackmail emergency relief organizations distributing food.[23]

Organized crime has become so powerful and generates so much money that national governments have been compromised and in some cases toppled because of it. Around the world the most significant forms of organized crime are characterized best by the term "political-criminal nexus:"

> A political-criminal nexus, the concentration and fusion of political and criminal power, is increasingly reaching the highest levels of many nation-states. Organized crime groups develop collaborative relationships with state authorities to gain access to, and to exploit for their own purposes, the political, economic, and social apparatus of the state. To increase the security of their operations, they also try to develop arrangements with local and/or national political and legal authorities. For their part, state authorities seek cooperative relationships with criminal elements for various reasons such as personal benefits, securing votes, money, or to control enemies.[24]

What has become increasingly obvious is that heads of state and other national leaders are themselves organized criminals. Treating national resources as if they were private treasure chests, "kleptocratic" rulers simply siphon national treasuries into their personal bank accounts. During his thirty year reign in Indonesia President Suharto amassed billions in personal wealth. Both Mobutu in Zaire and Daniel arap Moi of Kenya were born poor but were each worth $30 billion after years in power. Ferdinand and Imelda Marcos amassed $50 billion as rulers in the Phillippines, while peasant born Saddam Hussein of Iraq now has some $18 billion in personal assets. A so-called "corruption barometer" in South Africa claims that $4.5 billion has disappeared since Nelson Mandela took over. Countries like Nigeria, Sudan, Liberia, Pakistan, Sierra Leone, Cambodia, Somalia, Afghanistan, and Rwanda– nations also known, not coincidentally, for mass starvation and genocidal maniacs– are at the top of the Transparency Organization's world corruption index. The president of Brazil, Fernando Collor, and Carlos-Andres, the president of Venezuela, have both embezzled state money. Two former presidents of South Korea are serving time in jail for corruption and violence, and the former president of Mexico, Carlos Salinas, was forced to flee the country when his brother was charged with murder and money laundering in connection with Mexican drug cartels.[25]

The situation is especially bleak in what was the Soviet Union. With the collapse of communism, the weak and unstable former Soviet republics and satellites in Eastern Europe have witnessed the explosion of organized crime. The number of gangs thought to comprise the Russian "mafiya" had grown from 785 in 1990 to more than 8,000 by mid-1996, with more than one hundred of those groups operating in forty-four countries around the world.[26] Since the breakup of the old Soviet Empire, resources once controlled by the state have been plundered by the "nomenklatura" (Communist party elites), bureaucrats, KGB officers, and other organized crime elements, including Russian "mafiya" groups. Much of the process was and is a deliberate attempt by former members of the Communist party to maintain their power and wealth.[27] The privatization of the Soviet State has not led to a democracy or a free market, but was instead thwarted from the start by a political-criminal nexus, led by the nomenklatura. The organized crime that exists today in Russia, Georgia, Ukraine, and Kazakhstan is directed from the very top of the political leadership. Capital flight from Russia is endemic, with criminal elites laundering money into offshore accounts to the tune of $1.5 to $3 billion per month.[28] Most banks in Russia are almost entirely unregulated, and the Russian Institute for Banking and Financial Managers estimates that 70-80% of the private banks in Russia are owned or controlled by organized criminals.[29] It is no surprise that the region has become a global money laundering center.[30] Oleksandr Razumkov, former presidential economic advisor and expert at the Ukrainian Economic and Political Research Centre, has stated that the "shadow economy" in Ukraine had grown to 60% of the Gross Domestic Product in 1996.[31] Authorities estimate that about 40% of the entire Russian economy is linked to organized crime.[32]

Drug networks in Latin America control entire countries.[33] In Colombia, drug traffickers killed 1,000 public officials, over sixty justices including twelve Supreme Court judges, dozens of journalists, three presidential candidates, and more than 3,000 policemen and soldiers over an eight year period in the 1980's.[34] On the other hand, officials who "played ball" were rewarded well– computer records indicate that more than 2,800 politicians, judges, soldiers, journalists, and sportsmen were on the payroll of the Cali drug trafficking organization. The drug cartels had become so prosperous by the mid-80's that drug lords offered to pay off Colombia's $13 billion national debt if they were not extradited to the U.S.[35] Corruption and carnage have continued into the 1990's. According to Ernesto Samper's former campaign manager and Minister of Defense, the current president of Colombia accepted millions in campaign donations from drug traffickers.[36] In addition to political corruption and the murder of thousands of people, the influence of drug dollars has led to a re-valuation of the local currency, which has in turn resulted in the decline of Columbia's traditional industries. Drug trafficking has led to a climate of violence that has discouraged foreign investment, encouraged speculative and dangerous investments, and increased the overall costs of the business sector by forcing it to invest too heavily in securities.[37] In the 1980's and 1990's cocaine surpassed coffee as an earner of foreign exchange in Colombia. Meanwhile, the cartels are diversifying into opium cultivation and heroin refinement. The DEA estimates that the money flowing to the drug cartels is now close to $30 billion a year.[38]

In Japan, the debt crisis of the late 1990's is largely due to the influence of the Yakuza (a network of some 2,500 organized crime groups), which have refused to make payments on billions in overdue loans. In 1994, the manager of the Sumitomo Bank in Nagoya attempted to collect on a Yakuza loan, and was subsequently executed in his home– the message to the Japanese banking community was no doubt unmistakable. Most of Japan's unretrievable loans (close to $1 trillion) are in fact owned by the Yakuza, who have used the money to purchase real estate and move in on the stock market.[39] In 1997 two Japanese professors, Harnhiro Fukui and Shigeko N. Fukai described their country as "a haven for salaried thieves and crooks." It is said that in Japan, "fixing behind the scenes takes the place of messy parliamentary procedures."[40]

While the participation of government officials in criminal networks no doubt varies from country to country, the problem has been especially visible in Italy. While the "mafia" in Italy was originally merely a fragmented rural response to the power vacuum in Sicily resulting from the demise of feudalism, organized crime in Italy has grown to include several large criminal organizations (most notably the Sicilian Mafia or Cosa Nostra, the Calabrian N'drangheta, and the Neopolitan Camorra) and a network of criminals that have included the most powerful officials in Italian government. The most important party in Italian politics, the Christian Democratic Party, was founded in part by Giulio Andriotti, who has been perhaps the most influential man in Italian politics over the last fifty years (Andriotti has been referred to by the Italian mafia as "uncle"). Andriotti, who "served his country" as premier and prime minister on numerous occasions, has been implicated as a part of organized crime by at least eight different informants and his own personal diary. Through one time Italian Supreme Court Justice Carrado Carnevale, Andriotti fixed or reduced over 400 mafia convictions. Salvatore Lima, a close associate of Andriotti's and Sicily's one time Christian Democratic leader and representative to the European Parliament, has been linked to Stefano Bontade, Cosa Nostra's "capo di tutti capo" (boss of bosses). Lima was himself inducted into the Matteo Citardo crime family as a "Man of Honor." In late 1994 Gioacchion Pennino, former Palermo City Councillor and self-confessed Cosa Nostra member, told investigators that the ruling Christian Democrats in Sicily were practically a "family of the mafia."[41]

The Socialist Party of Italy has also been deeply enmeshed with organized crime in complex webs of corruption involving the pinnacle of Italian politics and commerce. Bettino Craxi, Socialist Party leader and Italian Prime Minister from 1983-1987, was forced to resign amid allegations of political corruption. Silvio Larini, a close friend of Craxi's, revealed that 4.9 million pounds had been channeled to the Socialist party by Roberto Calvi. Calvi, a banker for the Vatican, transferred the money on behalf of P2 grandmaster Liccio Gelli (P2 is a masonic lodge linked to the mafia). The money was a payment in thanks for a 50 million pound loan from the Socialist state-controlled energy conglomerate ENI (which supplied half of Italy's energy with an annual turnover in the neighborhood of 20 billion pounds) to the Banco Ambrosiano, a P2/mafia/Vatican entangled financial institution which eventually collapsed amid frauds of tremendous proportions (the ENI loan allowed the corrupt bank to stay afloat for several additional years). The largest bribery scandal in Italy to date was a 62 million pound payoff involving an attempted buy-out of ENI, with the money going to both the Christian Democrats and the Socialists. The president of ENI, Gabriele Cagliari, was arrested in 1993 and suffocated himself in his prison cell. These massive scandals led to the collapse of Italy's First Republic. Silvio Berlusconi, Italy's first premier of the Second Republic, resigned in 1994 when told he was under investigation for official corruption. Perhaps Palermo mayor Leoluca Orlando sums up the situation in Italy best: "For many years Italy didn't have a democratic government. Crime ran it."[42]

Transnational Criminal Enterprises

In a speech opening a conference on international organized crime in Naples in 1994, United Nations Secretary General Boutros Boutros Ghali noted that international crime gangs are prominently involved in not only narcotics trafficking, but also the worldwide sex trade, arms trafficking, money laundering, the traffic in human organs, and perhaps most frightening, the smuggling of nuclear materials and technology.[43] U.S. Representative Bill McCollum did not exaggerate when he spoke of the threat of international criminal networks in a 1996 hearing of the House Subcommittee on Crime:

> ...the dimensions and capacity for evil of global criminals boggles the mind. The great wealth they accumulate allows them to use technology, violence, and corruption to thwart law enforcement. Moreover, these criminals threaten emerging democracies and economic institutions throughout the world and pose a significant challenge to America's national security.[44]

International crime networks are now pooling their resources and developing "strategic alliances."[45] Drug lords in South America have formed joint ventures with criminal organizations in France and Italy, who have formed alliances with criminal entrepreneurs in Poland and Russia, who have completed the circle by establishing relations with organized criminals back in Latin America. Jamaican "yardies" in England enforce drug rule in England with Kalashnikovs (automatic weapons) provided by the Russian mob. Mobs from Russia, Poland, and Hungary smuggle young boys and girls into Europe to staff that continent's thriving sex market, while Serbian gangs transport young Croatian and Muslim girls (war refugees) to Holland and Germany for the same purpose. German pornographers have established arrangements with Chinese Triads to make child pornography films in Thailand and Sri Lanka, while American crime networks produce and export the same kind of filth to countries throughout the European Union.[46] The Czech police have stated that the Sicilian mafia has signed a deal with the Russian mafia for trafficking in nuclear materials as well as drugs.[47] Alfredo Biondi, the Italian Minister of Justice, has observed that conflict among different criminal organizations in Europe has been noticeably lacking, suggesting a considerable degree of international coordination.[48] Beginning in the late 1980's, international criminals have been convening "summit meetings:"

Italian Mafia members and Colombian drug lords met in Aruba in the late 1980's to follow up on discussions and arrangements made in Spain, some years earlier franchising cocaine distribution and money laundering in Europe. Russian and Italian mafia groups met in Prague in 1992. Now they are said to share ownership in a commercial bank in Yekaterinburg in the Urals. Colombians, Russians, and Italians are rumored to be holding "summit meetings," including one on a yacht off Monte Carlo in July 1993, where Colombian drug traffickers, Chinese Triad members, American La Cosa Nostra (LCN), and Israeli criminals were all reported to be present. The Colombian Cali drug "cartel" is said to have representatives in Hong Kong working with Chinese Triad groups to establish franchises for cocaine distribution in the Pacific rim. Mexican organized crime groups have become the silent and dominant partners over U.S. Outlaw Motorcycle gangs in the methamphetamine and precursor chemicals markets.[49]

Drug Trafficking

While coordinating their efforts on a global scale, organized criminals continue to involve themselves in a broad range of illicit activities. Perhaps the most pervasive of all criminal enterprises is the global narcotics trade, estimated to be a $500 billion a year industry.[50] In the United States, the "war on drugs," in addition to severely eroding civil liberties, has proven to be an unmitigated failure in terms of limiting drug abuse. Success in weakening the Colombian Medellin cocaine cartel has merely provided the impetus for the rise of the Cali cartel as well as Mexican traffickers. Mexicans now control the supply of 70% of the cocaine, 80% of the foreign grown marijuana, and 80% of the raw methamphetamine ingredients consumed in the United States.[51] Meanwhile, the Colombian groups have taken over the U.S. heroin market from Asia, moving a nearly 100% pure product through their previously established Caribbean cocaine routes.[52]

Worldwide the supply of heroin, cocaine, and cannabis continues to increase, precipitating a steady decline in retail prices.[53] The number of countries reporting cannabis seizures increased by a third between 1980 and 1994, while heroin and cocaine during the same time period witnessed the most rapid and consistent diffusion in terms of geography. The reasons for the growth in the international drug trade include the opening of new markets, increased global demand, and technological, socio-economic, and political changes which operate in tandem with the process of "globalization" to foster the industry.[54] Advances in agriculture such as new fertilizers, land management techniques, hydroponics, and selective breeding increase coca, opium poppy, and cannabis yields per hectare. Meanwhile, the increased trade in legal precursor chemicals, improved scientific equipment, new extraction techniques, and chemical product diversification have precipitated the formation of new psychoactive drugs, including the popular MDMA (ecstasy).[55] Socio-economic and political changes such as increases in migration, shipping, aviation, communications, and a general liberalization of trade policies provide cover and new markets for traffickers. Political integration in regions like Eastern Europe and South Africa similarly open up new markets and trafficking routes. The opening of economic and political borders in the European Union, the Central Asian Republics, and the former Soviet satellite countries has resulted in the production and distribution of not only opiates but also all manner of illicit commodities and services. By 1993, the volume of traffic moving between Germany, Austria, the Czech Republic, and Poland had increased by 20%, providing additional cover to smugglers. Free trade agreements also create new (but not unexpected) opportunities for drug traffickers as the increase in licit trade and the subsequent reduction in border checks provides additional cover. In North America, NAFTA "opened the floodgates" for drugs entering the U.S. from Mexico, and facilitated the rise of the Mexican drug cartels.[56]

One of the more disturbing aspects of the drug trade, and one of the factors which promotes drug traffic, is the "unholy alliance" between drug profits and war. Drugs have helped to finance wars, have provided alternative funding for covert operators seeking to avoid accountability, and have even presented solutions to international trade problems. In the 1800's Great Britain fought wars and turned China into a nation of opium addicts as a resolution to the trade imbalance that existed between the two countries.[57] The United States' political agenda of thwarting communism has facilitated world drug production and consumption since the CIA began supporting the Chinese Nationalist Kuomintang army in the 1950's. Front companies for the CIA like the Sea Supply Corporation provided military support for opium growing warlords in the Shan States and transported heroin to Southeast Asian markets. Many U.S. soldiers sent to fight communists in Vietnam became addicted to the same heroin supplied directly or indirectly by U.S. intelligence.[58] The pattern was repeated in the 1980's when the CIA helped to finance Mujahadeen guerillas in Afghanistan[59] and Contra "freedom fighters" in Nicaragua.[60] While thwarting communism to a degree, the legacy of those efforts also include the explosion of opium cultivation and heroin refinement in Southwest Asia, the facilitation of cocaine smuggling in Central America, and millions of additional drug addicts throughout the world.[61]

Arms Trafficking

The traffic in armaments is perhaps the most profitable of organized criminal endeavors, and is intimately linked to the illicit drug trade. The Ninth United Nations Congress on the Prevention of Crime and the Treatment of Offenders stated in a recent report:

> There is abundant evidence that organized crime is involved in the illegal arms trade and subversive activities that tamper with the rule of law in different parts of the world. The weight of the evidence indicates that it contributes to the political turmoil and upheaval occurring throughout the world. Drugs for weapons deals have become common in the world of organized crime, and many ethnic and political conflicts are aggravated by this unholy alliance.[62]

Armaments trafficking is complicated by the fact that the distinction between the legal and illegal supply of arms is not always clear. For example, transactions that may have been legal initially nevertheless circumvent the law because the end user is either a "rogue state that the international community is trying to isolate" or perhaps an ethnic group attempting to circumvent an arms embargo.[63] Worse, quasi-licit and illegal arms trafficking is sometimes sanctioned by nation-states. For example, Great Britain violated its own laws when it allowed Matrix Churchill to sell advanced machine tools to Saddam Hussein prior to the Gulf War and tacitly approved weapons sales to both sides in the Iran-Iraq War that lasted eight years and cost one million lives.[64] The link between the "legitimate" production and distribution of arms and organized crime war profiteers is exemplified by events surrounding the war in Yugoslavia in the early 1990's. In that conflict Croatian Anton Kikas forged alliances with manufacturers of conventional ordnance in South Africa and with a top ranking member of the Russian "mafiya," Aleksandr Kutzin. Kutzin chartered Boeing 707's to fly the convential weaponry to Croatia, and then used the same planes to transport nuclear cargo from former Soviet bloc countries to Zagreb, Yugoslavia.[65] The problem of arms trafficking in Russia is seen as especially severe:

> Weapons, munitions, and other equipment are stolen from storage sites by civilian criminals, often in collusion with military sentries and other service personnel. Facilities are also successfully attacked or breached by criminal groups that neutralize or kill sentries and seize arms... In addition, weapons are sold outright, individually and in lots of varying sizes, by officers and other military personnel stationed in Russia and abroad...[66]

Russian organized crime expert Louise Shelley has noted that a significant illicit trade in military equipment has supported armed conflicts in the former Soviet Republics and elsewhere throughout the world.[67]

Nuclear Theft and Smuggling

If organized crime's involvement in the trafficking of convential ordnance is troubling, then the smuggling of weapons-grade nuclear substances is downright terrifying. Between 1991 and 1995, approximately 440 incidents have been documented where attempts were made to smuggle nuclear materials into Germany,[68] considered to be the "hub of nuclear terrorism."[69] Russian "mafiya" gangs like the Chechens, Ukrainians, Georgians, and Dolgopruadnanskaya are prominet smugglers of nuclear materials. Smugglers also include former Red Army soldiers, former KGB agents, ex-officers of the Stasi (the East German secret service), German-based Russian "mafiya" gangs, the Italian mafia, South African groups, and the Serbian mafia, who transport or attempt to transport nuclear materials out of the former Soviet Republics through Eastern Europe, into Germany, and on to clients in Libya, Iraq, Iran, Algeria, and Pakistan.[70] Fortunately, most of the reported thefts consist of low-grade uranium, cesium-137, strontium-90, and cobalt-60– materials which are environmentally hazardous but cannot be used to make nuclear bombs. Nevertheless, radioactive substances such as these can be used quite effectively be terrorists. Rensselaer Lee has noted the seriousness of the problem:

1) A first and fundamental problem is that incentives and opportunities are rife in former Soviet Union nuclear complexes. Economic hardship creates an atmosphere ripe for diversion.

2) Supply chains and mechanisms to transport such materials over long distances and across international boundaries already are in reality in the former Soviet Union and in the West.

3) Established organized crime groups in Russia have displayed interest in commercial exports of dual-use isotopes– nonfissile materials which are important in the construction of atomic weapons but that are also used in civilian industrial manufacture. International markets for such substances are larger and better established than those for radioactive materials, and criminal penalties for dual-use trafficking are apparently less stringent.

4) The perception that the nuclear trade is dominated by bumbling amateurs may obscure important features of the diversion process. Linkages to organized crime are not necessarily the key issue. The archetypal modern nuclear criminal is more likely to be the chief engineer or chief bookkeeper of a nuclear enterprise or the head of an import-export firm.

5) Russian customs officials believe that the diversion of sensitive

74

materials... has occurred through ostensibly legal channels. In one scenario, a legal shipment of a radioactive isotope might be licensed and invoiced as cobalt-60 or cesium-137, but also contain an undisclosed quantity of HEU or plutonium.

6) An additional problem concerns non-traditional smuggling routes and banking connections. While most stolen nuclear materials still appear to move westward across Eastern Europe and the Baltic states, press reports suggest a growing number of smuggling incidents involving Russia's Southern tier, especially Chechnya, Georgia, Azerbaijan, and Kazakhstan... Borders are porous and customs checks are perfunctory... Reports abound that Turkish banks such as the Bank of Northern Cyprus play an important role in the illicit nuclear trade, financing purchases of dual-use and possibly radioactive materials on behalf of clients in the Islamic world.

7) Another concern is the increased incidence of nuclear theft at submarine bases of the Northern Fleet, where at least six attempted diversions of HEU in the Murmansk-Arkhangelsk area occurred between mid-1993 and early 1996. Targets included uranium fuel storehouses and submarine construction and repair facilities.

8) Recent reports cast doubt on the effectiveness of Russia's efforts against nuclear crime and proliferation. For instance, a reorganization of the MVD and FSB Economic Crimes Department in early 1995 reportedly cut the number of officials assigned to nuclear smuggling investigations... Some Russian officials obviously view counter-smuggling efforts as a low national priority.[71]

In 1994 thirteen hundred pounds of uranium originating in Kazakhstan that was intended for Saddam Hussein was successfully intercepted and is now stored in Tennessee.[72] This incident and hundreds of others like it suggest that the new "global village" may not be far removed from disaster.

Organized Theft– automobiles, art, etc.

In addition to stealing and smuggling nuclear materials, organized theft of more conventional goods is perhaps the most widespread of all criminal endeavors. The National Cargo Security Council has estimated that the losses due to air, ocean, and trucking cargo theft exceeded $30 billion from 1992-94.[73] Researchers have estimated that 90% of the dollar value of all objects which are stolen are swiped by professional burglary and hijacking rings.[74] For example, automobile theft is a multi-billion dollar industry with established international dimensions. Stolen vehicles are moved out of the United States on huge cargo ships for destinations around the world. U.S. officials have been aware of the magnitude of the problem for some time. In 1979 the U.S. Senate Permanent Subcommittee on Investigations held a series of hearings that detailed the nationwide spread of "chop shops," where stolen vehicles are broken down and sold for their parts.[75] More recently, a 1996 Congressional committee heard evidence of Russian criminals operating in the U.S. who export American cars to the Russian republics. Many vehicles are stolen in New York City, driven to Chicago, hidden in containers, and shipped to the former Soviet Union countries where they sell for three times their American value. Other criminal networks commonly export stolen vehicles to Venezuela, Ecuador, the Dominican Republic,[76] and Mexico.[77] In Hong Kong, luxury cars are stolen and transported to China on extremely fast motor boats. The problem is also extensive in some African countries and in Europe, where motor vehicle thefts tripled between 1989 and 1993.[78] A 1997 Chicago Crime Commission Report asserted that "if auto theft was legal, it would be number 50 on the Fortune 500 list."[79]

Art theft is also extremely lucrative, with many opportunities and little chance of getting caught. Formed in 1991, the Arts Loss Register in London immediately compiled a database of 650,000 stolen art objects, to which 2,000 new items are added each month. Moreover, it has been estimated that 40,000 pieces are stolen monthly in Great Britain alone. In Russia and the former Soviet satellites, art galleries are looted and their objects are shipped by the train load to Europe through Warsaw and Budapest. Fifteen thousand art objects valued at $32 million have been listed as stolen from the Czech Republic alone. Serbian forces looted forty-two art galleries, nine archives, and twenty-two libraries in Croatia during 1991 and 1992. Worldwide, the value of paintings and fine art stolen is estimated at over $4 billion annually.[80]

While piracy on the high seas is thought by many to be an anachronism, maritime crime has nevertheless increased dramatically, beginning in the late 1980's. The Strait of Malacca and the Phillip Channel south of Singapore have become especially dangerous for merchant ships, as have many of the waters around Indonesia, Thailand, China, Macao, and Hong Kong.[81] In March 1998, a Pakistani was killed off of Somalia's northeastern coast when his ship was attacked by several boats equipped with machine guns. In Brazil, shipping attacks have occurred in territorial waters and in port. Aside from acts of boarding and robbing, "phantom ships" and container fraud are common forms of maritime crime. Phantom ships sail under faked documents or change their identity while at sea, then sell their cargo to either unknowing or uncaring customers. The International Maritime Bureau has uncovered strong evidence of Chinese syndicate involvement in many maritime frauds.[82] The Regional Piracy Center (RPC), established in Kuala Lumpur, issues daily status reports on the most dangerous shipping areas and acts as a clearinghouse for all reports of piracy. The RPC reports that in the mid-1990's, the number of incidents of piracy increased every year: 92 in 1994, 170 in 1995, 228 in 1996, and 252 in 1997.[83]

Organized crooks have in no way limited themselves in what they will steal. In 1970 the National Crime Information Center estimated that at least $227 million in U.S. Government and private securities were stolen in that year. Cosa Nostra figures like Boston's Vincent Teresa obtained securities through inside operators at banks or brokerage houses, or by theft of registered mail at airports, and disposed of them through trusted associates like stockbrokers, attorneys, and other individuals who had the connections and the know-how to sell them or use them as collateral in financial transactions.[84] In 1971, a professional fence of stolen securities testified before a Congressional subcommittee that he had personally handled $50 million in stolen financial instruments.[85]

In the 1990's computer-related thefts have become increasingly common.

Commercial activity conducted over the Internet and the prodigious amount of sensitive information on the web have created new opportunities for thieves who swipe credit card numbers, social security numbers, and entire personal identities.[86] Software piracy and the theft of computers and computer components is highly profitable. Computers and components are in demand, are easy to sell, maintain a high black market value (central processing units are worth more money by weight than drugs), and are almost untraceable.[87] Officials have said that CPUs manufactured by the Intel Corporation are used as currency in certain parts of Mexico.[88]

The Traffic in Human Beings

Trafficking in people has several transnational criminal dimensions, including illegal migrations, the smuggling of women and children for the purposes of prostitution and pornography, and the trade in human body organs. Authorities believe that criminal organizations are smuggling as many as one million people a year from poor to wealthier nations– a business estimated to yield $3.5 billion annually.[89] Although the smuggling of Chinese people to Western countries like the United States has received the most attention[90] (since January 1993, the U.S. Coast Guard has intercepted eleven different ships carrying some 2,100 illegal Chinese),[91] some authorities estimate that Chinese migrants comprise only 20% of those in a global pipeline that stretches from China, India, Iraq, Iran, Pakistan, Romania, Sri Lanka, the Sudan, and on to Latin American countries and recipient countries in Europe as well as the United States. The United Nations believe that "those in transit include 60,000 Chinese in Moscow, 80,000 or more Asians, Africans, and people from the Middle East in Romania, and significant numbers in staging areas such as Guatemala, the Netherlands, and Spain."[92] Standard fees for different nationalities range from a couple hundred dollars for Central Americans up to $40,000 for Chinese. Criminal organizations which specialize in illegal immigrations operate with near impunity, since the practice is a crime in only a few recipient countries.

Moreover, the business of alien smuggling is made possible by "staggering levels of official corruption." Immigration officials in Belize, Guatemala, the Dominican Republic, and the United States have been implicated in the migrant smuggling trade.[93]

Trafficking in women and children for the purpose of prostitution is closely aligned with illegal migration networks. In fact, an insidious relationship exists between the demand for smuggling services and the need for laborers in the commercial sex industry. While many migrants are transferred to foreign lands with the full knowledge that they are to work as prostitutes, other highly vulnerable people indebted to smugglers are forced into sexual slavery. Moreover, the smuggling/prostitution industry "knows no geographic boundaries." Since the early 1990's there has been considerable growth in the trafficking of women from Eastern Europe to Western Europe, where as many as 500,000 foreign women work as prostitutes. To supply the prostitution industry, women from Eastern Europe and the former Soviet bloc are smuggled to the United States, Nigerians and Albanians are shipped to Italy, Thai women are moved illegally to Japan, and Dominican women are smuggled and work as prostitutes in Austria, Curacao, Germany, Greece, Haiti, Italy, the Netherlands, Panama, Puerto Rico, Spain, Switzerland, and Venezuela. One of the more significant trafficking routes is from Ukraine to Israel. The importance of prostitution to organized crime is exemplified in a study conducted by three Tai economists, who report that the sex trade generates $20 billion a year in Thailand alone (in that country, four times as much as drug sales).[94]

The demand for child prostitutes, driven by the growth in global tourism, fear of AIDS, and the exploitation of computer networks by pedophiles has been met by transnational criminal networks who exploit migrants and purchase children from desperate and impoverished parents. The United Nations reported in 1996 that child prostitution is very profitable and involves "highly organized syndicated networks" and the collusion of police and government officials. Since there is a global demand for child prostitutes, no part of the world is free of this affliction. Estimates of the number of children used for the purpose of commercial sex include 200,000 in Thailand, 650,000 in the Phillippines, 400,000 in India, 300,000 in the United States, and 2,000,000 in Brazil. The problem is present and growing in Benin, Nigeria, Senegal, Sudan, Kenya, Ghana, the Ivory Coast, Burkina Faso, Argentina, Bolivia, Chile, Colombia, Ecuador, Mexico, Peru, Nepal, Bangladesh, Sri Lanka, etc.[95] Children as young as five years old have been found prostituted in Sicily.[96]

The Traffic in Human Organs

The world is a place such that, if one looks in the right place and has money, anything can be purchased, including body parts. Children around the world are purchased or kidnapped, if not for sex, then for the high price their organs can fetch on the black market. The export of organs utilizing false documents and organ trafficking has been confirmed in Argentina, Brazil, Honduras, Mexico, and Peru, in most cases with Swiss, German, and Italian buyers. In February 1992, Argentina's Minister of Health announced that blood and organs had been removed from the inmates of a mental hospital.[97] In other cases doctors fabricated brain scans, declared patients brain dead, and then removed their corneas.[98] From 1989 to 1992, 4,000 children were shipped from Brazil to Italy, ostensibly for adoption; however, only 1,000 of those children have been accounted for in Italy. Authorities report that the Neopolitan Camorra places Mexican, Thai, and European children into clandestine clinics to have organs removed, and in Honduras, handicapped children are legally adopted and then sold like "spare parts." A Guatemalan police official has claimed that children in that country are sold to Americans as organ donors for $20,000. In Europe, organized criminals own clinics and hospitals through layers of shell companies and frontmen, making their access to human organs that much easier.[99] The problem may be especially severe in the Russian Federation:

> ...there are as many as 4,000 unclaimed bodies in Moscow morgues. One investigative report found one company that had extracted 700 major organs, kidneys, hearts and lungs, over 1,400 liver sections,

80

18,000 thymus organs, 2,000 eyes and over 3,000 pairs of testicles. Moreover, one Moscow forensic detective saw these activities as being firmly under the control of organized crime, which he suggested had "elaborate criminal structures for kidnapping children and adults, using their organs for transplants and for medical experiments.[100]

A similar market exists for fetal tissue, sought after for its research value. It has been reported that unborn fetuses are killed and lifted from their unsuspecting (or paid) mothers and then sold on the black market.[101]

Ecocrime

Ecocrime, or ecological crime, is "organized criminal activity that results in major harm to the environment."[102] The illegal disposal of hazardous wastes by organized crime groups has been well documented.[103] Both the export of toxic wastes to developing countries and a thriving black market in chlorofluorocarbons (CFCs) have emerged in the 1980's and 1990's. The combination of liberalized international trade policies and the rising cost of legal disposal in rich industrialized nations has spawned a burgeoning North to South trade in hazardous wastes, much of which is clandestine. In some cases international environmental treaties meant to protect the environment have instead worsened the problem. Initiatives like the Basel Convention failed to stop the export of toxins to the third world, but did precipitate a "moderate" black market in waste exports. In direct response to the Montreal Protocol's production and consumption control rules, the illegal trade in CFCs has exploded. Loss of tax revenue generated swift action in the United States, where an interagency task force confiscated 500 tons of illegal CFCs and recovered $40 million in lost tax revenues in its first year (1994). European Union countries, also a recipient of black market CFCs, have been slower to act.[104]

The illegal trade in exotic plants and animals is a huge global industry. In 1996 it was estimated that between $10 and $20 billion in exotic life forms were traded illegally, with the United States leading the list of purchasers. Fish and Wildlife officer Tom Striegler explained the lure: "a padded vest studded with 40 eggs from Australia's endangered black palm cockatoo, each worth $10,000, is far easier to smuggle than an equal-valued cache of cocaine, simply because custom officials aren't looking for cockatoo eggs." Snakes and tortoises are especially popular because of their ability to survive long trips, but the trade is no way limited, and includes all manner of species living and dead: Brazilian monkeys, Australian birds, the horns of endangered black rhinos, the bones of tigers, elephant tusks, and exotic skins used for designer clothing.[105] Scientists have said that the decimation of animals and their habitat could lead to the collapse of entire ecosystems.

The cultivation of illicit crops like coca and the opium poppy has serious environmental consequences, including deforestation and soil and water pollution. Slash and burn techniques for clearing land contribute to deforestation as well as soil erosion. In Peru, increased coca cultivation in the Upper Huallaga Valley is responsible for the stripping of one million hectares of tropical forest resources. Refiners of heroin and cocaine dump toxic chemicals and other waste by-products into countless streams and rivers, or else they bury it in the ground, contaminating the soil and groundwater sources. Each year in Colombia, 20 million liters of ethyl ether, acetone, ammonia, sulphuric acid, and hydrochloric acid used to produce cocaine are dumped from jungle laboratories into the headwaters of the Amazon and Orinoco rivers. Again, the effects can be devastating. In the Huallaga Basin, few fish are left, and many of those remaining are unfit for consumption. In addition to exterminating or mutating entire species, agro-chemicals decrease the quality of potable water and present a substantial health threat to native populations.[106]

Banks and Money Laundering

In no area is organized crime's wealth and growing sophistication more evident than in the realm of money laundering, a process whereby ill-gained profits are "washed," or made to look legal. In addition to disguising the source of illicit revenue, money laundering efforts involve, quite simply, the movement or conversion of money so that it is beyond the reach of law enforcement (a process intimately linked to creative forms of tax evasion).[107] Concealing the origins of dirty money and transferring money beyond the reach of legitimate authorities is also a process which exemplifies the symbiotic relationships among "underworld" and "upperworld" figures. Money laundering blurs if not totally eliminates the distinction between organized and white-collar crime, as the most important players in laundering schemes are bankers, accountants, tax lawyers, and public officials.[108] Criminal entrepreneurs like narcotics traffickers typically employ professional money brokers, who "differ little from corporate money managers."[109] Too often officials in tax-haven countries like Antigua, the Cayman Islands, Aruba, Switzerland, the Bahamas, Panama, Hong Kong, Montserratt, and Luxembourg (to name a few) welcome the absorption of dirty money into their banking systems, where the funds are hidden from investigators by bank secrecy laws.[110]

Techniques for laundering money range from the simple to the very complex. One of the most common forms of money laundering is the ownership of an legitimate business– drug dealers, professional gamblers, and extortionists use restaurants, food delivery services, and other cash businesses as a front and report their illegal profits as legal income. Casinos, largely unregulated in many countries, are commonly used to launder money because of the opportunity for large cash transactions which leave no paper trail.[111] A variety of other non-bank financial institutions are often used, including "foreign currency exchanges, check-cashing services, insurers, mortgagors, brokers, importers, exporters, trading companies, gold and precious metal dealers, casinos, express delivery services and other money movers of varying degrees of sophistication and capability."[112] Other criminals use import-export companies which invoice for non-existent purchases,[113] or incorporate strings of "shell companies," non-entities which produce no good or service, but which nevertheless provide crooks with an apparent source of legal revenue. Another relatively simple method is called the "loan-back," where a criminal deposits funds in a bank and is then "loaned" the money back– of course the phoney loan is never repaid, and the complicit banker merely "cooks the books." Even with the use of financial specialists and the development of more sophisticated methods, simply smuggling large amounts of bulk cash into countries with lenient banking regulations remains quite common.[114]

The Spence money laundering network in New York is illustrative of the scope and complexity of some money laundering schemes:

> It involved a network of 24 people including the honorary consul-general for Bulgaria, a New York city police officer, 2 lawyers, a stockbroker, an assistant bank manager in Citibank, 2 rabbis, a firefighter, and 2 banks in Zurich. A law firm provided the overall guidance for the laundering effort while both a trucking business and a beer distributorship were used as cover. The Bulgarian diplomat, the firefighter and the rabbi acted as couriers picking up drug trafficking proceeds in hotel rooms and parking lots, while money was also transported by Federal Express to a New York trucking business. The two lawyers subsequently placed the money into bank accounts with the assistance of a Citibank assistant manager. The money was then wired to banks in Europe including a private bank in Switzerland, at which two bankers ensured that it was remitted to accounts designated by drug traffickers. During 1993 and 1994 a sum of between $70 million and $100 million was laundered by the group.[115]

The methods for laundering money appear to be limited only by opportunity and the ingenuity of the crooks involved. Moreover, recent trends in money laundering do not bode well for law enforcement. New banking practices like "direct access banking" and the use of "cybercurrency" (micro-chip-based electronic money for financial transactions, via smart cards and the Internet) are rapidly emerging and have the potential to facilitate global money laundering.[116] In addition, Internet-based businesses make a perfect front for moving money around the world in phony transactions. The ability to transfer funds globally with great velocity and without end creates jurisdictional problems and makes it extremely difficult if not impossible for authorities to trace the flow of cash, even if they did have the resources to pursue a tenth of the largest transactions. Phil Williams of the Ridgway Center for International Security Studies has concluded that "the global financial system provides many more opportunities than law enforcement can ever hope to forestall or block."[117]

Regulators, money laundering investigators, and international policy making bodies like FATF[118] are facing profound challenges from a banking world which not only knows no geographic horizons and is open 24 hours a day, but is increasingly inter-connected, as large multinational banks extend their reach not only through branch and subsidiary networks but through correspondent relationships that cross the globe.[119]

Successful intervention is dependent on the cooperation of the international banking community. Even when bankers are immune from the huge fees for service offered by criminal entrepreneurs, the principle of "knowing your customer" is simply insufficient when the source of funds is hidden by multiple layers even before placement in the financial system occurs. Compounding the problem is alternative or "underground" banking systems such as the "hawala" in India and Pakistan and the "chit system" in China. Parallel illicit banking networks based on trust, family ties, gang affiliations, and local social structures are expedient, leave little trail for investigators, and virtually guarantee anonymity through the threat of retributive violence.[120]

Banks and other financial institutions are the linchpin which ensures the wheels of international organized crime continue to turn. The repatriation and reinvestment of organize crime profits is dependent on powerful world bankers in collusion with a shady assortment of lawyers, politicians, direct providers of illegal goods and services, power brokers, and members of the intelligence community.

Conclusion

The preceding description of criminal enterprises is in no way meant to be a comprehensive account– such a task would require many volumes. Counterfeiting (currency, art objects, furniture, etc.), industrial racketeering and extortion, kidnapping, arson and related insurance frauds, intellectual theft and software piracy, cattle rustling, illegal gambling, loansharking, trafficking in precious metals and diamonds, and the production of false documents are just a few activities not included in the previous discussion, but which are, nevertheless, significant criminal enterprises.

The world has witnessed monumental events since the late 1980's, not the least of which was the collapse of the Soviet empire. The vacuum left in its place was quickly exploited by organized criminals around the world, exemplifying one of the few features of organized crime which is truly axiomatic– crime manifests itself and is driven by opportunity. The liberalization of national markets and movements toward a "global economy" have presented opportunities for organized crime to thrive on a global scale. And while global crime syndicates are coordinating their ventures as never before, international cooperation in law enforcement has been slow to develop.

As we near the end of Part I of this volume, a brief recap is in order. First, it is important to recognize that organized crime thrives in part because ordinary citizens from around the world demand the goods and services it provides. Of course, criminal entrepreneurs are only too happy to exploit this demand by turning millions of people into drug addicts, debtors, and whoremongers. The second reason that organized crime flourishes is because the money generated is so great that public officials, law enforcers, and business executives are easily seduced into becoming participants and coordinators of criminal enterprises. The active participation and complicity of societal elites in criminal networks perpetuates and ensures the continuance of large-scale organized crime.

A comprehensive view of organized crime indicates that while important, the issue of ethnicity has been exaggerated and is not central to understanding coordinated criminal entrepreneurship. Rather, the most important feature of organized crime is the patron-client-like relationships which develop among "under-world" functionaries and so-called "legitimate society." Also, while legal, economic, and social realities indicate that criminal networks are far less formal or corporate-like than has been suggested in the past, this observation apparently does not preclude the possibility of significant and far-reaching criminal enterprises. While debate continues about the exact structure and functioning of criminal enterprises, organized crime experts agree that the threat of organized crime is not diminishing, and is a problem of global concern.

Endnotes

[1]William Chambliss (1988). "Vice, Corruption, Bureaucracy, and Power," in Criminal Justice: Law and Politics, ed. George F. Cole. Pacific Grove, CA: Brooks/Cole.

[2]Rensselaer Lee (1989). The White Labyrinth. New Brunswick, NJ: Transaction; Alfred McCoy (1972). The Politics of Heroin in Southeast Asia. New York: Harper and Row.

[3]Ivan Light (1977). "Numbers Gambling Among Blacks: A Financial Institution," American Sociological Review, Vol. 42, December: 892-904; Harold Lasswell and Jeremiah McKenna (1972). The Impact of Organized Crime on an Inner City Community. New York: The Policy Sciences Center.

[4]Annelise Anderson (1979). The Business of Organized Crime: A Cosa Nostra Family. Stanford, CA: Hoover Institution Press.

[5]Alan A. Block (1983). East Side-West Side: Organizing Crime in New York, 1930-1950. New Brunswick, NJ: Transaction. William Chambliss (1978). On the Take: From Petty Crooks to Presidents. Bloomington: Indiana University Press; Light, 1977.

[6]Block, 1983.

[7]Lasswell and McKenna, 1972. The researchers defined the "social process" as "the seamless web of life" which is comprised of eight "value categories." According to the researchers, the value categories that make up the social process of communities are power, wealth, enlightenment, well-being, skill, affection, respect, and rectitude. People associated with a given community seek to maximize their share of these "values."

[8]Lasswell and McKenna, 72:168.

[9]Lasswell and Mckenna, 72:161.

[10]Lasswell and McKenna, 1972.

[11]Michael D. Lyman and Gary W. Potter (1997). Organized Crime. Upper Saddle River, NJ: Prentice-Hall.

88

[12]Gary W. Potter and Larry K. Gaines (1992). "Country Comfort: Vice and Corruption in Rural Settings," Journal of Contemporary Criminal Justice, Vol. 8, No. 1. pp. 36-61.

[13]Stephen Handelman (1995). Comrade Criminal: Russia's New Mafiya. New Haven: Yale University Press.

[14]Lasswell and McKenna, 1972.

[15]Light, 1977.

[16]Lyman and Potter, 1997.

[17]Lyman and Potter, 97:88-89.

[18]Brian Freemantle (1995). The Octopus: Europe in the Grip of Organized Crime. London: Orion.

[19]Ibid.

[20]Ibid.

[21]Lyman and Potter, 1997.

[22]Brian Sullivan (1996). "International Organized Crime: A Growing National Security Threat." Institute for National Strategic Studies, No. 74, May.

[23]Ibid.

[24]Trends in Organized Crime, "Political Criminal Nexus," Vol. 3, No. 1, Fall 1997. p. 4.

[25]David Pryce-Jones (1997). "Corruption Rules the World." The American Spectator, December, pp. 22-25.

[26]Yuriy A. Voronin (1997). "The Emerging Criminal State: Economic and Political Aspects of Organized Crime," in Russian Organized Crime, Phil Williams (ed.). London: Frank Cass; Guy Dunn (1997). "Major Mafia Gangs in Russia," in Russian Organized Crime, Phil Williams (ed.). London: Frank Cass.

[27]Richard L. Palmer (1997). "The New Russian Oligarchy: the Nomenclature, the KGB and the Mafiya." Paper presented to the Working Group on Organized Crime, National Strategy Information Center, Washington D.C., May 1997– excerpted in Trends in Organized Crime, Vol. 3, No. 1, pp. 8-14.

[28]Timothy M. Burlingame (1997). "Criminal Activity in the Russian Banking System," Transnational Organized Crime, Vol. 3, No. 3, pp. 46-72.

[29]Ibid.

[30]Ibid.

[31]Taras Kuzio (1997). "Crime Still Ukraine's Greatest Enemy," Jane's Intelligence Review, Vol. 9, No. 1, January 1997: 10-13– excerpted in Trends in Organized Crime, Vol. 3, No. 1, pp. 27-30.

[32]Louise I. Shelley (1997). "The Price Tag of Russia's Organized Crime, " Transition, Vol. 8, No. 1. Feb. 1997: 7-8-- excerpted in Trends in Organized Crime, Vol. 3, No. 1, pp. 24-26.

[33]Rensselaer W. Lee III (1989). The White Labyrinth. New Brunswick, NJ: Transaction.

[34]Alex P. Schmid (1996). "Links Between Transnational Organized Crime and Terrorist Crimes," Transnational Organized Crime, Vol. 2, No. 4, pp. 41-81.

[35]Robert J. Kelly (1986). Organized Crime: A Global Perspective. Totowa, NJ: Rowman and Littlefield.

[36]Ibid.

[37]Schmid, 1996.

[38]Ibid.

[39]Ibid.

[40]Pryce-Jones, 1997.

[41]Freemantle, 1995.

[42]Ibid.

90

[43]Freemantle, 1995.

[44]The Growing Threat of International Organized Crime (1996).   House of Representatives Subcommittee on Crime, Committee on the Judiciary. Washington, D.C.: U.S. Government Printing Office. p. 2.

[45]Phil Williams and Ernesto U. Savona (1996).   The United Nations and Transnational Organized Crime. London: Frank Cass.

[46]Freemantle, 1995.

[47]Schmid, 1996.

[48]Ibid.

[49]Peter Lupsha (1996). "Transnational Organized Crime versus the Nation-State," Transnational Organized Crime, Vol. 2, No. 1., pp. 21-48.

[50]Pryce-Jones, 1997.

[51]Chris Eskridge and Brandon Paeper (1998). "The Mexican Cartels: A Challenge for the 21st Century," Criminal Organizations, Vol. 12, No.1&2, pp. 5-15.

[52]Lyman and Potter, 1997.

[53]Douglas Keh and Graham Farrell (1997).   "Trafficking Drugs in the Global Village," Transnational Organized Crime, Vol. 3, No.2, pp. 90-110.

[54]Ibid.

[55]Ibid.

[56]Keh and Farrell, 1997; Eskridge and Paeper, 1998.

[57]Alfred W. McCoy (1992).   "Heroin as a Global Commodity: A History of Southeast Asia's Opium Trade," in War on Drugs, Alan A. Block and Alfred W. McCoy (eds.). Boulder, CO: Westview Press.

[58]Ibid.

[59]Lawrence Lifschultz (1992). "Pakistan: The Empire of Heroin," in War on Drugs, Alan A. Block and Alfred W. McCoy (eds.). Bouder, CO: Westview Press.

[60]Peter Dale Scott (1992). "Honduras, the Contra Support Network, and Cocaine: How the U.S. Government Has Augmented America's Drug Crisis," in War on Drugs, Alan A. Block and Alfred W. McCoy (eds.). Boulder, CO: Westview Press.

[61]Lifschultz, 1992; Scott, 1992.

[62]Phil Williams (1996). "Problems and Dangers Posed by Organized Transnational Crime in the Various Regions of the World," in The United Nations and Transnational Organized Crime, Phil Williams and Ernesto U. Savona (eds.). London: Frank Cass. p. 23.

[63]Ibid.

[64]Freemantle, 1995.

[65]Ibid.

[66]Graham H. Turbiville (1997). "Weapons Proliferation and Organized Crime: The Russian Military and Security Force Dimension," Occasional Paper, U.S. Air Force Institute for National Security Studies (INSS), Colorado Springs, Colorado, 1996: 1-29– excerpted in Trends in Organized Crime, Vol. 3, No. 3, pp. 18-22.

[67]Joseph Albini, et. al. (1995). "Russian Organized Crime: Its History, Structure and Function," Journal of Contemporary Criminal Justice, Vol. 11, No. 4, pp. 213-243.

[68]Ibid.

[69]Freemantle, 1995.

[70]Ibid.

[71]Rensselaer Lee (1996). "Recent Trends in Nuclear Smuggling," Transnational Organized Crime, Vol. 2, No. 4, pp. 109-121.

[72]Albini et. al., 1995.

[73]Julie Salzano and Stephen W. Hartman (1998). "Cargo Crime," Transnational Organized Crime, Vol. 3, No. 1, p. 20.

[74]Ibid.

[75]Profile of Organized Crime: Mid-Atlantic Region (1983). Permanent Subcommittee on Investigations of the Committee on Governmental Affairs, the

92

United States Senate, 98th Congress, First Session. Washington D.C.: U.S. Government Printing Office.

[76]The Threat from Russian Organized Crime (1996). Hearing before the Committee on International Relations, House of Representatives, 104th Congress, 2nd session. Washington D.C.: U.S. Government Printing Office.

[77]Roslava Resendiz (1998). "International Auto Theft: An Exploratory Research of Organization and Organized Crime on the U.S./Mexico Border," Criminal Organizations, Vol. 12, No. 1&2, pp. 25-30.

[78]Williams and Savona, 96:28.

[79]"The Changing Faces of Organized Crime," Crime and Justice International: Worldwide News and Trends, Vol. 13, No. 10., Nov. 1997, p.22.

[80]Freemantle, 1995.

[81]"Maritime Crime," Trends in Organized Crime, Vol. 3, No. 4, Summer 1998, pp. 68-71.

[82]Ibid.

[83]Ibid.

[84]Humbert Nelli (1976). The Business of Crime: Italians and Syndicate Crime in the United States. New York: Oxford University Press; Matthew G. Yeager (1973). "The Gangster as White Collar Criminal: Organized Crime and Stolen Securities," in The Crime Society, Francis Ianni (ed.) New York: New American Library.

[85]The Pennsylvania Crime Commission (1980). A Decade of Change. St. David's, PA: Commonwealth of Pennsylvania.

[86]John E. Conklin (1998). Criminology, 6th ed. Needham Heights, MA: Allyn and Bacon.

[87]Salzano and Hartman, 1998.

[88]Ibid.

[89]Williams and Savona, 1996.

[90]See Zheng Wang (1996). "Ocean-Going Smuggling of Illegal Chinese Immigrants:

Operations, Causation and Policy Implications," Transnational Organized Crime, Vol. 2, No. 1, pp. 49-65.

[91]Jonathan M. Winer (1997). "Alien Smuggling: Elements of the Problem and the U.S. Response," Transnational Organized Crime, Vol. 3, No. 1, pp. 50-58.

[92]Williams and Savona, 1996; Winer, 1997.

[93]Winer, 1997.

[94]"Trafficking in Women and Children," Trends in Organized Crime, Vol. 3, No. 4, pp. 3-68.

[95]Ibid.

[96]Ibid.

[97]Freemantle, 1995.

[98]Williams and Savona, 1996.

[99]Freemantle, 1995.

[100]Williams and Savona, 96:27.

[101]Freemantle, 1995.

[102]"Organized Crime and the Environment," Trends in Organized Crime, Vol. 3, No. 2, pp. 4-5.

[103]Alan A. Block and Frank R. Scarpitti (1985). Poisoning for Profit: the Mafia and Toxic Waste Disposal in America. New York: William Morrow; Alan A. Block (1991). "Organized Crime and Toxic Waste: An Overview," in Space, Time, and Organized Crime, New Brunswick, NJ: Transaction, pp. 203-230; Maurice D. Hinchey (1991). "Criminal Infiltration of the Toxic and Solid Waste Disposal Industries in New York State," a preliminary report to the New York State Assembly Standing Committee on Environmental Conservation and the New York State Legislature, September 13, 1984, in The Business of Crime: A Documentary Study of Organized Crime in the American Economy, Alan A. Block (ed.). pp. 175-196. Boulder, CO: Westview; Organized Crime Links to the Waste Disposal Industry (1981). Subcommittee on Oversight and Investigations of the Committee on Energy and Commerce, House of Representatives, 97th Congress, First Session. Washington D.C.: U.S. Government Printing Office.

94

[104]Jennifer Clapp (1997). "The Illicit Trade in Hazardous Wastes and CFCs: International Responses to Environmental Bads." Paper prepared for SSRC-MacArthur Workshop on "Liberal Internationalism, the State, and the Illicit World Economy," Cornell University, Ithaca, New York, November 8-10, 1996: 1-42– excerpted in Trends in Organized Crime, Vol. 3, No. 2, pp. 14-18.

[105]Donovan Webster (1997). "The Looting and Smuggling and Fencing and Hoarding of Impossibly Precious, Feathered, and Scaly Wild Things," The New York Times Magazine, Section 6, Feb. 16, 1997: 26-33– excerpted in Trends in Organized Crime, Vol. 3, No. 2, pp. 9-10.

[106]United Nations International Drug Control Programme, World Drug Report, New York: Oxford Unviversity Press, 1997: 1-332– excerpted in Trends in Organized Crime, Vol. 3, No. 2, pp. 12-13.

[107]Phil Williams (1997). "Money Laundering," Criminal Organizations, Vol. 10, No. 4, pp. 18-27.

[108]Ibid.

[109]Ernesto Savona (1996). "European Money Trails," Transnational Organized Crime, Vol. 2, No. 4, pp. 1-20; Williams, 1997.

[110]Alan A. Block (1991). Masters of Paradise. New Brunswick, NJ: Transaction.

[111]Williams, 1997.

[112]Ibid.

[113]Ibid.

[114]Ibid.

[115]Williams, 97:20.

[116]"Financial Crimes and Money Laundering," The International Control Strategy Report, released by the Bureau for International Narcotics and Law Enforcement Affairs, U.S. Department of State in March 1997– excerpted in Transnational Organized Crime, Vol. 3, No. 1, pp. 87-113; Savona, 1996; Williams, 1997.

[117]Williams, 97:18.

[118]The G-7 Financial Action Task Force issued forty money laundering recommendations in April 1990.

[119]International Control Strategy Report, 96:95.

[120]Williams, 1997.

Chapter 4

Organized Crime in America: 1680-1945

A comprehensive history of organized crime in America is crucial to developing theoretical perspectives, research agendas, and law enforcement strategies that may adequately address the problem. Unfortunately, many of the historical efforts in this area are characterized by unsubstantiated claims and dubious secondary sources utilized by popular writers. Biographies of famous gangsters are quite popular, but the information contained in those works must be carefully sifted through and assessed for historical accuracy (a process which often reveals blatant impossibilities).[1] Other historical attempts based on government sources or written by former law enforcers at times have been misguided, ethnically biased, and shaped by historical naivete.[2]

Much of the history of organized crime as it is known is the history of organized crime in New York and Chicago, for it is in these cities that researchers have focused their energies. However, organized crime *should not* be mistaken as a phenomenon limited primarily to New York or Chicago– the work of Humbert Nelli is especially noteworthy in that he centers his study on twelve cities in various regions throughout the country.[3] As data and case studies continue to be slowly collated, it becomes more and more evident that organized crime permeates nearly every sector of American life and commerce, and can be found not only in large cities, but also in small towns, suburbia, and rural areas.[4]

Organized crime in America is, first and foremost, an *American* social phenomenon, created and perpetuated primarily by economic, political, and cultural variables indigenous to the United States. While it is certainly true that immigration has played a significant role in the development of criminal networks in America, organized crime is *not* the embodiment of an evil alien conspiracy, nor is it a singular bureaucratic super-organization (Cosa Nostra or Mafia) controlling illegal activities throughout the nation. Although Italians, the Irish, and Jews have at one time or another exhibited predominance in certain illicit spheres, illegal entrepreneurship transcends the participation of any one ethnic group.[5]

Early Forms of Organized Crime

The beginnings of organized crime in the United States can be traced back to colonial America. Organized prostitution and fencing networks were reported as early as the 1680's in Suffolk County and the Massachusetts Bay Colony (Boston).[6] Well-organized criminal enterprises operated in all of the major port cities of the American colonies prior to the Revolutionary War. Just like large-scale organized crime today, these early illicit enterprises were well-financed, and used "corporate buffers, bribery, political payoffs, and corruption" to further their goals.[7] A large East Coast smuggling syndicate was run by none other than the Declaration of Independence's most legible signer, John Hancock.[8]

After the Revolutionary War, land frauds and illegal speculations became widespread.[9] One of the largest of these crimes was the Yazoo land fraud of 1795, a scam which involved two U.S. Senators (James Gunn of Georgia and Robert Morris of Pennsylvania), U.S. Supreme Court justice James Wilson, two U.S. Congressmen (Thomas Carnes and Robert Harper), and dozens of Massachusetts and Connecticut bankers. These political and economic elites bribed the Georgia legislature to obtain title to 35 million acres of state and Indian lands at the price of one half cent per acre.[10] Another significant public corruption scandal occurred later during the Civil War, when directors of the Union Pacific Railroad, members of the Lincoln Cabinet, and a few members of Congress formed the Credit Mobilier Corporation of America. While the company was formed with the stated purpose of overseeing the construction of the first transcontinental railroad, "it operated to falsify invoices, overcharge, engage in kickbacks, issue dummy contracts, and bilk the taxpayers out of some $23 million dollars."[11]

As the new nation began to expand, so too did organized crime. The proliferation of early criminal enterprises has been linked to vice operators (gambling, prostitution, liquor), immigrant street gangs, and the development of urban political machines and corrupt police forces in northern cities like New York, Philadelphia, Chicago and Detroit.[12] The genesis and development of organized crime in Southern states was built upon political corruption as well, but also included elements indigenous to the South, and therefore took on a unique Southern "flavor." Syndicate crime in Southern states was dependent on the participation of large slave-owners and mercantile traders, while the river port cities became the vice districts of that region. The vices took on new forms, including the syndication of riverboat faro games, the kidnapping of young girls for the prostitution trade, and a highly organized liquor trade that involved production, smuggling, and tax evasion. "Slave stealing, land and river piracy, and piracy on the high seas were also integral to the development of Southern organized crime."[13]

On the western frontier, prostitution and gambling enterprises ensured that cattle and mining towns thrived in what was essentially a harsh and lawless environment. "Cow-towns" like Abilene and Dodge were lawless terminals for the millions of cattle driven up from Texas for shipment by rail east. H.C. Owens writes:

> These cow-towns, with only a few hundred actual inhabitants, would have a score or more of saloons and gambling-houses, and half a score of dance-halls, in which the girls were hostesses in the most generous sense.[14]

Faro, a game where "the dealer drew only two cards, paying off those who held similar cards on the first draw and collecting from card holders on the second,"[15] was extremely popular in the frontier west and has been credited with being one of the main reasons gambling was transformed into a widespread form of organized crime.[16]

Gambling was a very profitable and violent industry in the old west, and was widely accepted among frontier citizens. Prostitution was another important vice industry and was well-regulated in western communities; there were no "street-walkers," and while some women worked "freelance" in the saloons and gambling joints, most preferred "the security and status of the madam operated brothel." More than half of the profits from prostitution were passed up to the madam, who then took care of her silent partners– typically leading citizens of the boom towns.[17] Still, while the vices were integral to local western economies, cattle rustling was probably the most widespread, organized, and lucrative criminal enterprise.[18]

Back in the urban East, large-scale organized gambling could be found in major American cities by the early 1800's. Although Congress had declared gambling illegal, Washington D.C. hosted at least twelve gambling houses by 1825, many of which were important meeting places for politicians and lobbyists. Gambling houses first appeared in New York City in the early 1830's, and by 1850, about 6,000 gaming establishments were operating in addition to a thriving illegal lottery.[19] John "Old Smoke" Morrisey, a State Senator and member of Congress, was responsible for professionalizing gambling operations in New York City and New Orleans in the 1850's, demonstrating the use of organization, political contacts, and money to further illicit goals. Morrisey, a Tammany power, used his power position to collect "tribute" from his fellow gamblers. The funds were utilized to finance election campaigns and to buy protection from machine controlled police for his gambling interests.[20]

In the latter part of the nineteenth and into the early twentieth century, organized crime was characterized by its intimate association with municipal political machines. A kind of symbiosis existed between the two. "In exchange for a free hand in operating houses of prostitution, saloons, and gambling halls, criminal elements not only helped get out the vote on election day, but also kept as many opposition voters as possible from reaching the polling stations."[21] It was the world of patronage politics (infamous examples being the Tweed ring in New York and the Pendergast

Machine in Kansas City), where political bosses granted favors such as jobs, exemption from city ordinances, and, for their less savory clients, an unofficial license to practice breaking the law. Having emerged during the mid-nineteenth century, professional police forces soon fell under the aegis of municipal politicians, swelling the ranks of loyal clients. Historian Humbert Nelli has observed: "By the 1870's this connection had evolved into a working relationship among criminals, politicians, and the police, and it has plagued American cities ever since."[22]

Throughout much of the 19th century, organized crime at the street level was comprised of loosely coordinated "street gangs." Staffed by disenfranchised immigrant groups, street gangs often became "incubators for future organized criminals."[23] In New York City, many of the first gangs were comprised of Irish, who emigrated to New York and other East Coast cities because of Ireland's potato famine throughout the 1830's and 40's.[24] Some of the more famous (or infamous) gangs of New York were the Bowery Boys, the Dead Rabbits, the True Blue Americans, the American Guards, the O'Connel Guards, the Plug Uglies, the Shirt Tails, and the Atlantic Guards. Conflict between groups was not uncommon. The Bowery Boys and the Dead Rabbits fought for years until the Draft Riots of 1863, when "they combined with other gangs and criminals in an effort to sack and burn the city."[25] Herbert Asbury writes:

> Sometimes the battles waged for two or three days without cessation, while the streets of the gang area were barricaded with carts and paving stones, and the gangsters blazed away at each other with muskets and pistol, or engaged in close work with knives, brick-bats, bludgeons, teeth, and fists.[26]

Women were gang members too, inflicting "fiendish tortures" on policemen and soldiers captured by the mobs, "slicing their flesh with butcher knives, ripping out eyes and tongues, and applying the torch after the victims had been sprayed with oil and hanged from trees."[27] Perhaps the most notable of the female gang members was "Hell-Cat Maggie," who filed her teeth to points and wore artificially long fingernails made of brass to aid her fighting abilities. Not surprisingly, 1840's New York City residents became accustomed to seeing regiments of National Guardsmen marching through the streets to impose order.[28]

While many of the early gangs were no doubt formed as self-defense alliances, their proclivity for violence also made them very useful as bludgeons in municipal politics. In the first popular direct election for New York City mayor in 1834, both parties recruited gang members to vote "early and often" and to coerce the opposition. By the third day of the election, the resulting bloodshed required that the State Militia be called in to restore order.[29] New York's Democratic political machine in that era, known as "Tammany Hall," reigned supreme at the polls for decades in part because of the "muscle" provided by street gangs. The full significance of this relationship is noted by Peter Lupsha:

> ... an alliance that would last well into the 20th century was forged over the years between the Democratic party machine in New York and those who would rule various organized crime groups. New York City is not unique in this respect: organized crime held sway over First Ward politics and often the governance of the city of Chicago for more than eighty years.[30]

In the latter part of the 19th century, as new ethnic groups emigrated from Southern and Eastern Europe, the ethnic composition of some street gangs changed, but the often cozy relationships with municipal politicians did not. One of the more infamous groups was New York City's Five Points gang, led by Paolo Antonio Vaccarelli (Paul Kelly). Kelly commanded a loose network of gangs comprised of some 1,500 street thugs. Around the turn of the century, Kelly's battles with Monk Eastman (the brutal and somewhat colorful leader of another Five Points gang) are practically legendary. Kelly himself was associated with future organized crime notables such as Alphonse Capone, Salvatore "Lucky" Luciano, and John Torrio.[31]

Aside from relatively uncoordinated street gangs, one may conclude that the historical development of large-scale and corrupting organized crime in the United

States was created from the entrepreneurial politics of the nineteenth century, which through patronage, controlled criminal justice institutions. Professional criminals served their patrons as strike breakers and orchestrators of election frauds, while the profits from manufacturing and distributing illegal commodities and services helped to finance the political machines.[32]

While fostered by entrepreneurial politics, organized crime began to evolve further with the advent of three significant social events in the late 1800's. The Industrial Revolution, the urbanization of the populace, and the arrival of thirty million immigrants, primarily from Southern and Eastern Europe, provided the impetus for change.[33] First the Irish, followed by Eastern European Jews, and then Italians, the immigrants arrived in America's major seaports in the context of a rapidly expanding industrial, technological, and economic base. Some made their fortunes legally as longshoremen, stevedores, and merchants, while others chose illegal entrepreneurship, either as distributors of illegal goods and services, or as extortionists, preying upon their legitimate counterparts.[34]

In order to foster ethnic support, the machines would provide a variety of services and favors to each new wave of immigrants, primarily in the form of jobs. Beginning in the 1890's, the Nation witnessed the influx of Italians, Eastern European Jews, and other "new" immigrant groups who moved into neighborhoods previously dominated by natives of Northern and Western Europe. Once dominated by the Irish, New York's Tammany Hall bosses gave way but still maintained much of their power by the prudent distribution of favors and patronage. When Tammany boss Richard Croker promoted Timothy D. Sullivan to Bowery Assembly district leader in the early 1890's, Sullivan quickly granted to foremost criminals important functions within his political machine. Gambling entrepreneurs and organizers of prostitution were election district captains, responsible for bringing out the vote, or perhaps more appropriately, engineering election frauds. By the turn of the century, Italians dominated vice activities in the Bowery in return for their political support.[35]

Illegal business endeavors, characterized by symbiotic patron-client relationships among illegal entrepreneurs and municipal politicians, was not a phenomenon unique to New York City. In May of 1870 the press in New Orleans revealed that a formal system of payoffs existed in that city, whereby illegal gambling operators pooled their resources so as to ensure sufficient revenue to bribe police officers at all levels, from patrolman to commissioner.[36] A similar situation existed in Chicago, where syndicated crime first manifested itself in the 1870's. Gambling "dens" operated without interference from the police, who shared in the profits. Reform-minded mayors quickly went down to defeat in those years, with gamblers such as Michael Cassius McDonald, Harry Varnell, and the Hawkins brothers having developed a bookmaking syndicate which monopolized gambling throughout the Chicago and Indiana race tracks.[37]

By the turn of the twentieth century, prostitution was a widespread and open enterprise in every major American city, with the French importing young girls and coordinating business in the urban areas. One such organization centered in Chicago supplied prostitutes throughout the Mid-West, importing 3,000 women and clearing over $200,000 a year.[38] Prostitution rings existed in most large American cities. By 1900, San Francisco's Barbary Coast, the Tenderloins of New York and Philadelphia, the New Orleans French Quarter, and Chicago's Levee had all become "integrated within the local political machines."[39] Some organizations, like the Colosimo-Torrio gang, were well-organized and even developed a network for exchanging prostitutes with enterprises in other cities.[40] Some crooks successfully linked their political and economic interests over extended periods of time. Known as the "Lords of the Levee," Chicago aldermen Michael "Hinky Dink" Kenna and "Bathouse" John Coughlin served on the Chicago city council for nearly fifty years, overseeing vice activities in the Loop (Chicago's entertainment district) until the early 1940's.[41]

Just as organized criminal entrepreneurship was not limited to any one ethnic group or geographic area, illegal enterprises were not restricted to gambling and prostitution. In the years leading up to World War I, a budding drug market existed in the United States. Italians played a relatively minor role in the drug trade at this time, while Jews handled at least part of the business in New York City.[42] An analysis of New York City's cocaine trade from 1910 to 1917 revealed a market inhabited by a "web of small but efficient organizations," with criminal justice functionaries more often than not the suppliers.[43] Still, the narcotics industry did not become a large-scale enterprise until during and after Prohibition.[44]

Other important organized criminal activities in the late 1800's and early 1900's were counterfeiting and industrial racketeering. In New York City, Ignazio Saietta organized a group of Italian counterfeiters who sold two and five-dollar bills for thirty or forty cents to wholesalers, who in turn distributed the money throughout the country. Italian counterfeiters supplied bootleggers with fake liquor labels during Prohibition and operated in numerous cities, including Cleveland, Chicago, and Boston.[45] Although the full impact of labor and industrial racketeering would not be felt until the late 1920's, machine politicians as well as union leaders and businessmen utilized the services of organized crime "muscle" in the two decades before Prohibition. An early example of organized crime's role in activities related to the restraint of trade are the newspaper wars which raged in many American cities at the turn of the twentieth century. In Chicago, both sides in the circulation battle between the *Tribune* and the *Examiner* employed underworld thugs to counter the opposition, suppling a "training ground for the system of gang warfare and racketeering that would emerge in the city during the 1920's and 30's."[46] In the first decade of the 20th century New York's Paul Kelly joined with Cera Terranova in East Harlem to take over the rag-pickers union, where the gangsters extorted money from businessmen and rag-pickers alike.[47]

The Development of a Myth

An examination of organized crime in the earlier part of the United States' history would not be complete without a discussion of the factors which have led to the formation of what has been called the "Mafia myth." Against the backdrop of vice, counterfeiting, and racketeering which proliferated around the turn of the century, the influx of Italian immigrants and misconceptions associated with certain events first precipitated a mythology characterized as an "evil Alien Conspiracy" directed by secret predatory societies like the "Mafia," the "Black Hand," and the "Camorra." The murder of popular New Orleans police chief David Hennessey in 1890 was attributed to the "Mafia," a state within a state, "with laws that are surer of execution than the decrees of the state."[48]   False assumptions, rumor, and inaccurate reporting, combined with widespread anti-immigrant sentiment, fueled the fanciful perception that a singular powerful criminal *organization* comprised of southern Italians had somehow been transplanted from the Old-World, and was involved in a conspiracy not just in New Orleans, but in Italian communities throughout the nation.[49]   The far-reaching power of the "Mafia" seemed to be affirmed when a New York City police lieutenant, Joseph Petrosino, was murdered in 1909 after being dispatched to Palermo– his mission, the investigation of some 5,000 Italians in New York with old-world criminal records. During that era, any murder involving Italians was generally attributed to the "Mafia."[50]

While myths about the ultimate powerfulness of Italian criminals were rampant during this period, it is nevertheless clear that "by 1891 criminal bands were at work in any American city that contained sizable Southern Italian immigrant populations."[51] However, as opposed to a large, secret, and ultra-powerful organization called the Mafia, early forms of Italian organized crime involved small groups whose principle criminal endeavor was extortion, *usually perpetrated against members of the Italian community*. As early as 1878, a band of Sicilian extortionists preyed upon members of the Southern Italian community in San Francisco and surrounding towns. After his arrival in New Orleans in 1880, Giuseppe Esposito organized a group of some seventy-five "cut-throats," who specialized in kidnapping. Even before that, law-abiding Italian settlers in New Orleans were plagued by unorganized blackmailers who utilized their reputation from the homeland to extort monies.[52]

In Manhattan and Brooklyn, gangs of extortionists and black-mailers had begun to operate on a large-scale by 1901. From about 1903 and continuing into the 1920's, extortion and blackmail among Italians came to be known as the "Black Hand," and usually involved the "work of individuals or small groups who came together only briefly to carry out a single job or a limited number of jobs."[53] Typically, a semi-prosperous Italian businessman would receive a note demanding money. The consequences of ignoring a Black Hand note included the kidnapping of a loved one, a bombing, or the murder of the uncooperative victim. Interestingly, extortion was not limited to legal Italian businessmen– some prominent criminals were also known to receive Black Hand notes. James Colosimo, who dominated vice activities in Chicago's Near South Side Italian District, was forced to bring in John Torrio from New York in order to thwart extortion attempts (which he did successfully). Torrio went on to become the dominant figure in organized crime in early 1920's Chicago.[54]

Prohibition

On January 16, 1920, the Eighteenth Amendment and the Volstead Act were implemented, proscribing the "manufacture, sale, or transportation of intoxicating liquors" (Interestingly, the *consumption* of alcohol was not prohibited). The "noble experiment" is perhaps viewed best as an exercise in social control, an extension of sentiments founded in the Progressive Reform period dating back to the 1870's.[55] Progressive reformers believed the ward boss, political corruption, and the liquor industry were bound together, and that their mission was to regain control of the inner city areas, where the political machines utilized the immigrant vote and the proceeds from vice to remain in power. Liquor was one of the few industries of that time which was not dominated by White-Anglo-Saxon-Protestants (WASPs). The passage of the Volstead Act, then, may be interpreted, quite simply, as an effort on the part of middle-class WASPs to impose their will on the latest wave of immigrants.[56]

The failure of Prohibition to curb the liquor business was due to an uncoordinated and inadequate enforcement effort, and the continued demand for alcohol by millions of Americans. Opportunistic and ambitious young entrepreneurs (many of the significant bootleggers in the 1920's were young street gang thugs in the 1910's) met the demand, and made a fortune doing it. In fact, the prohibition of the manufacture and distribution of alcoholic beverages was the catalyst which transformed criminal syndicates into something new, while the money accrued during those propitious years served as the foundation for future large-scale syndicate enterprises.[57] So while the passage of the Volstead Act not only failed to curb the manufacture, distribution, and sale of alcohol, it also precipitated the "full flowering of entrepreneurial crime in America."[58] Moreover, the proliferation of gangs specializing in alcohol distribution should not have been a surprise to authorities, since bootlegging had occurred in twenty-seven dry states prior to 1920. In Denver, aspiring bootleggers who later became prominent gangland figures made their start as early as 1914, when Colorado became a dry state. Italian bootleggers were operating as early as 1919 in Detroit, fighting among themselves for control of that market.[59]

Criminal businessmen could obtain their alcohol supplies from a number of sources. Under the Eighteenth Amendment, doctors and druggists could still prescribe and dispense intoxicating liquors, thereby granting an informal license for many professionals to enhance their income. A larger source of revenue derived from the conversion of industrial alcohol to alcohol suitable for consumption. The production of denatured alcohol expanded from 28 million gallons in 1920 to 180 million gallons per year throughout the 1920's, a third of which was utilized for bootlegging purposes.[60] Perhaps the largest source of alcohol during the Prohibition years were legitimate brewers and distillers who leased their operations to enterprising hoods. The distillers and owners of liquor warehouses arranged for the "robbery" of their own stockpiles, while brewers utilized gangsters as fronts while they continued to operate in apparent compliance with Volstead restrictions. Joseph Stenson, a prominent brewer in Chicago and a silent partner in John Torrio's bootlegging operation, was reputed to have cleared $12 million over a four year period from the syndicated beer racket.[61] Interestingly, many pre-Prohibition brewers obtained their options back and started to operate just after repeal in 1933, indicating that they had merely brought in criminal elements to manage their businesses during the years in which the Volstead Act was in effect.[62]

Smuggling was another primary source of illicit alcohol. A large volume of liquor was brought in by land, sea, and air, with bootleggers employing any means available to transport their product. The Reinfield syndicate of New Jersey, in order to avoid the Coast Guard, would anchor their cargo ships one hundred yards offshore, while a motorboat would transport a rubber hose out to the main vessel– Canadian whiskey was then pumped to oaken tanks concealed in an onshore house. In another case, smugglers used a World War I German submarine.[63] By far, most of the distilled liquor smuggled into the United States originated in Canada. In fact, the Canadian liquor industry was highly dependent on American bootleggers, with 80% of Canada's whiskey output finding its way into the U.S. during Prohibition.[64]

By the late 1920's, however, the primary source of liquor consumed in the United States was the domestic liquor industry. In 1929, illicit stills produced more than 63 million gallons of alcohol. Stills varied in size from the huge factory operations producing as much as 2,000 gallons daily, to the small homemade variety with a one-gallon capacity. Small home-centered production was very common, as many formerly law-abiding citizens scrambled to reap the proceeds made available by the Prohibition law. Small one-gallon stills were easy and inexpensive to construct or buy, while instructions on how to manufacture alcohol could be obtained in any public library as well as a number of Department of Agriculture bulletins.[65] Even small home operations, however, were subject to the organizing presence of the larger entrepreneurs. The Genna brothers of Chicago saw great potential in the home liquor industry, and distributed hundreds of portable stills to residents in the Near West Side Italian community with orders to produce, resulting in gross sales of about $350,000 a month. In New York City, former Black Hander Frank Yale organized the home industry in Brooklyn's Bay Ridge section. Whole neighborhoods were comprised of home stills producing 350 gallons of raw alcohol per week. The individual operators supplemented their own income (as much as fifteen dollars a day), while the criminal syndicates provided protection and dispensed payments to local officials.[66]

Many of the leading bootleggers were young men in their twenties, first generation immigrants. During the early years of Prohibition, the liquor trade was dominated by Irish criminals like Dan Carroll and Joe Kennedy in Boston, and Owney Madden in New York.[67] By the mid-1920's, however, syndicated crime and bootlegging had come to be controlled by Jewish criminals, then Italians.[68] In New York City by the late 1920's, approximately half of the bootleggers were Jewish, twenty-five percent were Italian, and the rest were Irish or Poles.[69] The pattern was not limited to one city or area. Nationwide, the Jewish criminal element had become prominent during the Prohibition years.[70]

Large-scale Jewish bootlegging may have begun with the Bronfman brothers of Canada. Originally brothel owners in Saskatchewan and Manitoba, the Bronfmans became importers, then manufacturers of alcohol. After moving to Montreal in 1924, the Bronfman's became major suppliers for bootleg syndicates nationwide, making enough money from their illegal ventures to buy Joseph E. Seagram and Sons in 1928. In Cleveland, Jewish gangsters Moe Dalitz, Sam Tucker, Morris Kleinman, and Louis Rathkopf made a fortune smuggling Canadian liquor across Lake Erie. Bootlegging in Detroit was dominated by the notoriously violent "Purple Gang," led by Sammy Purple Cohen and Abe Bernstein. For a number of years the Purple Gang supplied Canadian whiskey for the Capone organization in Chicago, but by the end of the 20's the Jewish syndicate had been pushed out by Italian criminals such as Joseph Zerilli, Angelo Meli, and Pete Licavoli, who emerged as the dominant power in Detroit's underworld. Philadelphia was riddled with gangland violence during the Prohibition era, with bootlegging in that city controlled by the former Jewish prizefighter, Max "Boo Boo" Hoff.[71]

The greatest number of Jewish bootleggers were found in New York City and New Jersey, the center of American Jewry. A legitimate liquor dealer for fifteen years prior to Prohibition, Mannie Kessler was perhaps the best known Jewish bootlegger in New York City in the early 1920's. Arnold Rothstein, professional gambler and financier to many illegal entrepreneurs, began bankrolling bootleg activities as early as the Fall of 1920. Middle-aged and well-to-do at the outset of Prohibition, Rothstein was not typical of most Jewish bootleggers, who were very young and fresh out of the street gangs and lesser rackets of pre-1920's New York. Arnold Rothstein was the mentor for young organized crooks like Meyer Lansky and Benjamin Siegel, and provided political protection and financial backing for the enterprises of Irving Wexler (Waxey Gordon), Frank Costello, "Big Bill" Dwyer, Louis "Lepke" Buchalter, Albert Anastasia, and Jack "Legs" Diamond. A loan from Rothstein started Waxey Gordon in the bootlegging business along with his associates Max Greenberg and Max Hassel. Gordon, a cocaine distributor prior to Prohibition, acquired interests in at least thirteen breweries scattered about New York, New Jersey, and Pennsylvania. In conjunction with Longie Zwillman of Newark, Gordon acquired a 50% interest in the Reinfeld syndicate, a large bootlegging enterprise with operations throughout New Jersey. By 1929, this operation had emerged as the leading beer syndicate in the nation, procuring most of their supply from the Bronfmans in Montreal.[72]

That Italian John Torrio should be the person largely responsible for centralizing the East Coast liquor trade is perhaps indicative of the changing ethnic structure of the underworld in the late 1920's. Although the greatest number of bootleggers appear to have been Eastern European Jews, by the latter portion of the Prohibition era the Italians had become increasingly prominent in the illicit liquor industry. Fighting for shares in the liquor market was widespread in cities like Kansas City, Denver, and Los Angeles, where Italian gangsters emerged victorious by the end of the 1920's.[73] In New York City, murders and mergers had consolidated the Italian criminal element into five gangs: in the Bronx, Gaetano Reina, Gaetano Gagliano, and Thomas Lucchese; Giuseppe Magliocco and Joseph Profaci in Staten Island and Brooklyn; Alfred Mineo, Carlo Gambino, Albert Anastasia, and Vincent Mangano, with interests in Brooklyn and Manhattan; the Castellammarese immigrants, Salvatore Maranzano and his apprentice, Joe Bonnano; and the most powerful group, led by Joe "the Boss" Masseria, included Frank Costello, Vito Genovese, Charles "Lucky" Luciano, Joe Adonis, and Willie Moretti.[74] Toward the end of the Prohibition era a power struggle among the Italian factions, commonly referred to as the "Castellammarrese War," led to the deaths of both Maranzano and Masseria. This event allegedly coordinated by Lucky Luciano is credited with "Americanizing" the "mob," a process characterized by Italian-Jewish joint ventures and a measure of regional and intra-city cooperation. (The Castellammarrese War has also been cited widely in government/law enforcement circles as the birth of Cosa Nostra, the singular and corporate-like criminal organization that operates throughout the United States– the hyperbole in this perspective was discussed in chapter I of this volume).

While the bootlegging industry was characterized by intense competition and violence, the overall trend was towards centralization and cooperation. Recognizing that unrestrained competition and violence was not good for business, groups of bootleggers emerged as dominant forces in cities throughout the nation in the latter portion of the Prohibition era.[75] In Chicago, cooperation materialized early under the leadership of John Torrio, an alumnus of New York's Five Points gang. The coming to power of a hostile municipal administration in 1923, however, resulted in disunity and a gang war which lasted several years and resulted in over two hundred murders. Torrio's successor, Al Capone, continued the war which included factions led by Dion O'Banion, Hymie Weiss, and later, George "Bugs" Moran. The war culminated in the infamous St. Valentine's Day Massacre in 1929, in which Capone successfully eliminated much of his competition and assumed a measure of central control over Chicago's underworld.[76]

Following Arnold Rothstein's murder in 1928, it was John Torrio who once again surfaced as a leader and financier for underworld operations in New York City. Torrio organized the liquor trade along the East Coast just as he had done earlier in Chicago. An association of the seven largest bootlegging enterprises agreed to rationally divide the Eastern market and share profits. Prices were fixed, and each group was allocated a specified quantity of liquor it could purchase from Canadian sources. Functioning as an oligopoly, the association was comprised of the Luciano group, which included Joe Adonis and Frank Costello, the Meyer Lansky/Bugsy Siegel gang, Nig Rosen in Philadelphia, Longie Zwillman and the Reinfeld syndicate centered in Newark, Charles "King" Solomon of Boston, Daniel Walsh in Rhode Island, Yasha Katzenberg of New York, and the Torrio group. Dutch Schultz, who controlled the beer industry in the Bronx and who was generally disliked among his underworld associates, refused to join. An IRS investigative report concluded that this association controlled the sale of liquor from Boston south to Philadelphia, and that a commission had been formed in Canada among the prominent liquor distributors who agreed to export liquor only to those enterprises belonging to the "Big Seven."[77]

Just how much money bootleggers made from 1920 to 1933 is impossible to determine. However, Internal Revenue Service and Prohibition Bureau reports indicate that profits were in the hundreds of millions. A Department of Commerce Report in 1925 estimated liquor smuggling proceeds at $40 million, an admittedly low figure. Other sources believed that the Capone/Torrio organization alone was thought to gross anywhere from $60 to $240 million annually from liquor sales.[78]

With the passage of the Twenty-first Amendment in 1933 Prohibition ended, and the lucrative bootlegging rackets soon went into decline. Organized criminals had amassed fortunes and developed complex and binding ties with legitimate business and government. After repeal, former bootleggers lent themselves to the task of investing the millions they had earned.

After Prohibition: Expansion of Illicit Enterprises

The repeal of Prohibition did not put organized criminals out of business, or even slow them down. "Nest eggs" amassed during the Prohibition years provided the financial base for the expansion of other illicit business ventures, primarily gambling, narcotics trafficking, and the rapidly expanding realm of business and labor racketeering. Of course, these activities had not been abandoned during Prohibition.

Narcotics was an expanding business even during Prohibition. Drugs were manufactured in Swiss and German labs and smuggled into the United States through New York, Tampa, and New Orleans, and from those points to Kansas City. During the 1920's and 1930's, Kansas City was the major transshipment center for illicit narcotics distributed throughout the Mid-west, from Chicago to Denver and Laramie. The Joseph Roma organization in Denver dealt not only in booze, but was responsible for distributing narcotics throughout the Rocky Mountain States.[79] Perhaps the most active drug syndicate was centered in New York City, and consisted of Jewish gangsters Waxey Gordon, Lepke Buchalter, Saul Gelb, and Mandy Weiss. This syndicate brought in Japanese heroin by way of Tientsin. From New York, it was distributed across the country to wholesalers like Louis Oppleman in Baltimore and Kitty Gilhooley in Chicago. Although narcotics was not the money-maker it would become in later decades, it has been estimated that organized crime profits from drug trafficking were in the area of $500 million per year during the 1930's. In New Orleans, future syndicate leader Carlos Marcello became one of that city's busiest drug wholesalers by the late 1930's. In New York, Lucky Luciano dispatched Vito Genovese to Fascist Italy in 1933 to establish a smuggling ring under the protection of the Italian government.[80] Still, throughout the 1930's narcotics trafficking was dispersed among many individual gangs, with little coordination.[81]

In addition to the distribution of narcotics, many former bootleggers never abandoned the liquor industry. The two largest illicit stills known to authorities were discovered *after* the passage of the Twenty-first Amendment, one in Cleveland, and the other in New Jersey.[82] Shrewd bootleggers who anticipated the demise of Prohibition had already signed importing and distribution contracts with distillers before repeal took effect. For example, the exclusive distributorship for Seagram products in Kansas City was given to the Midwest Distributing Company, a wholesale liquor firm headed by Kansas City mob figures Vincent and Joseph Di Giovanni. In New York, Frank Costello and his associate "Dandy Phil" Kastel incorporated Alliance Distributors, Inc. at the time of repeal for the purpose of importing liquor from Canada and Europe. Alliance Distributors handled whiskey produced by Whiteley Distilleries of London, a company which Costello and Kastel eventually controlled. John Torrio was one of the more prominent legal liquor promoters, who, through a complex series of frontmen, owned and operated the importing firm of Prendergast and Davies.[83] Just before Prohibition ended, Joe Reinfeld and other members of his organization spent six weeks in Europe cultivating the grounds for a licit importation business with White Horse, one of the "Big Five Scotches." The Reinfeld syndicate became Browne Vintners, which controlled the largest selling scotch in America. Joe Kennedy, with his upper-world connections and business ties, also went to Europe seeking liquor franchises, and came away with the best of the lot. In any city, the main prizes were the Seagram and Schenley distributorships, controlled by Samuel Bronfman and Lewis Rosenstiel, respectively. Over forty years after the end of Prohibition, the head of the New York State Liquor Authority, upon surveying the businessmen he was supposed to regulate, stated "All those guys were in bootlegging. That's how they got into the wholesale liquor business."[84]

Although liquor and narcotics were big income producers after 1933, the most profitable enterprise for organized criminals was gambling, including the numbers racket (an illegal daily lottery), casino gambling, horse and dog racing, and slot machines. Numbers gambling had replaced the old policy game in many American cities by the 1920's and 1930's, and was thought to bring in at least $100 million a year in New York City alone. Cities like New York, Philadelphia, Chicago, and Detroit witnessed the infiltration of ex-bootleggers into the numbers game, an industry which was characterized at that time by the prevalence of African-American entrepreneurs.[85] Rising stars in the world of organized crime like Vito Genovese and Willie Moretti operated a large numbers enterprise in Bergen and Passaic Counties, and later invested in the slot machine business with the help of Frank Costello. Frank Costello and his partner Phil Kastel grossed $18 to $36 million annually from the slot machines they placed in bars, cigar stores, candy stores, and groceries throughout New York City. When a reform fervor pervaded New York upon the election of mayor Fiorello La Guardia, Costello relocated his machines in New Orleans after an invitation from U. S. Senator Huey Long.[86] Meanwhile, at the height of Dutch Schultz's centralization effort in Harlem, his numbers enterprise contributed $20 million to his annual income.[87]

At about the same time that former bootleggers were discovering the immense profits to be had in the lottery business and slot machines, horse and dog racing became lucrative investments for criminal entrepreneurs. After 1930, horse racing gained a national following, with the tracks owned through front men but controlled by underworld figures. In conjunction with the syndicate-controlled dog and horse tracks, bookmaking operations exploded on a national level. Meyer Lansky, the alleged financial mastermind of mob-connected activities after the murder of Arnold Rothstein, was thought to have operated the largest bookmaking establishment in New York City during the 1930's.[88] The rapid growth in the bookmaking industry was largely made possible by the wire service provided by former Hearst circulation manager, Moe Annenberg. Bookmaking operations depended on the timely dissemination of track odds, scratches, and race results, and Annenberg amassed a fortune providing the service, monopolizing the telegraph service from race tracks in the United States, Mexico, Cuba, and Canada. Trial transcripts indicate that Annenberg's wire service was the American Telephone and Telegraph Company's fifth largest customer.[89]

Gambling casinos also became a major source of syndicate revenue during and after Prohibition. While not on the grand scale of the luxury hotel casinos of post-World War II Las Vegas, gambling houses could be found in American cities large and small throughout the 1930's, from Miami and New Orleans to Hot Springs, Arkansas, Newport, Kentucky, and Maple Heights near Cleveland.[90] Meyer Lansky was often a principal entrepreneur in these new gambling ventures. In Florida, ex-bootleggers cultivated the market and contributed to the region's growing status as a resort center. Mob money was invested in hotels, race tracks, nightclubs, and real estate. Lansky, Nig Rutkin, Longie Zwillman, and Jack Dempsey formed a partnership and opened a glitzy hotel-casino in Miami Beach. Lansky continued to orchestrate casino ventures in Florida after World War II, drawing upon his political contacts and a wide range of ethnically diverse investors to ensure the success of glamorous resorts like the Colonial Inn in Hallendale.[91]

A friendly government (to organized criminals) ninety miles away in Cuba was also the site of mob-controlled gambling enterprises. In the 1920's, Havanna was a major center of operations for American smugglers dealing in liquor and narcotics. By the mid-30's, friendly relations with Fulgencio Batista and other Cuban politicians facilitated the leasing of a racetrack and the opening of the Hotel Nacional in Havanna by a group of investors led by Meyer Lansky. Batista's return to power in 1952 ensured the rapid expansion of luxuriant casinos backed by a variety of mobsters, including Lansky, Moe Dalitz, Phil Kastel, and Frank Costello.[92]

Intimately associated with gambling activities, loan-sharking had also become a lucrative syndicate activity by the mid-1930's. A study by the Russell Sage Foundation estimated the gross annual income from loan-sharking in New York to be in excess of $10 million at that time.[93]

In addition to the huge profits associated with drug and alcohol distribution, the provision of gambling services, and extortion in a number of vital industries, the oldest vice of them all still provided vast wealth for syndicate leaders after Prohibition. In San Francisco, prostitution was so abundant that residents of the North Beach area had to put signs on their doors informing eager clients that their homes were not whorehouses. While no one group exercised dominance over prostitution in San Francisco, the French syndicate was thought to be predominant, while a sizable portion of the city's police force collected their dues through the ever-present McDonough brothers. In Chicago, organized prostitution was conducted by Capone's successors without interference from the law, and was accepted as a business reality in that city.[94] In New York City, the prostitution industry had been set up much like a factory system, with organization facilitated by the process of "booking" women in brothels. Half of all earnings went to the madam of the house, while 10% went to the "booker," usually a syndicate functionary. Medical exams, arrest costs, and other fees were typically subtracted from workers' earnings and administered by the organizers. In 1933, Lucky Luciano attempted to centralize the industry by extorting from both prostitutes and madams, who retaliated by cheating the organization. At that time the prostitution industry was about as organized as it was going to get, and the Luciano effort was largely a failure.[95]

Gambling, booze, narcotics, prostitution– all had their place in the growing weal of organized crime in the decades following the repeal of the Volstead Act. Perhaps the activity which best characterizes organized crime's intimate relationship with municipal political and local market structures, however, is labor and industrial racketeering, an activity distinguished by the act of extortion and the sometimes violent exercise of power.

Although New York City is unique in many ways, an examination of corruption and reform in that city's political history from near the end of repeal to post-World War II does provide a vivid depiction of the symbiosis between local political and economic processes, organized crime, and industrial racketeering in its most noteworthy manifestations. With the murder of Arnold Rothstein in 1928, corruption again became an issue in New York City, precipitating law enforcement pressure on the corrupt Tammany Hall political machine. The subsequent investigation into the city's magistrates courts by Samuel Seabury uncovered a vast sea of graft and abuse. The magistrates owed their appointments to the District leaders, who controlled the administration of justice and essentially granted franchises to local judicial officers who saw their role as entrepreneurial as opposed to legal or administrative. Making payments to political patrons in order to secure their appointments, magistrates and court clerks, in collusion with the police, would arrest innocent people who had to arrange for their release by bribing officials at every step of the criminal justice process. Meanwhile, organized criminals providing vice services were permitted to operate in exchange for a cut of the profits.[96]

The role of organized criminals in the structure of economic and political life in 1930's New York City was much like their role in other places and at other times: that of power broker, or political middleman– people who were willing to utilize private violence in order to mediate and control given situations. In the case of the New York City Magistrates' Courts in the 1920's and early 1930's, the roles of organized criminals, judicial officers, and political officials had become utterly blurred. The organizational hierarchy of the courts played no part in administrative decisions or the allocation of authority, with those decision processes instead directed by a jumble of county politicians and illegal entrepreneurs. City employees and organized criminals were often one and the same.[97] With justice for sale, it was the bail bondsmen who emerged as power brokers, directing the course of court administration and serving as mediators in the patronage system. Essentially, bondsmen controlled the criminal justice process, negotiating the price illegal entrepreneurs had to pay their political patrons in order to operate with impunity. The career of Anthony Iamascia, city employee and bail bondsmen, may be viewed as a microcosm of the organized crime/municipal political system. Iamascia served as a representative of the Bronx political machine, while controlling 95% of the bailbond industry in that borough.[98]

It was in this atmosphere of political corruption and collusive relationships that the maturation of industrial, business and labor racketeering transpired. Labor racketeering flourished in conjunction with trade associations created and maintained in demoralized industries. These employer or trade associations were nothing more than devices utilized by owners to restrain trade by limiting production, stabilizing competition, and raising commodity prices. The racketeer/extortionist stepped in when uncooperative owners were lured by the attraction of price cutting. Intimidation of union leaders as well as partnerships with corrupt trade unionists allowed organized crime power brokers to coerce fractious employers to abide by agreed upon prices. Of course, the whole system was made easier when organized criminals actually held positions as union officials, which was too often the case. As officials in union locals, extortionists could control and exploit the rank and file workers, collecting dues and stealing pension fund monies. Corrupt union officials often sold out the rank and file by engaging in "sweetheart contracts" with employers, where the savings from the bogus contract was split between the union officials and the employer. Labor racketeering was, however, a two-edged sword– extortionists could coerce unions or employers. For example, an employer, threatened with a strike or picket, could be forced to pay "strike insurance" for the privilege of continuing to do business. In the final analysis, however, it was most often employers in cahoots with organized criminals specializing in extortion and private violence who prospered at the expense of workers.[99]

No where was the racketeering as great as on the New York waterfront. The New York State Crime Commission uncovered criminality on the Brooklyn docks, concluding that organized crime controlled the waterfront from the 1930's through the 1950's. The poor physical condition of the port and the structure of the labor market contributed to organized crime's prevalence on the docks, while the vulnerability of the labor supply and the crucial element of timely unloading and loading of goods placed the corrupt officials of the International Longshoremen's Association (ILA) in a good position to dictate terms and extort from the shippers.[100] While an indebted labor force was used to exact payoffs from the shipping firms, the dock workers themselves were subjected to exploitation at the hands of loan-sharks, gamblers, and corrupt union officers.[101] Called the "shape-up," only those workers willing to kick back a portion of their wages to the hiring boss were permitted to work on any given day.

The ILA had a long history of corruption dating back to pre-Prohibition times, when Five Points gang leader Paul Kelly was responsible for the influx of waterfront hoods. It was Irishman John P. Ryan, however, who became president of the ILA in

1927 and ruled for twenty-five years, solidifying the position of the racketeer in waterfront economics. While the Irish controlled the northern, or Hudson River piers, Italian criminals reigned supreme on the Brooklyn waterfront. The Red Hook neighborhood in Brooklyn was controlled by six ILA locals under the dominion of a power syndicate centered in the City Democratic Club, members of which included Vincent Mangano, Joe Adonis, Joe Profaci, Emil Camarda, Giocchino Parisi, and Albert Anastasia. Directed by Anastasia, waterfront rackets included the theft of goods and the hijacking of goods between the piers and inland terminals, kickbacks from employers in exchange for the timely movement of goods, and a $200,000 a year loan-shark business. On some piers, workers would be hired only if they first agreed to borrow money from the local syndicate loan-shark.[102] William O'Dwyer, the District Attorney of Kings County who later became the mayor of New York City, ordered an investigation in 1949 into the ILA locals in Brooklyn. Although some charters were revoked, no significant reforms were enacted, and O'Dwyer eventually dismissed the investigation. Interestingly, O'Dwyer's brother Paul had been counsel for the ILA locals in question.[103]

The use of manpower by syndicates like the one in Red Hook was not the only method by which racketeers shaped corruption on the waterfront. Aside from the structure of the labor market, criminal networks were highly adaptive and expressed themselves through private enterprises set up in the service sector of particular economic zones of industries. For example, Vito Genovese controlled the Erb Strapping Company, CC Lumber, and Newbrook enterprises, companies which provided services and products essential to the port industry. By controlling labor unions, then, well-placed racketeers could steer contracts to mob-run enterprises, which also conveniently served as money-laundering vehicles for the profits derived from gambling, prostitution, and the distribution of narcotics.[104]

Of course, racketeering was in no way limited to waterfront industries. A list of industries confirmed as being controlled by organized crime in New York City in the 1930's includes "bead, cinder, cloth, shrinking, clothing, construction, flower shops,

122

Fulton Market (fish), funeral, fur, dressing, grape, hod carriers, ice, Kosher butcher, laundry, leather, live poultry, master barbers, milk, milling, musical, night patrol, neckwear, newsstands, operating engineers, overall, paper box, paper hangers, shirt makers, taxicabs, and window cleaners."[105] Beginning in the late 1920's, Lepke Buchalter and Jacob Shapiro maintained complete control over New York City's garment industry, extorting at least $15 million from garment manufacturers and associated industries.[106] In addition, Buchalter helped to organize the Flour Truckmen's Association, a trade association of truck owners and self-employed drivers which immediately raised cartage costs.   Buchalter extorted union membership fees and monies from the flour trucking and baking companies in return for his "services."   Shapiro and Buchalter also established dominance over the fur industry, the shoe trade, the taxicab business, and the poultry market, sometimes in partnership with associates like Bugsy Siegel, Meyer Lansky, and Lucky Luciano.[107]

A major organized crime success story is that of Joseph "Socks" Lanza, who organized the Fulton Fish Market workers into the United Seafood Workers' Union. By the late 1920's, the USWU had become affiliated with the AFL and maintained a thousand man membership.   Lanza collected tribute from every retailer and wholesaler at the Fulton Market, an enterprise which endowed him with $20 million per year, and a racket which affected the price of fish nationwide. Despite a two year prison sentence served in violation of the Sherman Anti-Trust Act, Lanza maintained control of the Fulton Market until his death in 1968.[108]

Just as industrial and labor racketeering was not limited to any one industry or market, the location of extortionate enterprises was virtually unbounded by the 1930's. In Chicago, some fifty rackets were openly flourishing in a diverse range of occupations and industries such as candy jobbers, garage owners, glazers, bootblacks, and physicians. By 1931, racketeering dominated by the Capone organization was thought to produce $200 million for the criminal syndicates. Similar estimates placed the figures at $100 million in Philadelphia, $75 million in Detroit, $50 million in Los Angeles, and $25 million each in Pittsburgh and Cleveland.[109]

One of the more notorious union infiltrations was that of the International Alliance of Theatrical, Stage Employees, and Motion Picture Operators. George Brown and William Bioff, with the backing of Frank Nitti, Lepke Buchalter, Lucky Luciano, Longie Zwillman, and other mobsters from Midwestern and Eastern power syndicates, took over the IATSE with the objective of extorting as much as possible from theater owners with the threat of strikes and shutdowns. The IATSE eventually won the right to represent 12,000 Hollywood employees, placing Bioff and his associates in a position to collect over $1 million dollars from the major Hollywood movie studios between 1936 and 1940.[110]

An infamous industrial and labor racketeers was Arthur Fleggenheimer, aka Dutch Schultz, who managed an extortion racket in the New York City restaurant industry from 1932 to 1936. Employers were forced to join the Metropolitan Restaurant and Cafeteria Association and sign contracts with one of two locals controlled by Schultz. Although the restaurant owners were forced to pay into the Association, they ultimately saved money as sweetheart contacts were arranged and true unionization was thwarted. The losers were consumers and the restaurant workers, as prices were fixed, wages were frozen, and the rank and file were otherwise exploited. The beauty of the arrangement for the Schultz syndicate was that it also controlled the restaurant employer's association in such a way that not only the workers, but also the employers were victims of extortion.[111]

Another prime example where unions were used as vehicles to restrain trade was in the construction industry. In the late 1920's the incorporation of the Plasterer's Information Bureau was used to force plastering contractors in the Bronx to join the Bureau and pay fees. Created by Tomasso Gagliano and Antonio Monforte, the United Lathing Company gained control of the lathing industry by hiring a "walking delegate" of the Lathers Union, which meant that the union representative could walk onto any construction site and order a work stoppage. Upon payment of a percentage of the contract fee, the strike would be called off. If the contractors decided not to pay, the building site would invariably suffer from a destructive fire. The

Intelligence Unit of the Internal Revenue Service determined that in 1929 alone, Monforte and Gagliano extorted over $457,000 from intimidated building contractors.[112]

Illusory Successes and New Opportunities

Against the backdrop of vice, corruption, and racketeering in American cities, organized crime during and after Prohibition was in actuality an "agent of political change." Periodic reform movements and the successes of special prosecutors made careers and altered the constitution of local municipal politics. In New York City, the political career of Mayor James Walker was ruined as a result of the Seabury investigation, which uncovered widespread corruption and bribe-taking under the Walker administration. Appointed as a special prosecutor in Manhattan, Thomas E. Dewey successfully prosecuted a number of well-known gangsters, including Lucky Luciano, Dutch Schultz, Jacob Shapiro, Louis Buchalter, James Plumeri, and Johnny Dioguardi. Dewey went on to become governor of New York and almost the President of the United States, largely because of the good press he received as a result of his organized crime-fighting efforts. William O'Dwyer, who went on to become mayor of New York City, was credited with breaking up the infamous Murder Inc. ring of extortionists led by Albert Anastasia.[113]

With the imprisonment of many significant organized crime leaders– men like John Torrio, Lepke Buchalter, Lucky Luciano, and Tammany Hall political ally Jimmy Hines– the impression that real progress was being made in the fight against organized crime came to be widely accepted as the nation moved into the World War II era. Real reform, however, was either elusive or illusory. In New York City, under the administration of mayor Fiorello La Guardia, reform was limited by the still considerable power of the county governments backed by corrupt district attorneys. Bill O'Dwyer came under fire for his inability (or lack of desire) to prosecute so many of the Murder Inc. crowd, and notable gangsters like Joe Adonis escaped indictments unscathed. Lucky Luciano had his sentence commuted for aiding the U.S. naval intelligence effort during World War II.[114]

While the control of organized crime was illusory, new events provided a catalyst just as Prohibition had. As historian Humbert Nelli observed, "World War II, with its diversion of public attention from the activities of crime syndicates, its shortages, its needs for cooperation at any price between capital and labor, and its frenzied emphasis on pleasure to compensate for the pains of sacrifice, ushered in a new and even more profitable era for America's criminal entrepreneurs."[115] Organized criminals nationwide took advantage of the increased demand for illegal goods and services, as well as the new opportunities the War provided for illegal entrepreneurs and extortionists in the realm of labor/management relations.[116] When the U.S. Government rationed essential supplies during the War, a huge and pervasive black market developed, supplying American consumers with meat, tin, rubber, gasoline, and other scarce commodities. Underworld soldier Joseph Valachi, later of McClellan Committee fame, made over $200,000 from 1942 to 1945 from the sale of gas ration stamps, while Joe Adonis specialized in black market automobile deals from his King County Buick Company in Brooklyn. Black marketeers operated with little interference from the law, with employees of the Office of Price Administration (which administered wartime rationing) often acting in collusion with underworld associates by stealing and selling ration stamps. Black market operations were very lucrative. The OPA estimated that 2.5 million gallons of gasoline alone were sold illegally every day.[117]

World War II did little to alter in any meaningful way the close relationship enjoyed by both illegal entrepreneurs and public officials. Perennial power broker Frank Costello helped elect his man Michael Kennedy to the Tammany Hall leadership in 1942, and subsequently arranged for the nomination and election of Thomas Aurelio to the New York State Supreme Court.[118] In many cases, police forces stepped over the line as protectors or regulators of illicit activities into the role of extorters and managers. For example, the extensive bookmaking and numbers syndicate of Harry Gross was actually bankrolled by the New York City police department in the late 1940's.[119]

Conclusion

While the illicit business activities of organized criminals and public officials continued unimpeded through the decades of the 1930's and 1940's, the *perception* of organized crime and what it was did change as the American nation approached the 1950's and a new era. A Communist scare, anti-immigrant feelings, and a pervasive atmosphere of paranoia apparently conditioned public officials as well as the general public to perceive the organized crime phenomenon in terms of a great "alien conspiracy," as opposed to deriving from economic and social realities indigenous to the United States.

Propelled by the televised Congressional Kefauver Committee hearings in 1951, the government, the law enforcement community, the media, and the general public increasingly viewed organized crime as synonymous with a secret underworld organization called "The Mafia."[120] The infamous meeting of organized criminals in Appalachin New York in 1957 fueled the idea that the Mafia was national in scope and very well-organized. A few years later, Joe Valachi revealed to the McClellan Committee a new name for the secret criminal society– Cosa Nostra (translated as "our thing/this thing of ours"). Valachi's testimony and other government files formed the basis for the conclusions of President Johnson's Task Force Report on Organized Crime in 1967: that organized crime was virtually synonymous with Cosa Nostra, a national corporate-like crime organization comprised of Italian-Americans.[121] Legislative initiatives that grew out of the 1967 report have targeted Italian criminal enterprises with great success, particularly in the 1980's and 1990's.[122] Nevertheless, the law enforcement perspective and approach has been misguided in several important ways (implicitly minimizing the role of political and economic elites being one prime example). Also, while the government and the criminal justice system mobilized their attack on organized criminals, organized crime itself was changing, adapting, and proliferating.

128

Endnotes

[1]Alan A. Block (1994). <u>Space, Time, and Organized Crime</u>. New Brunswick, NJ: Transaction Publishers; Jay Albanese (1985). <u>Organized Crime in America</u>. Cincinnatti: Anderson Publishing Company.

[2]Block, 1994.

[3]Humbert Nelli (1976). <u>The Business of Crime: Italians and Syndicate Crime in the United States</u>. New York: Oxford University Press.

[4]The reports of the Pennsylvania Crime Commission (1970-1993) provide excellent examples of organized crime in smaller cities. Also see Gary Potter and Larry K. Gaines (1993). "Country Comfort: vice and corruption in rural settings." <u>Journal of Contemporary Criminal Justice</u>, Vol. 8, No. 1, pp. 36-61.

[5]Francis A.J. Ianni (1972). <u>A Family Business: Kinship and Social Control in Organized Crime</u>. New York: Russell Sage Foundation; President's Commission on Organized Crime (1986). <u>The Impact</u>. Washington D.C.: U.S. Government Printing Office.

[6]Peter Lupsha (1986). "Organized Crime in the United States," in <u>Organized Crime: A Global Perspective</u>, Robert J. Kelly (ed.). Totowa, N.J.: Rowman and Littlefield.

[7]Ibid.

[8]Ibid.

[9]Ibid.

[10]Ibid.

[11]Lupsha, 86:42.

[12]David R. Johnson (1977). "A Sinful Business: The Origins of Gambling Syndicates in the United States, 1840-1887," in <u>Police and Society</u>, ed. David H. Bayley. Beverly Hills: Sage; Gary W. Potter (1997). "The Antecedents of Southern Organized Crime." Paper presented at the 1997 ACJS conference, March 1997, Louisville, Kentucky.

[13]Potter, 97:1-2.

[14]H.C. Owen (1932). Excerpt from King Crime, in Organized Crime in America: A Book of Readings, Gus Tyler (ed.) Ann Arbor, Michigan: University of Michigan Press. p. 112.

[15] James N. Gilbert (1996). "Organized Crime on the Western Frontier," Criminal Organizations, Vol. 10, No. 2, p.9.

[16]David R. Johnson (1981). American Law Enforcement: A History, cited in Gilbert (1996).

[17]Gilbert, 96:11.

[18]Gilbert, 1996.

[19]Mark Haller (1976). "Gambling in Perspective," in Gambling in America, The Commission on the Review of the National Policy Towards Gambling. Washington D.C.: U.S. Government Printing Office.

[20]Haller, 1976; Nelli, 1976.

[21]Nelli, 76:112.

[22]Ibid.

[23]Lupsha, 86:42.

[24]Lupsha, 1986.

[25]Herbert Asbury (1928). Excerpt from The Gangs of New York, in Tyler (1976), p. 97.

[26]Asbury (excerpted in Tyler,1976), p. 97.

[27]Ibid.

[28]Ibid.

[29]Lupsha, 1976.

[30]Ibid.

[31]Ibid.

130

[32]Alan A. Block (1983). East Side-West Side: Organizing Crime in New York, 1930-1950. New Brunswick, NJ: Transaction; Lupsha, 1986.

[33]Stephen Fox (1989). Blood and Power. New York: William Morrow.

[34]Nelli, 1976.

[35]Ibid.

[36]Ibid.

[37]Ibid.

[38]Ibid.

[39]Mark Haller (1990). "Illegal Enterprise: A Theoretical and Historical Interpretation," Criminology, 28: 207-235.

[40]Nelli, 1976.

[41]Haller, 1990.

[42]Nelli, 1976.

[43]Alan A. Block (1979). "The Snowman Cometh: Coke in Progressive New York," Criminology, 17:94.

[44]Nelli, 1976.

[45]Ibid.

[46]Nelli, 76:111.

[47]Lupsha, 1986.

[48]Nelli, 76:51.

[49]Nelli, 1976.

[50]Ibid.

[51]Nelli, 76:70.

[52]Nelli, 1976.

[53]Nelli, 76:77.

[54]Nelli, 1976.

[55]Fox, 1989; Nelli, 1976.

[56]Fox, 1989.

[57]Fox, 1989; Nelli, 1976.

[58]Nelli, 1976.

[59]Ibid.

[60]Ibid.

[61]Ibid.

[62]Block, 1983.

[63]Nelli, 1976; Fox, 1989.

[64]Nelli, 1976.

[65]Ibid.

[66]Ibid.

[67]Fox, 1989.

[68]Stephen Fox (1989) has observed that alcohol bootlegging had a distinct "ethnic flavor" to it. The WASP population contributed a few notable bootleggers such as Roy Olmstead in Seattle and the Shelton brothers in East St. Louis, but the most significant suppliers were Irish, Easter European Jews, and Italians. Still, while the Irish followed by the Jews followed by the Italians were the dominant forces in the illicit liquor industry, many of the criminal syndicates were characterized by ethnic diversity. For example, the Capone organization in Chicago contained large numbers of Italians, but was not limited to any one ethnic group. In some cities ethnicity was not a central feature in the organization of the illicit booze industry. In New Orleans for example, no single group was able to establish control– U.S. Senator Huey Long along with state and local politicians coordinated the rackets throughout Louisiana.

132

A similar situation existed in San Francisco, where police regulated and directed bootlegging operations.

[69]Mark Haller (1979). "The Changing Structure of American gambling in the Twentieth Century," Journal of Social Issues, Volume 35, No. 3, pp. 87-111.

[70]Nelli, 1976.

[71]Ibid.

[72]Block, 1983; Fox, 1989.

[73]Nelli, 1976.

[74]Fox, 1989.

[75]Nelli, 1976.

[76]Virgil Peterson (1952). Excerpt from The Barbarians in Our Midst, in Tyler (1973); Edward D. Sullivan (1930). Excerpt from Chicago Surrenders, in Tyler (1973); Nelli, 1976; Fox, 1989.

[77]Nelli, 1976.

[78]Ibid.

[79]Ibid.

[80]Ibid.

[81]Fox, 1989.

[82]Nelli, 1976.

[83]Nelli, 1976; Fox, 1989.

[84]Fox, 89:57.

[85]Haller, 1979.

[86]Nelli, 1976.

[87]Nelli, 1976; Block, 1983.

[88]Fox, 1989.

[89]Nelli, 1976; Fox, 1989.

[90]Nelli, 1976.

[91]Haller, 1979; 1990.

[92]Haller, 1979.

[93]Nelli, 1976.

[94]Ibid.

[95]Block, 1983.

[96]Ibid.

[97]Ibid.

[98]Ibid.

[99]Ibid.

[100]Ibid.

[101]Nelli, 1976.

[102]Block, 1983; Nelli, 1976.

[103]Ibid.

[104]Block, 1983.

[105]Block, 83:163.

[106]Nelli, 1976.

[107]Ibid.

[108]Ibid.

134

[109]Ibid.

[110]Ibid.

[111]Ibid.

[112]Ibid.

[113]Ibid.

[114]Block, 1983; Block in Kelly, 1986.

[115]Nelli, 76:253.

[116]William Howard Moore (1974). The Kefauver Committee and the Politics of Crime. Columbia: University of Missouri Press.

[117]Nelli, 1976.

[118]Moore, 1974.

[119]Block, 1983.

[120]Moore, 1974.

[121]President's Commission on Law Enforcement and the Administration of Justice (1967). Task Force Report: Organized Crime. Washington D.C.: U.S. Government Printing Office.

[122]James B. Jacobs, Christopher Panarella, and Jay Worthington (1994). Busting the Mob: U.S. v. Cosa Nostra. New York: New York University Press.

Chapter 5

Organized Crime in America: 1945-1998

Post-World War II America has witnessed events even more revolutionary than the rapid urbanization and industrialization of the late nineteenth century. An explosion in population and the incredible expansion of the technological base has altered American society forever. Naturally, rapid transportation, space-age communications, and the expeditious management of information has had an impact on the nature of organized crime as well. While the law enforcement community has employed new and better techniques in their fight against organized criminals, illegal entrepreneurs have countered with increasingly sophisticated methods and an expansion of their illicit activities. From the illegal disposal of hazardous waste, to the laundering of illicit profits through commercial banks, to fuel-related tax scams, organized crime has expanded its scope and evolved into something new.

Industrial Racketeering

In addition to its increasing sophistication, what seems most clear in the latter half of the twentieth century is that organized crime is virtually unbounded and hopelessly intertwined with legitimate commerce. No where is this statement more true than in the realm of industrial, labor, and business racketeering. Ever since the Gilded Age of the 1890's, organized crime has been "deeply enmeshed" with both credit structures and distribution facilities. Whether by extortion or through legal ownership, organized criminal elements have in the past and to this day continue to impact American business and commerce in profound ways. The racketeers' legacy in labor and business is the systematic restraint of trade, the pillaging of union benefit funds, and the laundering of illicit revenue through otherwise legitimate business and financial institutions. The costs to consumers and businessmen is beyond measure. Worse, there appears to be no limit to the commercial activities organized criminals involve themselves in. A partial list of legitimate industries infiltrated by organized crooks include: advertising, appliances, automobiles, banking, coal, construction, pharmaceuticals, electrical equipment, florists, meat, seafood, dairy products, groceries, cheese, olive oil, fruit, garments, import-export businesses, insurance, liquor, news services, newspapers, oil, paper products, radio, ranching, real estate, restaurants, scrap metal, shipping, steel, television, theaters, and transportation. It seems that the list of possibilities is bounded only by opportunity.[1] In 1979, the U.S. Justice Department estimated that Cosa Nostra members (representing only a fraction of all organized criminals in the U.S.) owned 10,000 legitimate businesses which generated approximately $12 billion annually.[2]

The racketeering side of organized criminal endeavors has traditionally involved the creation and control of employer trade associations and the infiltration of labor unions. Since the 1950's, labor racketeering, or perhaps more appropriately, *industrial* racketeering, has permeated the industrial economy of the United States, especially in those markets where 1) labor costs are significant competitive factors, 2) the industry is characterized by a local rather than a national product market, and 3) the market is characterized by many under-capitalized firms which are vulnerable to labor strife. The official response to industrial racketeering has fallen well short of success. For example, collective bargaining contracts are not subject to the Sherman Anti-Trust Act, enforcement under the Hobbs Act is not applicable to labor unions, and authorities have failed to consider all of the options (mainly civil) available to them under the federal RICO statute.[3] Modern racketeers, in collusion with government officials, have infiltrated numerous industrial sectors and overwhelmed the regulatory role of the government, most notably in those economic zones involving the protection of the environment and the construction of buildings.[4] Unsafe (and overpriced) structures, spoiled food, higher prices on countless goods, exploited workers, and a poisoned environment have been organized crime's greatest contributions.

A good example of the prevailing quality of industrial racketeering involves the International Longshoreman's Association (ILA). In 1954 the New York State Waterfront Commission reported on years of criminal activities and forced the expulsion of the ILA from the American Federation of Labor (AFL). However, the ILA eventually prevailed over the new union, the International Brotherhood of Longshoremen, and re-entered the AFL. After the infamous racketeer Albert Anastasia was murdered in 1957, his brother Anthony wielded great power in the ILA and consolidated the Brooklyn locals along with Joe Biondo, Vito Genovese, and Carlo Gambino. From the 1960's through the mid-70's, the power of the Waterfront Commission was largely circumscribed. In 1978, the federal UNIRAC probe revealed that New York City mobsters affiliated with the ILA (Mike Clemente, Tino Fiumara, and Anthony Scotto, with close ties to New York Governor Hugh Carey) had set up shop in Miami, confirming that while its power had been weakened somewhat during a transitional period in the mid-1950's, organized crime's grip on the waterfront is not limited geographically and is distinguished by its continuity.[5]

Another industry unable to break the grip of organized crime is garment manufacturing. Due largely to a decrease in overseas competition and a cheap supply of labor from illegal aliens, the number of garment sweatshops has rapidly increased in New York City.[6] Trucking firms, many of which are controlled by the Gambino and Lucchese "families," finance and set up "sweatshops" favored by the 7th Avenue manufacturers who find it easier and cheaper to contract work out to criminal elements. The losers are the workers (sometimes children), who are paid extremely low wages and are forced to work in harsh conditions violative of OSHA regulations. The winners in the scheme are trucking outfits which elevate cartage rates, 7th Avenue "jobbers" who produce their wares more cheaply, and retailers who mark up clothing which has been produced quite inexpensively. Manufacturers cannot switch to trucking firms with lower rates because the market is controlled. Deregulation has ensured that 90% of trucking in the New York City region is not subject to ICC regulations.[7]

The construction industry in New York City has been dominated by organized criminals since at least the 1920's. In 1922, the Lockwood Commission (the New York State Joint Legislative Committee on Housing) found "extensive union extortion of builders and contractors, expressed amazement at the extent of collusive agreements among contractors and suppliers, and documented racketeers using their control over construction unions to extort large tribute payments from builders and contractors by threatening to withhold labor unless the payments were made. The Commission also reported that contractors and suppliers had substantially eliminated competition by forming cartels or "combinations."[8] Seventy years later, the New York State Organized Crime Task Force found that the New York City construction industry had not changed, and concluded that the industry's susceptibility to racketeer domination was a result of five factors: 1) the nature of the labor market (controlled by mob-infiltrated unions); 2) the structure of collective bargaining (including the balkanization of bargaining units and the weakness of employer associations); 3) the competitive business environment; 4) the high cost of construction delays; and 5) the fragility of the construction process.[9] The industry has been and remains characterized by extortion, bribery, theft (from building sites), various frauds (related to billing, pension funds, tax evasion, and performance bonds), sabotage (of construction sites), and bid-rigging. The following excerpts are just a few of many examples:

> George Boylan, business manager of Local 5 of the International Brotherhood of Boilermakers, was convicted of extorting more than $1 million over a fifteen year period from six construction companies working on electrical power plants. Boylan threatened a strike if the payments were not made. His demands were allegedly supported by Pittsburgh organized crime figures.[10]

On June 4, 1987, two operators of a Long Island pipe supply company pleaded guilty to stealing $1 million worth of pipes from New York City's pipeyards...the scheme involved cash payments of $250,000 in cash bribes to employees of the City's Department of Environmental Protection to obtain their assistance in stealing the pipes and pipe fittings. The defendants sold the stolen pipes to contractors working on the City's sewer and water mains. In effect, the defendants thus stole the pipes from the City and then sold them back to the City.[11]

As the Marriott Marquis Hotel neared completion, work kept getting done and undone, electrical work was put in and pulled out, and cement was poured down toilets...one week before the opening of the South Street Seaport in 1983, all wiring on Schermerhorn Row was cut. Workers were then paid overtime to repair the damages.[12]

...recent federal prosecutions proved the existence of a "concrete contractor's club" which conspired to rig bids and allocate markets for all poured concrete used in New York City construction. Nonclub members were prevented from submitting bids on concrete contracts totaling more than $2 million through union threats of labor problems, concrete supply difficulties and physical harm. The conspiracy was policed by Ralph Scopo, a member of the Colombo Crime family and president of the District Council of Cement and Concrete Workers, and by three other New York City organized crime families. The four families divided equally approximately two percent of the price of every contract.[13]

The scope of organized crime's power is exemplified in the last example, where essentially any major construction project in New York City was subject to a two percent "tax" by the mob.[14]

While racketeering on the part of organized criminals has not been limited to any one industry or trade union, the International Brotherhood of Teamsters is exemplary. The International Brotherhood of Teamsters, Chauffeurs, Warehousemen, Stablemen, and Helpers of America was founded and given an AFL charter in 1898. The first Teamsters president, Cornelius P. Shea, was indicted for extorting money from team owners, and was followed by Dan Tobin, who controlled the union for the next forty years. The first significant infiltration of organized crime into the union may have occurred in 1941, when Jimmy Hoffa, at that time the negotiating chairman of the

Central States Driver's Council, called in mob muscle to drive Denny Lewis and the CIO out of Detroit. Although Dave Beck was elected president of the Teamsters in 1951, it was Hoffa and his supporters who were running the union by the mid-1950's. By that time Hoffa had developed relationships with many organized crime figures, including Morris Dalitz in Las Vegas, Paul DeLucia, Sam Giancana, Joseph Glimco, and Paul Dorfman in Chicago, Nick Civella in Kansas City, and Tony Provenzano, Frank Plumeri, and the Dioguardi brothers in the East. It was Jimmy Hoffa who helped set up the Michigan Conference of Teamsters Welfare Fund and the Central States Health and Welfare Fund, which came to be administered by the Union Casualty Insurance Company, owned by Paul "Red" Dorfman's wife Rose and his stepson, Allen.

As president of the Chicago Scrap Hauler's Union, Paul Dorfman (previously a Capone associate) maintained an intimate association with Chicago's underworld. After the Reconstruction Finance Corporation outlived its legitimate purpose and could no longer be plundered by organized criminals, it was the Central States Pension Fund, administered by Allen Dorfman, which became the "mob's bank." Through Dorfman, hundreds of millions of dollars were funneled to criminal entrepreneur's for real estate investments in south Florida, resorts in southern California, and hotel/casinos in Las Vegas.[15]

The McClellan Committee hearings, spearheaded by soon-to-be Attorney General Robert Kennedy, brought corruption in the Teamsters Union into the light in the late 1950's. Former IBT president Dave Beck was convicted in 1959 for violating federal income tax laws, while Hoffa, after dodging Kennedy bullets for a number of years, was convicted of jury tampering in 1964. Governmental reform efforts had a minimal impact, however, as labor leasing schemes (where workers were fired and then rehired without seniority or benefits), "white paper contracts" meant to undermine master freight agreements, and "sweetheart" deals continued to characterize union-employer relationships. And, as always, benefit funds, administered by corrupt trustees and executors, continued to be plundered at the expense of the rank and file. Asset managers and service providers like Allen Dorfman paid themselves exorbitant salaries while billing for non-existent or unnecessary administrative fees. While drafting governing by-laws intended to ensure the accumulation of large cash reserves, trustees directed payments to organized crime businesses for fictitious services and placed organized crime associates and friends on the union payroll for "no-show" jobs. Of course, criminal entrepreneurs in need of a loan for licit and illicit business ventures could always depend on the Central States "bank."[16]

Organized criminals nationwide cashed in on some of the nation's largest union health and welfare funds through fraudulent health plans. As is often the case, the provider of services which contracts with the union is not the end provider, but merely handles the claims. Payments on behalf of workers go to insurance companies or prepaid health plans which charge inflated fees and bill for services never rendered. In many cases, the service provider is merely a corporate shell, while fund administrators, asset managers, insurance executives, lawyers, doctors, dentists, and accountants front for organized criminals who funnel union funds. For example, a Laborers' Union health benefit administrator with ties to the Chicago underworld diverted 68% of the money paid out for dental care to third party providers for "administrative costs."[17] In another case, a provider charged the union $100,000 for a *list* of dentists.[18]

After Hoffa's disappearance in 1975, the Teamsters came under close scrutiny by the Special Investigations Staff (SIS) of the Department of Labor as well as the Internal Revenue Service. Aside from a large number of questionable loans made to companies on the verge of bankruptcy, $418 million in pension fund loans had been made to seven entities controlled by three men, all of whom were known to have organized crime connections. These three men were David Glick, a front for organized criminals in the ownership of several Las Vegas casinos, Meyer Lansky protégé Alvin Malnik, and Morris Shenker, former attorney for Jimmy Hoffa and the recipient of $40 million in questionable pension fund loans on behalf of the Dunes

Hotel and Casino. With the fraudulent manipulation of the Central States, Southeast, and Southwest Areas Pension Funds as their target, federal investigators equipped with the new Employment Retirement Income Security Act (ERISA) found themselves in a unique position to break the hold racketeers had over the Teamsters. Unfortunately, the opportunity to reform pension fund mismanagement/theft was largely squandered as the IRS refused to coordinate with the Department of Labor by unexpectedly revoking the pension fund's tax exempt status, while the Department of Labor handcuffed the SIS by ordering investigators not to pursue a third part investigation. Ultimately, the government failed to attain an enforceable agreement, so when the fund's tax exempt status was reinstated, the union Board of Trustees soon discontinued their cooperation with many of the original reform conditions never having been met.[19]

With the death of Hoffa's successor Frank Fitzsimmons in 1981, organized crime entered into negotiations to determine who would be the new IBT president. Roy Lee Williams, who maintained close ties to Nick Civella in Kansas City and had the support of the Chicago "family," was elected. Williams' ultimate deferral to mob power is evidenced by his later testimony stating that he dared not interfere with the affairs of powerful locals such as Anthony Provenzano's 560 in New Jersey. Williams, Dorfman, and Chicago organized crime boss Joey Lombardo were convicted in 1982 of conspiring to bribe United States Senator Howard Cannon of Nevada for his influence in blocking or delaying the deregulation of trucking freight rates. A month later, Dorfman was murdered.[20]

Abuses in the Teamsters union continued under the presidency of Jackie Presser, who was simultaneously controlled by organized criminals while serving as a secret FBI informant. Presser's information led to over seventy convictions, yet miraculously, he died of natural causes. Successes against the mobster elements in the Teamsters continued throughout the 1980's. The first large scale application of the federal RICO statute was utilized in 1984 when Provenzano's Local 560 was placed under a trusteeship. The Teamsters and the government also negotiated important consent decrees meant to direct the legal investment of pension fund monies.[21] Still, abuse and organized crime control of IBT locals continued under Presser and his successor, Bill McCarthy.[22] The latest IBT president, Ron Carey, has been praised for "cleaning up" the Teamsters, yet his own re-election was invalidated in late 1997 by a federal overseer.[23] Carey's campaign manager Jere Nash and campaign consultants Martin Davis and Michael Ansara have pled guilty to charges involving "donation swaps" with the Democratic National Committee (DNC). The scheme involved a diversion of money from the ailing Teamsters' treasury to the DNC, the AFL-CIO, and various "political advocacy organizations." In return, those groups would steer money back to the Carey campaign through an organization called, ironically, Teamsters for a Corruption Free Union.[24] Carey was subsequently prohibited from running in the rerun election, and James Hoffa Jr. was elected to the Teamsters presidency in 1998.

Gambling and Illicit Sex

Exploiting certain highly competitive markets through the utilization of ill-gained leverage is but one segment of organized crime's role in the changing environment of the modern American political economy. While mass production and urbanization have created the need for broader credit structures, larger distribution facilities, an expansion of the education system, and the requirement for new governmental roles, the advancing technological base has also precipitated higher standards of living and made possible the enhanced pursuit of leisure activities. The proliferation of businesses catering to the human pleasures has been tightly regulated by the state, "creating a climate for criminal conspiracies that thrive on the systematic avoidance of regulation."[25] Not surprising, then, is organized crime's continued dominance of the vice industries– gambling, prostitution, and illicit drugs.

At the end of World War II, Las Vegas had a population of 20,000 persons and little going for it economically. Twenty years later, Las Vegas had grown to ten times its post World War II size, nurtured and built by enterprising mobsters like

Benjamin Siegel, Frank Costello, Hyman Abrams, and Meyer Lansky. Benjamin "Bugsy" Siegel recognized the potential in Las Vegas early, establishing himself in Los Angeles as a representative of the Trans-America wire service, which he utilized to gain a foothold in the Las Vegas bookmaking industry. Siegel's vision of a massive hotel-casino complex in Vegas was realized in the decade of the 1950's, as ex-bootleggers from the Mid-west and the East Coast invested their money and Teamster Union pension funds in the highly lucrative Las Vegas strip.[26]

Organized criminals have generated tremendous profits through their hidden ownership of legal casinos in Las Vegas and Atlantic City. Front men like Allen Glick were given huge pension fund loans in order to acquire casinos– deals which were arranged, of course, by organized crooks in the Teamsters.[27] In addition to direct or indirect ownership, organized criminals have skimmed large amounts of cash from the casinos by miscalibrating the scales used to weigh coins, or through elaborate scams involving confederates working as casino employees. In Atlantic City infiltration of labor unions integral to the functioning of hotel/casinos (security guards, restaurant workers, bartenders, etc.) have allowed criminals to use that leverage profitably, to the detriment of legal owners.[28] Organized criminals have also involved themselves in enterprises peripheral to the casino business, including the collection of credit "markers" and the operation of junket services. After relocating in Arizona, New York City's Bonnano family grossed $13 million in one year from just one licensed junket operation.[29]

Despite organized crime's overwhelming dominance of gambling enterprises, authorities now believe that legal casinos are free of mob control. Large-scale gambling is heavily regulated and has now become part of corporate America. Still, experts agree that continued vigilance is required, as not all governmental interventions have been successful. A case in point is the Bicycle Club Casino, a legal enterprise in California that was used by Asian organized crime groups to launder illicit drug profits. A 1996 Senate Governmental Affairs hearing heard testimony that revealed the U.S. Marshal Service had been running the casino since it was seized under the federal asset forfeiture program in 1990. Worse, the casino lost money and illegality continued after the Marshal Service took over. Four years after the Government seized control, the highest paid employee of the casino was convicted of conspiracy, loan sharking, and extortion of casino patrons.[30] Another reason for concern is the under-regulation of casinos on Indian reservations. Indian gaming is a $6 billion a year industry, and must be an attractive target for criminals. While officials have asserted that there is absolutely no evidence that Indian casinos have been infiltrated by organized crime, Nevada's Senator Harry Reid has pointed out that since the federal government has neither the mechanism nor the expertise to regulate class III gaming, it is shortsighted to suggest there is no organized crime involvement– authorities simply don't know.[31]

Even if legal casinos are truly free of criminal involvement, organized crime continues to operate illegal casinos, numbers games, and bookmaking enterprises. The numbers racket has not diminished as a result of legal lotteries, and continues to generate large profits for African-American, Puerto-Rican, Cuban, and Italian numbers enterprises.[32] In addition to numbers, one of the largest income producers for organized crime is the taking of bets on sporting events. Although off-track betting on horses continues to be quite popular, it is the ever-growing popularity of professional as well as amateur sports like football, basketball, and baseball which provides the bookmaking industry with multi-billion dollar profits. In conjunction with their bookmaking interests, organized crime has a long history of infiltrating and corrupting professional and amateur athletics, including point-shaving scams and the virtual ownership of some professional boxers.[33]

A relatively new gambling enterprise for organized crime is the placement of video poker games into bars and restaurants. In New Jersey, state police seized five video poker machines which had generated $500,000 over a fifteen month period. Still, the wave of the future in illegal gaming may be the Internet, where "virtual casino" websites are growing exponentially. As of mid-1998, about 140 Internet sites offered pay-to-play casino type games.[34]

Like gambling, the sex trade continues to flourish in the United States. In 1976, federal officials estimated the dollar volume of the pornography industry at $4 billion annually.[35] Huge profits are generated from significant mark-ups on sexually explicit movies, books, and paraphernalia. For example, a 1980's era porn magazine might cost about fifty cents to make, but wholesale at five dollars and retail at ten. The Pennsylvania Crime Commission asserts that organized crime involvement in pornography began in the late 1960's, when John Franzese recognized the potential in supplying and operating "peep show" machines in Times Square adult bookstores. Soon thereafter, organized crime figures from the Colombo, DeCalvacante, and Galante families created pornographic film production and distribution companies like Allstate Film Labs and Bryanston Productions.[36] Since then, pornography rings have become national in scope and vertically integrated, controlling in many cases production, distribution, and retailing. Competitive advantages in the porn industry are typically engineered through "strong arm tactics," and include requiring producers to process film at organized crime controlled labs, forcing producers to distribute through organized crime controlled companies under threat of piracy, burglarizing independent retail outlets, and intimidating theater owners screening pirated versions of organized crime controlled films.[37]

Pornography rings have been characterized by their sophistication and geographic scope. The career of Pennsylvania pornographer John Krasner is illustrative. At the time of his death in 1979 (he was shot in Florida by porn competitors from California), Krasner was associated with over fifty companies which employed more than one hundred people. The porn merchant controlled his chain of adult bookstores from a five story warehouse in Allentown. The scope of Krasner's pornography empire included Pennsylvania, New York, New Jersey, and Virginia, with interests in other states including Florida and Colorado. The following excerpt from the 1980 Pennsylvania Crime Commission Report underscores the sophistication and breadth of Krasner's operation:

A bookstore run by Krasner was masked behind a veil of corporations and changing faces. According to former Krasner employees, a typical Krasner store includes multiple corporations which are formed using "straw parties." Information received by the Crime Commission indicated at least one person to whom Krasner paid monthly fees for using her name on various corporate papers. New stores were generally formed in the name of a corporation by someone from Krasner's Allentown headquarters. Many times, the corporation was formed exclusively for the purpose of opening that store. One source explained that this was done so a court injunction against a single corporation would affect only one store, rather than several. Once the store was opened, a manager, employed by a second corporation, assumed control of the store. The clerks were usually local people employed by the manager.Certain supplies for the stores were packaged by a third corporation and delivered by a fourth. The peep-show booths were constructed by a fifth enterprise, while the projectors and films in the booths, along with the collection of all the quarters customers paid for the peep shows, were handled by a sixth corporation. The money from the sale of magazines and other products was forwarded to Allentown, where a seventh corporation administered the accounting duties. An eighth corporation handled the acquisition and licensing of the vehicles used in Krasner's operation.[38]

Of course, Krasner's enterprise represents just one of many in the national pornography industry. In Los Angeles for example, officials believe that 80% of the production and distribution of pornographic materials is controlled by organized criminals.[39]

Trafficking in pornography over the Internet has quickly grown into an international problem and is extremely difficult to regulate. In September 1995 FBI agents arrested twelve people involved in an "on-line" child pornography ring. The criminals used America Online, the nation's largest Internet service provider, to transmit pornographic pictures and computer simulated images of children ages two to thirteen nude or having sex. In September 1998 authorities in twelve countries including the United States collaborated in a sting that netted almost four dozen members of the "Wonderland Club," a network of pedophiles that traded images of sexually exploited children "like baseball cards." The Wonderland case is an offshoot of an investigation into the San Jose-based "Orchid Club," which led to the arrest of men who raped an eleven year old girl and transmitted pictures of the assault over the World Wide Web.[40] The unlimited geographic scope of the Internet is also used by pedophiles (and organizations which provide children to pedophiles) to identify and lure young children.

Naturally prostitution continues to be significant and has become an increasingly sophisticated organized crime activity. For example, Richard Toner, who has been dubbed the "computerized pimp," ran a prostitution ring from his home using a computer program to profile potential customers for his "out-call massage service." By feeding data into his computer, Toner weeded out potentially dangerous clients or those who fit the profile of law enforcement agents. Like many massage parlor operations today, Toner accepted Visa and MasterCard and advertised in the local newspaper. Prostitutes carried portable credit card processors, while customers were billed under the name of a fictitious sewing machine company. A "switchboard madam" handled incoming calls and assignments, and contacted "company employees" by beeper.[41]

"Call-girl" operations like Toner's are proliferating, as are massage parlors which typically front for prostitution operations. Most of them also offer legal services (non-sexual massages, body tanning, etc.) in addition to illicit sex. These enterprises operate much like any legitimate business, accepting credit card payments, maintaining a payroll, paying taxes, advertising, and even providing benefits for employees. A quick perusal of any small, medium, or big city yellow pages reveals scores of massage and out-call services, most of which are fronts. Prostitution businesses of this sort are typically links in a chain of operations run by the same "business-person."[42] Law enforcers are of course cognizant of these quasi-legal enterprises, but generally take a "hands-off" approach so long as the criminals maintain a low profile (and presumably, make regular payments to the police). While the typical massage parlor operation may seem relatively innocuous, sex services offered by crime networks range from the "conventional" to the deviant, meeting every type of demand. For example, child pornography and prostitution services are provided by organized crime networks to pedophiles around the world. In fact, the United States is one of the chief suppliers of "kiddie" porn to countries of the European Union.[43]

Drugs and Tobacco

Trafficking in illicit drugs remains one of the most significant criminal industries in the United States. In 1995 Americans spent about $57 billion on illegal drugs, much of which is smuggled into the United States by international crime networks.[44] Profits from the distribution of illicit drugs (as well as other criminal enterprises) have become so great that the very nature of organized crime has been altered. The direct providers of illegal goods have become increasingly dependent on the services of upper-world professionals to handle and launder the staggering amounts of cash produced by the narcotics trade. Authorities estimate that worldwide, between $300 billion and $500 billion are laundered through financial institutions every year.[45] More than ever before, collusive arrangements, partnerships, and patron-client relationships bind the purveyors of vice to prominent lawyers, accountants, politicians, and bankers attracted by drug dollars. In fact, the money involved in the global narcotics industry is so great that the economies of some nations are largely dependent on the flow of narco-dollars, while how to regulate or control the industry has become the domain of international politics. With the profits from narcotics distribution rivaling those of the world's largest corporations, illegal entrepreneurship has now become the province of governments and nation-states.[46]

A look at contemporary narcotics trafficking in the United States begins with the Cotroni brothers, who established the "French connection" in the 1950's. At that time, opium was cultivated in Turkey, refined in Marseilles, and shipped to major American ports, especially New York City. With additional connections in Montreal through Carmine Galante and in Cuba with Santos Trafficante, the supply of heroin to U.S. addicts was assured.[47] Responding to the growing number of addicts returning from war in Vietnam, President Nixon declared the first "war on drugs" in 1972. This effort successfully eliminated opium cultivation in Turkey's Anatolian Plateau. Unfortunately, the U.S. was to learn a hard lesson in the global supply and demand of commodities, as the suppression in Turkey stimulated increased production in Southeast and eventually Southwest Asia along the mountainous highlands from Pakistan to Laos. Asian syndicates responded to Nixon's drug war by exporting their heroin to Europe and Australia, while the American market was captured by Mexico.[48]

By the late 1970's cocaine had become the drug of choice for millions of Americans. From 1977 to 1987, cocaine imports increased tenfold, precipitating a tremendous criminal justice and medical problem.[49] Using the Bahamas as a major transshipment point for cocaine as well as marijuana, the Colombian Medellin and Cali "cartels," (through men like Jorge Ochoa, Pablo Escobar, and Joe Lehder) were importing 72 tons of cocaine a year into the United States by 1985.[50] Grown in the poor South American countries of Bolivia and Peru, the cultivation of coca has been intimately tied with the economic fortunes of those nations. Naturally then, the supply oriented suppression efforts of the United States have not been welcomed by the Bolivian or Peruvian governments. Similarly, syndicates involved in the refinement and distribution of cocaine have consistently corrupted the Colombian government. Experts agree that the American supply side approach to decrease the consumption of illicit drugs has failed time and again, and that the only way to remove drug profits from illegal entrepreneurs is through the elimination of demand.[51]

While policies aimed at curbing drug use in the U.S. have been an utter failure, the matter is exacerbated by the fact that certain elements of the U.S. Government have fostered narcotics production and distribution. For example, the CIA's complicity in the global drug trade has been well-documented. Before the creation of the Central Intelligence Agency, U.S. covert operations were largely the province of the Office of Strategic Services (OSS). Through its corporate front, the Sea

Supply Corporation, the OSS was responsible for bolstering the Southeast Asian opium trade, helping the opium dealing Chief of Police in Thailand to create a police force which surpassed the Thai Army in strength. Having re-armed remnants of the Chinese Kuomintang Army in the early 1950's for warfare against the Communist Chinese, the CIA, faced with budgetary constraints, developed relationships with warlords of the local hill tribes in the Shan States. Alliances forged by the CIA tied the Nationalist Chinese opium supply in Burma with demand in Bangkok and Hong Kong, thereby financing the war effort.[52]

The CIA's promotion of poppy cultivation in the Shan States set a precedent for the financing of future covert operations. Over its fifty year history, CIA missions worldwide have stimulated the trade in opium, opium derivatives, and cocaine. From Burma to Laos to Afghanistan to Central America, the cultivation of the poppy and coca have financed the political agendas of numerous U.S. administrations. Washington D.C., responding to the epidemic use of cocaine throughout the 1980's, declared a "war on drugs," simultaneously protecting and financing political allies who supplied the drug to American users.[53] While elements of the Reagan and Bush Administrations covertly financed the Contras in Honduras through the sale of cocaine, official White House policy involved the allocation of funds to South American countries to *limit* the cultivation of coca. At about the same time, the Bush Administration overlooked the threefold increase in world opium production between 1982 and 1990.[54] As Alfred McCoy has observed, "the increasing opium harvests in Afghanistan and Burma were, in part, the legacy of CIA covert operations past and present... Just as CIA support for KMT troops in the Shan States had increased Burma's opium crop in the 1950's, so the Agency's aid to mujaheddin guerillas in the 1980's expanded opium production in Afghanistan and linked Pakistan's nearby heroin laboratories to the world market."[55]

While contradictions in U.S. foreign policy have for years fostered global narcotics distribution, domestic supply networks have been equally detrimental. Alan Block observes that "U.S. intelligence agencies have either merged with drug enforcement agencies enrolling key drug agents and officials in counterintelligence work as with the Federal Bureau of Narcotics, or later created cells of CIA agents within the DEA."[56] So, in addition to outright corruption, the enforcement of drug laws has often taken a backseat to intelligence concerns. To further exacerbate the failure of U.S. drug policy, stateside distribution of narcotics has frequently become the realm of entrepreneurs within the criminal justice system. Recent examples in major American cities like New York, Philadelphia, and New Orleans demonstrate that some of the more significant drug dealers are police officers, while arrest quotas merely produce an emphasis on low-level dealers and users.[57]

Recently, the emphasis on narcotics importation to the U.S. has focused on the activities of the Mexican drug cartels. Drug transshipment routes have shifted somewhat from the eastern Caribbean Sea to land routes through Mexico and the porous U.S.-Mexico border.[58] Many blame the North American Free Trade Agreement (NAFTA) for the increase in Mexican drug trafficking– before NAFTA in 1993, 1.9 million trucks crossed the border, but after passage of the agreement the number immediately rose to 2.8 million in 1994, with those numbers increasing yearly. The Mexican cartels (the Gulf Cartel, the Juarez Cartel, the Sinaloa Cartel, the Sonora Cartel, and the Tijuana Cartel) are investing in Mexican trucking firms and warehouses to use as fronts for their smuggling operations.[59]

Juarez Cartel leader Amado Carillo Fuentes revolutionized the Mexican drug trafficking industry by utilizing Boeing 727s for bulk shipments of up to fifteen tons of cocaine.[60] Mexico has now become the main conduit for Colombian cocaine bound for the U.S. In fact, about 70% of all cocaine, 25% of all heroin, and 80% of all marijuana consumed in the United States enters the country from Mexico.[61] In addition, Mexican traffickers have replaced outlaw motorcycle gangs as the primary manufacturers and distributors of methamphetamine, and are now responsible for about 80% of all "speed" consumed in the U.S.[62] Like drug trafficking throughout the world, the industry in Mexico has resulted in endemic corruption at all levels of government. The brother of ex-Mexican-president Carlos Salinas (now in exile) has been tied to the Gulf Cartel (Raul Salinas is believed to have funneled some $300 million in drug money into Swiss accounts.)[63] Meanwhile, the Colombian traffickers have moved into heroin production and distribution with a product that is estimated to be 80% to 100% pure.[64] In November 1998, Defense Minister Rodrigo Lloreda stated that the Colombian Air Force had been "seriously infiltrated" by drug traffickers, this coming just four days after a Colombian Hercules C-130 transport plane was seized in Fort Lauderdale with 1,639 pounds of cocaine and 13 pounds of heroin on board.[65]

While trafficking in heroin, cocaine, marijuana, and other illicit drugs receive greater attention, at least one organized crime scholar has suggested that the smuggling of tobacco products and the evasion of taxes on those products may rival the illicit narcotics trade in profitability.[66] In the United States, the smuggling of cigarettes is driven by disparate tax rates between the states. For example, a truck that can haul 1,000 cases of cigarettes bought legally in North Carolina (where the tax is two cents per pack) can realize a gross profit of $100,000 for just that one truck load if the cigarettes are smuggled and sold at retail prices in Connecticut or Massachusetts (where the tax is twenty-one cents per pack).[67] Smuggling into New York City is even more profitable, since the city adds a seven cents per pack tax to the New York State tax of fifteen cents.[68] Organized smugglers often steal or counterfeit cigarette tax stamps (called "fusons," these stamps let authorities know that the tax has been paid). Metered cigarette stamping machines are stolen, tampered with, and reproduced so that cigarettes can be stamped without state taxes ever having been collected. Wholesalers in North Carolina have aided smugglers by running their stamping meters without actually stamping the cigarettes. A 1976 report from the Organized Crime Desk of the Law Enforcement Assistance Administration estimated that the tax revenue lost from just ten U.S. states was $10 million.[69] Aside from the lost tax revenue, legitimate cigarette wholesalers, distributors, transporters, and retailers are placed at a competitive disadvantage by the activities of smugglers, and some are forced out of business. A New York State

Commission of Investigation reported that one-hundred tobacco retailers had succumbed due to smuggling in 1971 alone, while at least one trucking company went under as a result of repeated hijackings.[70]

The problem of cigarette smuggling, like so many other organized crime activities, is exacerbated by the participation of public officials. Beginning in March 1972, a Philadelphia based cigarette smuggling ring brought in four million cartons of contraband cigarettes from North Carolina– the total loss to Pennsylvania in tax revenue was about $7.5 million. In the indictment of Pennsylvania's largest cigarette wholesalers, information was released which indicated that the defendants had made weekly payments of $1,000 to officials in the Pennsylvania Department of Revenue. In return, the revenue officials kept the defendants informed of confidential state and federal investigations. Other cigarette smuggling activities in the early 1970's involved members of the Democratic City Committee in Philadelphia and members of the Cigarette Tax Bureau. In order to evade payment of the Pennsylvania tax, the smugglers paid an employee of Pitney-Bowes $10 a case to alter tax meter machines to conceal the fact that many cigarettes had been stamped illegally with a counterfeit stamp. Today, as many states and now the federal government continue to levy so-called "sin taxes" on items like cigarettes (increasing the state to state disparity in tax rates), opportunities for organized smugglers and crooked officials will likely increase.

Organized Theft

In addition to the plethora of vice and racketeering activities perpetuated by organized criminals, organized thefts may well be the largest of criminal "industries" worldwide. Mob control of air, rail, and water freight terminals (through union infiltrations and employer associations) has provided crooks with billions of dollars in easily plundered cargo. The 1970 report of the Pennsylvania Crime Commission provides an explicit example:

At New York's Kennedy Airport, where billions of dollars of air freight passes each year, $3.4 million in cargo was stolen in 1969 in 545 major thefts. All trucking companies which carry freight from Kennedy Airport must belong to the Metropolitan Import Truckmen's Association. In 1965 the New York Commission of Investigation concluded that Cosa Nostra leader John Masiello was the "behind the scenes" power of the association. Soon thereafter he relinquished his control, and it passed to Anthony DiLorenzo, a rising member of the Vito Genovese family. (DiLorenzo was convicted in 1969 of interstate transportation of stolen stocks from New York to Gettysburg). Teamsters Union Local 295, which holds a monopoly over all air freight labor at Kennedy, has been controlled by such Cosa Nostra leaders as John Dioguardia and Anthony Corallo. When such organized crime infiltration of both labor and management associations comes to light, it is more easy to understand the multi-million dollar annual thefts at Kennedy Airport.[71]

Tractor-trailer hijackings are commonly arranged by groups of organized criminals. Researchers have observed that "most hijackings today are give-ups in which drivers, in accordance with prior arrangements, deliver the merchandise to thieves and then claim they were hijacked." As an example of how lucrative hijacking can be, in 1975 "Izzy" Hubsshman hijacked one tractor trailer of *beef* valued at $100,000.[72]

Large-scale theft relies on professional fences who move quantities of stolen goods, mix hot items with legitimate stock, and even provide technical support and coordination services for thieves.[73] A Senate Committee in 1974 heard testimony which suggested that many goods are "stolen for order." The witness asserted that "the markets are already established and the property is absorbed into our economic system just like a huge dry sponge."[74] Blakey and Goldsmith write:

> The Syndicate's connections with master and professional fences, and the influence it exerts over many legitimate businesses, have enabled it to develop a redistribution system capable of funneling stolen goods through interstate commerce with great ease.[75]

In the United States in 1974, losses from transportation theft alone were estimated to be $1 *billion*.[76]

New Scams and Increasing Sophistication

While never abandoning their highly lucrative vice, theft, and racketeering endeavors, organized criminals have expanded their business activities into a vast number of legal and illegal enterprises virtually spanning the spectrum of U.S. commerce. One of the more disturbing developments in organized crime has been its participation in the disposal of hazardous wastes. In recent decades, the governmental response to the hazardous waste dilemma has been to legislate and regulate the industry, in effect making it very expensive for establishments to safely dispose of waste material. In addition to those firms content to handle the problem on their own through midnight dumping, other criminals have provided a cheap alternative to abiding by stiff regulations.[77] For example, many organized criminals formerly involved in attempts to monopolize the private sanitation industry incorporated hazardous waste disposal firms, which were utilized to dump toxic and solid waste illegally. In New York, companies like the All County Environmental Service Corporation and the Ra-Mar Waste Management Corporation were merely fronts for organized criminals who used a variety of means to inexpensively dispose of chemical and solid waste. Chemicals have been mixed with household garbage and dumped in municipal landfills, hidden in sludge and spread on the land, flushed out on city streets and down sewers, and added to waste oil to be sold as fuel.[78] A popular method of disposal is described in an Associated Press article:

> One operation that allegedly runs out of Hartford, Connecticut only works in foul weather. A driver watches the forecast for rain or snow, then picks up a tanker load of chemicals. With the discharge valve open he drives on an interstate until 6,800 gallons of hot cargo have dribbled out. "About 60 miles is all it takes to get rid of a load," boasted the driver, "and the only way I can get caught is if the windshield wipers or the tires of the car behind me start melting."[79]

Similar rackets were "endemic" and continued through the 1970's and 1980's. One of the principal locations for "toxic blending" was Long Island's Mattituck terminal, owned by the brother of former Governor Hugh Carey. In 1982, Maryland authorities discovered PCBs in fuel tanks at a large truck stop, and the New Jersey Attorney General indicted five corporations on charges that they mixed hazardous wastes with an "oil blend" and sold it throughout New England and the Middle Atlantic region.[80] Additional corruption, ineptness, and collusion with public officials in agencies like the EPA have ensured massive profits for those elements willing to poison the environment.[81] The recent spate of well-meaning environmental regulations have continued to create highly lucrative black markets. For example, approximately 10,000 to 20,000 metric tons of chloroflourocarbons (which deplete ozone from the atmosphere) are smuggled into the United States every year.[82]

Escalating energy costs have provided new opportunities for organized crooks as well. The Leviticus Project, an investigation of coal fraud in states from New York south to Alabama, concluded in 1980 that "organized crime figures are in the process of acquiring substantial interests in the American coal industry."[83] Project investigators stated:

> Organized crime figures are defrauding foreign buyers and bankrupting domestic coal producers through the use of foreign coal purchase contracts.
>
> Organized crime figures are defrauding investors and facilitating massive tax frauds through the sale of limited partnership interests in coal and mining ventures.
>
> Organized crime figures are heavily involved in both the theft and interstate transportation of stolen coal mining equipment and the fraudulent financing of non-existent or over-valued mining equipment.[84]

The Leviticus Project noted that activities being investigated in association with coal fraud included: "securities fraud, tax fraud, bank fraud, insurance fraud, political and commercial corruption, bribery, murder, extortion, theft of equipment, loan-sharking, advance fee loan schemes, narcotics trafficking, and price-fixing."[85] The racketeers' sophistication and expansion into white-collar-crime-like offenses is exemplified by two Pennsylvania promoters who managed to obtain a $35 million loan from a mid-western bank with only $300,000 worth of coal reserves.[86]

Racketeering in fuels has not been limited to coal, but prominently includes abuses in the fuel oil and gasoline industry. The loss of excise fuel tax revenue is estimated at $1 million dollars a day in California alone, with about half of the profits going to American-based Russian organized crime groups.[87] In circumstances where excise taxes are to be paid by gas retailers, criminal responses include price-fixing by gas station owners, the delivery of "unbranded" fuel to "branded" stations like Mobil or Exxon (called "cross hauling"), the manipulation of gas pump registers, the purchase of smuggled fuel in order to circumvent reporting, and the over-reporting of fuel oil sales to government subsidized housing. Another common practice of fuel racketeers is to mix inexpensive waste oil with heating oil, or mix low-grade fuels with butane in order to increase the octane level. Attempts to collect fuel excise taxes by shifting the responsibility for payment to wholesalers has merely generated new tax evasion scams, principally in the form of false transfers among wholesale firms– when authorities are unable to trace the final "transfer," fuel is sold to retailers and the wholesalers pay no tax.[88]

The expansion of organized crime into new realms in the latter half of the twentieth century has been coupled with a significant increase in the sophistication of its methods. Not only are criminal methods and techniques more complex, but it is increasingly difficult to differentiate between organized crime and white-collar crime. A case in point is the manipulation of the stock market. Over a ten month period in 1971-72, organized criminals artificially inflated the price of Magic Marker stock from $6.50 a share to about $30 a share.[89] More recently, a 1997 *Business Week* article reported that organized crime groups had infiltrated Wall Street, running up stock prices, cashing out early, and extorting money from Wall Street brokers and traders. Organized crime thugs have physically assaulted brokers and traders to "persuade" them to stay away from certain stocks and artificially inflate others. Through the use of front-men, it is estimated that the mob controls as many as two dozen brokerage firms and influences many others.[90] Another good example of merging organized and white-collar crime activities is the infamous savings and loan debacle of the 1980's and 1990's. At least twenty-two failed S&L's can be "tied to joint money-laundering ventures by the CIA and organized crime figures."[91] Spoils from plundered savings and loan institutions were even the subject of "sit-downs" between some of New York City's organized crime families.[92]

The infiltration of "white-collar" industries by the mob has increased its presence in boardrooms and in politics. One prominent example of this trend involves the Genovese Crime family, which has established a health care brokerage company that arranges medical, dental and eye care group plans to over one million people nationwide. The motivation has not been to ensure health coverage for Americans who need it, but to maximize profits by overcharging group health care providers, intimidating health care administrators to approve the overcharges, bribing and intimidating people into bringing business to the company, and accessing private medical records for extortion and blackmail purposes. Experts have noted that this is the only documented case of this type of health care fraud, but also agree that such activity is consistent with the trend toward mob infiltration of "white collar" industries.[93]

In the 1990's computer related crimes have become a growing concern. Organized criminals use computers to perpetuate a variety of crimes, including credit card theft, identity theft, on-line gambling, trafficking in child pornography, money laundering, and the transmission of directions for manufacturing drugs and building bombs. In just the first half of 1998, at least several hundred government agencies, corporations, financial institutions, and universities suffered computer related security break-ins, with losses totaling hundreds of millions of dollars.[94] The need to protect vital systems and sensitive communications have generated "unbreakable" encryption technologies. While necessary and useful, the problem with encryption is the trend to integrate encryption technologies into desktop applications and networks, creating a potential shift in power from government and law enforcement to criminals intent on concealing their activities. In fact, recent events indicate that organized criminals are using encryption technology to further their illicit goals. F.B.I. director Louis Freeh testified before a 1997 Senate committee that an international drug trafficking suspect used a telephone encryption device to frustrate electronic surveillance, while a pedophile used encryption in transmitting child pornography over the Internet.[95] While the use of encryption by criminals is in the early stages, the growth rate is rapid and includes about 1,000 to 1,500 cases worldwide every year.[96]

Evolution of the Mob/Fighting Back

Increasing sophistication and expansion into new and lucrative enterprises were not the only ways that organized crime changed after World War II. Men who were in their twenties during Prohibition realized their full power in the decade of the 1950's and after, while as time wore one, new entrepreneurs and new alliances were forged and destroyed. What has come to be called La Cosa Nostra underwent major changes in the mid-1950's. Meyer Lansky moved from New York to Miami to more closely supervise his interests there and in Cuba, while Vito Genovese assumed control for Frank Costello in what had been the Luciano organization. Albert Anastasia had become the head of the Mangano family and was himself murdered in 1957. Meanwhile, marriages between the Bonnanno and Profaci families pulled the New York and Detroit mobs closer together.[97]

The 1950's and 1960's witnessed the heyday of Italian syndicated crime, yet it was events occurring at roughly the same time which foreshadowed its decline. The coordination of local, state, and federal law enforcement efforts, especially in the Kennedy Administration, internal power struggles evidenced by the murder of Anastasia and the attempted murder of Costello, and the inability to recruit new young members opened the door for a new wave of criminal entrepreneurs.[98] Through the 1960's and into the 1970's, Italian syndicates responded to increasing competition from African-Americans and Hispanic-Americans by importing new blood from Sicily in an attempt to forcefully regain control of certain markets.[99] The 1960's was also a decade which witnessed important power shifts among Italian criminal networks, stemming from the attempted assassination of Carlo Gambino and Thomas Lucchese by Joe Bonnano. The "Bannana Wars" from 1963-1969 in New York ended with Bonnano's expulsion and his realignment with Santos Trafficante of Florida and Carlos Marcello of Louisiana.[100] Although the southern and western triumvirate of Marcello-Trafficante-Bonnano was said to rival the influence of the New York families, it was evident that by the mid-1970's Italian organized crime was in decline.[101] While competition from other groups may have played some part, probably the single greatest factor in the evisceration of the Italian mobs has been a massive and unprecedented effort by the U.S. Government.[102]

While Robert Kennedy's Justice Department did undertake a serious federal crusade against the Italian syndicates, the first sustained attack on Cosa Nostra began in the late 1960's with the passage of appropriate legislation. Title III of the Omnibus Crime Control and Safe Streets Act of 1968 provided for judicially approved electronic surveillance by federal, state, and local law enforcement officials. Amendments in 1986 authorized "roving surveillance," strengthening the government's legal authority to monitor criminal activities. Intercepted conversations have been a component of nearly every major organized crime prosecution in the last thirty years, and have provided law enforcers and scholars with thousands of pages of transcripts which reveal much about the inner workings of Italian syndicated crime.[103]

The "most substantive and procedural law tool in the history of organized-crime control" is the Racketeer Influenced and Corrupt Organizations Act (RICO), itself a part of the Organized Crime Control Act of 1970.[104] RICO makes it a crime to participate in or conduct the affairs of an enterprise through a "pattern of racketeering activity."[105] Before the RICO law the guilt of organized crime figures had to be established individually, which made it very difficult to present a comprehensive picture of organized criminal violations in a single prosecution.[106] RICO removed the constraints on prosecutors, allowing them to try in a single case multiple criminal defendants as a group– in short, law enforcement was no longer attacking distinct criminal acts, but entire *patterns* of criminal activity.[107] In addition to hefty criminal penalties for individual defendants (twenty years for each RICO violation, twenty years for a RICO conspiracy, and additional prison sentences for each predicate offense– in *U.S. v. Salerno*, Cosa Nostra bosses were sentenced to one hundred years each, and could have been sentenced to *three hundred years*), RICO and the Continuing Criminal Enterprise (CCE) provisions of Title II of the Comprehensive Drug Abuse Prevention and Control Act of 1970 also provide for the forfeiture of property (including businesses, offices, jobs, personal property, cars, boats, planes, and real estate) and severe fines (up to $250,000).[108] The RICO statute also contains civil provisions which allow the Government to obtain injunctions to prevent organized criminals from controlling legitimate enterprises. Courts may place enterprises (like labor unions) under a Government trusteeship which bans organized crime members from holding office in or associating with the victim enterprise.[109] However, the success of court-appointed trustees in ridding labor unions of organized crime influence has been mixed. The use of Civil RICO against Teamsters Local 560 is a case in point, as the Government and trustees have found themselves back in court time and again seeking relief against "obstructionist union tactics" or defending themselves against litigation engineered by mob lawyers.[110]

Along with the widespread use of electronic surveillance, the Continuing Criminal Enterprise provisions, and the civil and criminal provisions of the RICO statute, the Witness Security Program has been a significant component in recent successes against organized crime. Authorized by the Organized Crime Control Act of 1970 and implemented by the U.S. Marshal Service, the program protects organized criminals who agree to testify for the government in mob trials. With the

Government's promise of new identities, re-location, jobs, and homes, famous snitches like Sammy Gravano, Thomas Buscetta, Jimmy Fratianno, and Angelo Lonardo have broken Cosa Nostra's code of silence (omerta) repeatedly in major prosecutions beginning in the 1980's.[111]

With the right tools, the Government's attack on Cosa Nostra has been impressive. While there exists no precise figure on how many criminal and civil cases were brought against organized crime in the 1980's, FBI Director William Sessions testified before a Senate subcommittee that between 1981 and 1988 nineteen bosses, thirteen underbosses, and forty-three capos (crew chiefs/captains) had been convicted. At the same hearing, the director of the GAO's Office of Special Investigations stated that between 1983 and 1986, there had been 2,500 indictments of Cosa Nostra figures.[112] One of the more significant cases was *U.S. v. Salerno* (also called the Commission case because the mobsters were charged with operating "The Commission," viewed as a "national board of directors" for Cosa Nostra), in which four of the five New York City bosses were convicted. Another major law enforcement success was the federal UNIRAC investigation of the International Longshoremen's Association, which led to the conviction of 130 businessmen, union officials, and Cosa Nostra figures. Other significant efforts against organized crime during this period were the civil RICO suits filed against Local 560 (controlled by the Genovese family since the 1950's) and against the International Brotherhood of Teamsters, its executive board, and the board's incumbents. Various consent decrees in those cases have had some success in purging racketeer elements from the Teamsters.[113] Other initiatives have taken on international dimensions, one of the most notable being *U.S. v. Badalamenti*, commonly referred to as the "Pizza Connection" case. In that case, a cooperative effort among American, Italian, Swiss, Brazilian, and Spanish law enforcement agencies broke up a network of American Cosa Nostra and Sicilian Mafia groups who had been using state-side pizzerias as fronts for their $1.6 billion heroin and money laundering enterprise.[114] Prosecutions of Cosa Nostra members have continued well into the 1990's, with recent cases including the conviction of crime bosses Vincent "The Chin" Gigante in 1997 and John Gotti Jr. in 1999.

Has this massive law enforcement effort generated the demise of Cosa Nostra? Law enforcers have predicted it, but the Italian syndicates have proven to be extremely durable. In fact, it is probably "premature to predict that the investigations and trials of the 1980's constitute the beginning and last chapter in the history of Cosa Nostra."[115] One notable example is the LaRocca/Genovese family in western Pennsylvania, which is as powerful now as it has ever been.[116] Of course, even if one accepts the notion that the Government has weakened Cosa Nostra, the reality is that Cosa Nostra is but one small part of organized crime in its entirety. The 1980's and 1990's have been characterized by the increasing prominence of numerous organized crime groups operating in the U.S., including African-American, Latino, Chinese, Jamaican, Korean, Vietnamese, Japanese, Nigerian, Colombian, and Russian networks.[117] If Cosa Nostra is in decline, then it seems fairly obvious that other groups are filling the void. In New York City, it has been suggested that Asian street gangs such as "Born to Kill" have become the most significant heroin traffickers.[118] Prison gangs and outlaw motorcycle gangs have also coordinated large scale criminal enterprises nationwide. The Hell's Angels, Pagans, Warlocks, and Outlaws have been especially active in the distribution of illicit drugs (especially methamphetamines), the porn industry, and contract killings.[119] It seems obvious that the law enforcement attack against Cosa Nostra, while impressive, has been directed at only one tentacle of what has been appropriately described as an octopus.[120]

The hydra which is organized crime has many heads– merely chopping one off fails to deal with the others or addresses the social, legal, political, and economic factors which give rise to criminal networks. A glance at the nation reveals that vice crimes continue to flourish because many Americans demand illicit sex, drugs, and gambling. Likewise, business racketeering continues because of the desire to restrain competition and the inseparable nature of legitimate and illicit commerce. What is even more obvious (and disheartening) is the fact that organized crime is something which continues to permeate all levels of government, from the municipal to the federal.

Organized Crime and the White House

In addition to those instances when federal officials have themselves become illegal entrepreneurs, as with the DEA or the CIA, cooperative arrangements and associations between organized criminals and the U.S. Government have not been uncommon, and date back to at least World War II, when Lucky Luciano and "Socks" Lanza aided naval intelligence in securing the New York waterfront. Organized criminals including Vito Genovese were also instrumental in the invasion of Sicily, where they provided intelligence and guidance.[121] Another infamous example of a cooperative effort between organized criminals and the federal government was the attempted assassination of Fidel Castro. When Castro overthrew Batista in 1959, the mob lost many lucrative investments in Cuba. With IBT president Jimmy Hoffa as the liaison (Hoffa had also used a Teamster pension fund to finance arm sales on both sides of the Cuban Revolution), Santos Trafficante, Carlos Marcello, Russell Buffalino, Johnny Rosselli and Sam Giancana allegedly worked for the CIA in an attempt to poison Castro. Hoffa and Giancana were murdered within a month of each other in 1975, possibly to silence them concerning their role in the assassination attempt.[122]

Although speculative, the assassination of President John F. Kennedy may have been orchestrated by organized criminals. Consider the following: 1) The President's father Joe Kennedy was a bootlegger and organized crime associate; 2) Oswald assassin Jack Ruby was an organized criminal with ties to the Chicago underworld (Oswald himself had close ties to his uncle, a bookmaker in the Marcello organization); 3) witnesses have said Carlos Marcello planned to kill Kennedy; 4) telephone records indicate that Ruby talked to numerous mobsters before the Oswald hit; 5) Chicago mobster Sam Giancana had ties to the CIA and to President Kennedy (remember that Giancana was allegedly hired by the CIA to kill Castro, while both

Giancana and Kennedy had a relationship with the same woman who claims to have moved money between the two); 6) Giancana is also believed to have orchestrated an election fraud in the very close 1960 presidential election on behalf of Kennedy; 7) John Kennedy appointed his brother Robert Attorney General in 1960– RFK immediately set about attacking the very people who, through his father Joe, helped to put John Kennedy in the White House. A preponderance of facts suggest that organized criminals had plenty of motivation to want the President dead. Still, while a conspiracy of some sort seems probable to many people, who actually ordered the hit may never be established and remains a matter of speculation.[123]

On the other hand, direct links between organized crime and recent White House administrations are not speculative, but have been well-documented. Criminality in the Nixon White House has come to epitomize public corruption. For example, when the Teamsters backed Richard Nixon in the 1960 election, Jimmy Hoffa funneled a $500,000 contribution from New Orleans mob boss Carlos Marcello to the Nixon campaign fund. A land fraud indictment against Hoffa in Florida was subsequently dismissed. Later, a contribution to Nixon's reelection campaign in 1972 got Hoffa out of prison.[124] During his presidency, Nixon developed a pattern of aiding his organized crime associates and supporters, intervening on behalf of mob figures like Leonard Bursten, Carl Kovens, and Morris Shenker. Nixon Administration attorney generals John Mitchell and Richard Kleindienst derailed numerous Department of Justice organized crime investigations during their tenures, as did Nixon campaign manager Murray Choitner. When the Watergate burglars began blackmailing the White House, it was IBT president Frank Fitzsimmons, Central States asset manager Allen Dorfman, and New York racketeer Tony Provenzano who allegedly delivered $100,000 in hush money.[125] And, when the IRS was closing in on organized crime profits hidden in the Bahamas, it was Nixon appointee Donald Alexander who dismantled the Investigative Division of the IRS– whether because of personal philosophy or otherwise, certain Nixon associates were no doubt pleased that the IRS hounds were called off the trail of their money stowed in offshore tax havens. President Nixon's name was also spotted on an account list belonging to Castle Bank, the conduit by which attorneys from Chicago and Miami funneled untaxed profits into the Bahamas.[126] Nixon had close ties to the Mary Carter Paint Company, which eventually became Resorts International, an amusement and casino conglomerate with ties to the Lansky syndicate. An IRS investigation in the 1960's and early 1970's uncovered relationships between Nixon and persons associated with Resorts International and Castle Bank, including international financial swindler Robert Vesco and Las Vegas casino owner Howard Hughes. Central to the investigation of tax evaders, casino operators, and common organized crime hoods were illegal Nixon campaign contributions funneled through Charles "Bebe" Rebozo. Nixon's closest friend and confidant, Rebozo maintained a close association with the head of Resorts International.[127]

The unseemly relationship between organized crime and the White House continued prominently under the Reagan Administration. Reagan's closest friend and advisor, Nevada Senator Paul Laxalt, was described by Las Vegas FBI agents as a "tool of organized crime." Laxalt associates and political fund-raisers included organized figures such as Allen Dorfman, Moe Dalitz, Morris Schenker, Allen Glick, and "Lefty" Rosenthal. Laxalt himself operated a gambling casino that was backed by organized criminals and was used as a major "skimming" enterprise.[128] Aside from Laxalt, high-level corruption in the Reagan Administration was endemic, as forty-five presidential appointees resigned as a result of criminal or ethics investigations in just the first four years of the Reagan presidency.[129]

The most egregious criminality in the Reagan years involved what has come to be called the "Iran-Contra Affair." The scandal involved the executive branch of the United States by-passing the will of Congress by continuing to illicitly support the Contra rebels in Honduras and Nicaragua. While the support of the Contras may be framed as a patriotic fight against Marxism in Nicaragua, the manner in which the covert operation was funded included a "gun-for-drugs scheme" involving cocaine cartels, the direct traffic in cocaine by Contra leaders, and the diversion of funds from

168

covert arms sales to Iran. Worse, high-ranking officials in the CIA as well as the National Security Council (NSC) orchestrated or were fully complicit in the various schemes which included the smuggling of cocaine into the United States. In an internal study released by the CIA in July 1998, one CIA official synthesized the Agency's position: "In some cases, we knew that the people we were dealing with would not qualify as Vienna choirboys, but we dealt with them nonetheless because of the value they brought."[130] The various investigations into Iran-Contra led to the conviction (now overturned) of the highest ranking public official to be convicted since Watergate, National Security Adviser John Pointdexter.[131] President Reagan's complicity in the scandal seems probable. Regarding a plan to use Israel to deal 100 TOW missiles to Iran in exchange for the release of American hostages, Reagan first acknowledged that he authorized the sale, reversed himself and said that he had not authorized the sale, and finally claimed that he had no specific memory one way or the other. In any event, the missiles were transferred to Iran, but no hostages were released.[132]

Organized criminality and the Clinton White House appear to be indistinguishable. The abuse of power, manipulation and intimidation of potential witnesses, campaign finance violations, misuse of confidential FBI files, and numerous federal Privacy Act violations (not a complete list) perpetuated by President Clinton, some of his associates, and other officials in the Clinton Administration could have been taken from a page of the Nixon "how-to" book.[133] The most well known case of criminality involving the President and the First Lady is the growing number of Clinton business associates and friends who have been convicted of various charges centered around the looting of the Madison Guarantee Savings and Loan. The Clintons' business partners, Jim and Susan McDougal, former governor of Arkansas Jim Guy Tucker (Clinton's former Lt. governor), and Hillary Rodham Clinton's former law firm associate Webster Hubbell have all been incarcerated as a result of what has come to be called the "Whitewater" scandal. The bank scam involved the funneling of money from Madison Guarantee Savings and

Loan into various fraudulent real estate deals (Whitewater land development project/Castle Grande) involving the Clintons. The bank fraud and obstruction of justice surrounding the Whitewater scandal has been well documented in the press and in Government hearings.[134] Although the Clintons have not been charged with any crime, an even-handed PBS *Frontline* documentary aired in 1997 leaves little doubt that both President Clinton and especially Hillary Rodham Clinton were complicit in the savings and loan rip-off and cover-up that ultimately cost tax-payers some $60 million.[135]

In addition to the Whitewater scandal, President Clinton has a number of disturbing links to organized crime dating back to his days as governor of Arkansas. Dan Lasater, who was an important fund raiser for Clinton in Arkansas, went to jail on cocaine charges at about the same time that the President's brother Roger Clinton was also convicted of cocaine trafficking. After his release from jail, Bill Clinton pardoned Lasater, who then paid off Roger Clinton's debts. Lasater's cocaine smuggling activities have been corroborated by Arkansas state trooper L.D. Brown, who flew with the now infamous cocaine smuggler and government informant Barry Seal to Central America at Governor Clinton's request. When Brown discovered that Seal was taking guns to Central America and bringing cocaine back in through Mena, Arkansas, he confronted then Governor Clinton who reportedly said "that's Lasater's deal."[136] Clinton also approved $664 million in state bonds to be handled by Lasater's bond company, this while Lasater was under indictment on the cocaine charges. Clinton appointed three board members suggested by Lasater to head the Arkansas Development Finance Authority (ADFA– the agency set up by Clinton to issue the bonds), thus stacking the deck in Lasater's favor and assuring that Lasater's company would handle the bonds. Three different confidential informants and a former employee of the ADFA have stated that the state agency was used by Clinton and Lasater to launder drug money ($100 million was laundered through an unsuspecting court clerk in Arkansas). This activity ceased within days of the murder of Barry Seal, who had been set to testify before a grand jury in an ongoing Mena investigation. U.S. Customs has estimated that 75% of all aircraft used in drug smuggling operations have passed through Mena, Arkansas at one time or another.[137] (In fairness, drug smuggling at Mena is believed to date back at least to the early 1980's, and may very well be a legacy of the CIA during the Bush years).

The Arkansas Development Finance Authority (ADFA) was also used to payoff Clinton campaign contributors and channel money to Clinton's friends and business associates. For example, ADFA channeled some $10 million to Don Tyson, the owner of Tyson Foods, which is the largest industry in Arkansas. As governor, Clinton himself drafted regulations favorable to Tyson's growth as a business. Not surprisingly, Tyson Foods gave to the Clinton gubernatorial campaign some $600,000. Investigative police files also indicate that Don Tyson is a significant drug trafficker.[138] However, as has been the case in many criminal investigations involving close Clinton associates, probes into Tyson's alleged drug dealing, money laundering, and contract killings have been sabotaged and de-railed. When evidence was brought to Clinton Attorney General Janet Reno, she declined to widen the investigation into Tyson's activities.[139] Tyson has nevertheless been implicated in the bribing of U.S. Agriculture Secretary Mike Espy. (Espy was incredibly acquitted of all charges in December 1998 despite the fact that Independent Prosecutor Smaltz had secured fifteen convictions involving the giving of illegal gratuities to Espy– Tyson executives were among those who pled guilty to the bribery charges.)[140] Interestingly, Don Tyson's attorney is the same man who advised Hillary Clinton in her now infamous cattle futures deal where she made $100,000 on a $1000 investment. Although unproven, this may have been a payoff from Tyson to Clinton.[141]

Another glaring example of President Clinton's ties to organized crime is his very close relationship with Arthur Coia, president of the "mobbed up" Laborers' International Union of North America. A report issued by the House Judiciary's Subcommittee on Crime released a report in 1997 that documented Coia as a close friend of the President and First Lady. Coia and Clinton have exchanged personal gifts and various notes and invitations relating to their mutual attendance at "dinners, special events, and flights aboard Air Force One." Coia was also considered for an appointment to the prestigious President's Council on Competitiveness. President Clinton must have been aware of the memorandum sent to the White House by the FBI stating: "Coia is a criminal associate of the Patriarca organized crime family" and "Coia is a person we feel has, through past associations, shown a nexus and affiliation with Cosa Nostra..." While Coia was enjoying his "unusually close relationship" with the First Couple, he managed to have discontinued a Department of Justice investigation of his union by negotiating a settlement of racketeering charges against himself and the Laborers' International. In that settlement, Janet Reno's Justice Department agreed to allow Coia and the union to handle their own mob cleanup efforts.[142]

One need not speculate why Coia was treated like a royal guest in the White House, or why a number of international criminals like Roger Tamraz (an international embezzler wanted by INTERPOL) and Grigori Loutchansky (a leader of the Russian "mafiya") have had tremendous access to the Clinton White House. Tamraz openly admitted to the Senate Governmental Affairs Committee investigating campaign fund-raising abuses that he donated $300,000 to gain access to the President, and said that next time he would be smarter and give $600,000.[143] After Johnny Chung, a Democratic Party fund-raiser, was described by National Security personnel as a "hustler," the White House granted him access more than fifty times.[144] Incredibly, White House spin-doctors have stated that the reason for Chung's access was because the White House felt sorry for him and that he had a crush on the First Lady. The real reason must have something to do with the hundreds of thousands of dollars donated by or arranged by Chung to be illegally donated to the Democratic National Committee (DNC) and Clinton's 1996 re-election campaign. Government investigators have discovered that at least $110,000 delivered by Chung came directly from the Communist Chinese government and a "Chinese aerospace official,"[145] an interesting revelation considering the approval by Clinton of a waiver which resulted in an American company (Loral) exporting sensitive missile technology to the Chinese[146] (at the time of this writing, several Congressional committees are investigating possible wrongdoing in the Clinton Administration regarding the transfer of encryption and missile technology). Coincidentally or not, the CEO of Loral, Bernard Schwartz, was also the single largest contributor to the DNC in 1996.[147]

The web of criminality associated with the campaign finance abuses of the 1996 presidential election includes an infusion of communist Chinese money into the Democratic National Committee and President Clinton's private legal defense fund.[148] At the core of the scandal lies the Lippo Group, an international banking conglomerate run by Mochtar and James Riady of Indonesia. The Riadys and the Lippo Group have important economic ties with the Chinese Communist Party, are partially owned by the People's Liberation Army (PLA), and as reported by the CIA, are "participating agents of the Chinese Communist Party (CCP) and its intelligence services."[149] The Riady family also happens to be President Clinton's most important patron, and was "the leading source of money for the Democrats in 1992."[150] From 1991 to 1993, at least $800,000 of Lippo-based contributions were illegally laundered by John Huang through three Riady shell companies, Hip Hing Holdings, San Jose Holdings, and Toy Center Holdings.[151] The Riadys were also quite generous in providing $100,000 to Clinton crony Webster Hubbell in June 1994. Hubbell, a former Rose Law Firm associate of Hillary Rodham Clinton's, had just resigned from the number three spot in the Clinton Justice Department and was about to be indicted by independent counsel Kenneth Starr for bilking Rose clients. Hubbell subsequently became very uncooperative with Starr's Whitewater investigation, suggesting that the $100,000 payment from Hong Kong China, Ltd. (a Riady company) was "hush money." In all, Hubbell received over $600,000 from Democratic donors and Clinton benefactors for doing "little or no work," all during a time when Starr was pressuring Hubbell to cooperate in his Whitewater investigation. Washington Post columnist Michael Kelly observed (sarcastically) "perhaps the $600,000 was not hush money to the sole witness who could, perhaps, personally implicate Mrs. Clinton for involvement in a fraud and for perjury."[152]

In return for all their support, the Riadys were permitted to place in the Commerce Department a man who has every appearance of being a Communist Chinese spy. Moreover, John Huang's appointment to the International Trade Division (ITA) was arranged by Hillary Rodham Clinton, a fact that was "common knowledge" at Commerce.[153] While at ITA in 1994 and 1995, Huang was given an unprecedented (unprecedented at his level of employment) top secret security clearance. CIA testimony before a 1997 Senate Governmental Affairs hearing (the "Thompson Committee"[154]) further revealed that Huang had received thirty-seven classified one-on-one briefings and an estimated 370 to 550 sensitive CIA-produced pieces of intelligence directly related to Chinese economic and political affairs. Immediately after receiving classified CIA briefings at his Commerce office, Huang regularly walked across the street to a private office of Stephens Inc. (the owner of Stephens Inc. is Jackson Stephens, who in the 1980's co-owned the largest bank in Arkansas with James Riady), where he delivered faxes to Lippo subsidiaries in Hong Kong and Jakarta. At the Thompson hearings a secretary in Huang's secret office testified that the head of the Stephens Inc. office in D.C., Vernon Weaver, directed her to disguise the Huang-Stephens link, and that Weaver told her to call Huang on his behalf "because he didn't want his name to show up on the message logs of the Department of Commerce."[155] Huang's appointment to Commerce in July 1994 occurred less than one month after a series of week long meetings between President Clinton, James Riady, John Huang, Ng Lapseng (an organized criminal and DNC contributor from Macao), and Charlie Trie (a member of the Four Seas "triad" society and DNC fundraiser) which culminated in the delivery of 100,000 Lippo dollars to Webster Hubbell.[156]

In the Fall of 1995 the Clinton White House, strapped for campaign cash, decided to move Lippo bag man John Huang from the Commerce Department to the Democratic National Committee. Officials at the DNC including Chairman Don

Fowler were aware of Huang's shady background and opposed the move. James Riady traveled to Washington to lobby Fowler for Huang's appointment, and Huang himself visited the White House sixteen times between September 13 and November 13, 1995. Fowler finally gave in when President Clinton himself spoke to him on Huang's behalf. Between November 1995 and July 1996, Huang subsequently raised close to $3 million in illegal foreign contributions for the Democrats, most of which was returned by the DNC in 1997 (*after* Clinton's re-election and the exposure of DNC campaign finance illegalities).[157] Central figures in the funneling of foreign donations have been described by the CIA as Communist Chinese agents. Huang associates Maria Hsia and Ted Sioeng "solicited contributions from Chinese nationals" and "worked together to identify non-U.S. citizens who might contribute money to Democratic causes."[158] Pauline Kanchanalak, an associate of China's Peoples Liberation Army (PLA), organized what has been perhaps the most infamous Clinton fund-raiser, a "coffee" event in which international arms smugglers were solicited by John Huang in the White House Map Room:

> One month after Norinco was caught by federal agents smuggling one thousand fully automatic machine guns into the United States for sale to drug gangs on the West Coast, its business associates were in the White House receiving an illegal campaign solicitation from John Huang. Norinco's agents, in turn, made a brazen pitch for more militarily useful American high-tech exports to China. All of this was made in front of and to the President of the United States![159]

Additional illegal contributions flowed from Chinese arms smuggler Wang Jun (who also had "coffee" with the President), PLA Lieutenant Colonel Liu Chaoying (daughter of the PLAs former top uniformed officer and a graduate of the PLA's "high-tech spy academy"), and international organized crime figures Ng Lapseng and Charlie "Yah Lin" Trie.[160] Ng and Trie laundered at least $645,000 to the DNC, an unknown amount of which originated with drug trafficking, prostitution, and gambling enterprises.[161]

In sum, President Bill Clinton and DNC officials knowingly accepted illegal campaign contributions.[162] In at least one case Clinton personally observed a violation of federal law and did nothing (at the Norinco "coffee").[163] Whether Communist Chinese donations actually influenced U.S. foreign policy is, of course, a matter of speculation and is virtually unprovable. Nevertheless, in addition to John Huang's faxes immediately following classified CIA briefings, Clinton administration policies have coddled and benefited a foreign government which has been targeting the U.S. government for infiltration since at least the 1980's.[164] U.S. Defense officials have stated in unequivocal terms that the recent transfer of U.S. satellite technology to China has improved the capabilities of Chinese rockets aimed at the U.S.[165]

Despite government hearings in both the Senate and the House of Representatives concerning campaign finance illegalities in the 1996 election cycle, justice has been denied. Over one hundred witnesses have either fled the country or pled the fifth, including special assistant to the President Mark Middleton.[166] The Clinton Justice Department under Janet Reno has been pursuing its own investigation, but the sincerity of these efforts is highly questionable.[167] Charlie Trie has been indicted on charges of "defrauding the DNC," transparently framing the DNC and the White House as unknowing victims. Reno has refused to appoint an independent counsel despite being advised to do so by top ranking Justice Department subordinates including FBI director Louis Freeh. John Huang has pled the fifth and appears to be untouchable.[168]

Perhaps the symbiotic relationship between organized crime and recent White House Administrations has been characterized best by Johnny Chung, who said: "I see the White House is like a subway-- you have to put in coins to open gates."[169]

Conclusion

Certainly organized crime is evolving in even more sinister directions. From relatively uncoordinated urban street gangs, to machine-politics, to modern day networks spanning international boundaries, coordinated criminal ventures have become the province of societal elites. Organized crime is no longer primarily a local or municipal phenomenon. Civil service reform, police unionization, and decentralized municipal political structures have greatly decreased the ability of local politicians to protect and control organized criminal activities. While in the past police were totally controlled by municipal politicians in the management of vice enterprises, today police act more so on their own. A de-emphasis on gambling and an increased effort to curb narcotics means that the highly routinized "pads" (where entire police commands received bi-monthly payoffs) are largely a thing of the past. Presently, it seems that corrupt police now act in small groups very much like street gangs. Perhaps more insidious is the point made in preceding sections– that organized crime has grown to the point where it routinely compromises not only local but also state and federal governmental units as never before.

History teaches us that the corruption of otherwise law-abiding public officials by criminal entrepreneurs is perhaps a dangerous and misleading conceptualization of the organized crime phenomenon. Time and again, events demonstrate that far too often elected public officials and functionaries within the criminal justice system, whether they be local prosecutors or the presidents of nations, *are* the organizers and entrepreneurs of crime. The history provided in the previous chapters supports the position of William Chambliss, who said that organized crime in the United States may be seen as a symptom of bureaucracy, corruption, and power indigenous to American civil society. As for the rest of the world the pattern is similar regardless of economic or political system, and remains one where organized crime at its most virulent is nearly synonymous with powerful elites in both private and public sectors.

Endnotes

[1]Humbert Nelli (1976). The Business of Crime: Italians and Syndicate Crime in the United States. New York: Oxford University Press.

[2]The Pennsylvania Crime Commission (1980). A Decade of Organized Crime. St. David's PA: Commonwealth of Pennsylvania.

[3]Alan A. Block (1991a). The Business of Crime. Boulder, CO: Westview Press.

[4]New York State Organized Crime Task Force (1990). Corruption and Racketeering in the New York City Construction Industry. New York: New York University Press; Block, 1991.

[5]Alan A. Block (1983). East Side-West Side: Organizing Crime in New York, 1930-1950. New Brunswick, NJ: Transaction; Profile of Organized Crime: Mid-Atlantic Region (1983). Permanent Subcommittee on Investigations of the Committee on Governmental Affairs, the United States Senate, 98th Congress, First Session. Washington D.C.: U.S. Government Printing Office; Waterfront Corruption (1981). Hearings before the Permanent Subcommittee on Investigations of the Committee on Governmental Affairs, U.S. Senate, 97th Congress, 1st session. Washington D.C.: U.S. Government Printing Office.

[6]Block, 1991a.

[7]Ibid.

[8]The New York State Organized Crime Task Force, 1990.

[9]Ibid.

[10]Ibid, p. 20.

[11]Ibid, p. 25.

[12]Ibid, p. 34.

[13]Ibid, p. 36.

[14]Michael D. Lyman and Gary W. Potter (1997). Organized Crime. Upper Saddle River, NJ: Prentice Hall.

178

[15]Dan E. Moldea (1978). The Hoffa Wars. New York: Shapolsky.

[16]President's Commissionon Organized Crime (1986). The Impact. Washington D.C.: U.S. Goverment Printing Office; Moldea, 1978.

[17]President's Commission, 1986.

[18]Block, 1991a.

[19]Ibid.

[20]Moldea, 1978; President's Commission, 1986.

[21]James B. Jacobs, Christopher Panarella, and Jay Worthington (1994). Busting the Mob: U.S. v. Cosa Nostra. New York: New York University Press.

[22]James Neff (1989). Mobbed Up. New York: Dell.

[23]"Carey disqualified from Teamsters' rerun election," The Pittsburgh Tribune Review, November 18, 1997, p. A1.

[24]"Fund-raising scheme uncovered," The Pittsburgh Tribune Review, January 25, 1998, A11.

[25]Block, 91:15.

[26]Mark Haller (1979). "The Changing Structure of American gambling in the Twentieth Century," Journal of Social Issues, Volume 35, No. 3, pp. 87-111.

[27]Block, 1991a.

[28]Profile of Organized Crime: Mid-Atlantic Region, 1983.

[29]President's Commission on Organized Crime (1985). Organized Crime and Gambling. Washington D.C.: U.S. Government Printing Office.

[30]William V. Roth (1997). Statement before U.S. Senate Permanent Subcommittee on Investigations, Committee on Governmental Affairs hearing on "The Asset Forfeiture Program- A Case Study of the Bicycle Club Casino," March 19, 1996– excerpted in Trends in Organized Crime, Vol. 3, No.2, pp. 36-38.

[31]Statement of Hon. Harry Reid, U.S. Senator from Nevada. U.S. Senate Committee on Indian Affairs Oversight Hearing on the Need for Amendments to the Indian Gaming Regulatory Act, April 20, 1994– excerpted in Trends in Organized Crime, Vol. 3, No. 2, pp. 39-42.

[32]Don Liddick (1999). The Mob's Daily Number: Organized Crime and the Numbers Gambling Industry. Lanham, MD: University Press of America.

[33]Organized Crime in Boxing: Final Report (1986). Trenton, NJ: New Jersey Committee on Investigation; President's Commission, 1985.

[34]"Senate Targets Internet Gambling," The Pittsburgh Tribune Review, July 24, 1998, p. A10.

[35]PA Crime Commission, 1980.

[36]Ibid.

[37]Ibid.

[38]PA Crime Commission, 80:119.

[39]PA Crime Commission, 1980.

[40]"Sting targets child porn on "Net," The Pittsburgh Tribune Review, September 3, 1998, p. A4; "Suicides follow raid on child porno ring," The Pittsburgh Tribune Review, October 24, 1998, p. A10.

[41]PA Crime Commission, 1980.

[42]Gary W. Potter (1994). Criminal Organizations: Vice, Racketeering, and Politics in an American City. Prospect Heights, IL: Waveland Press, Inc.

[43]Brian Freemantle (1995). The Octopus: Europe in the Grip of Organized Crime. London: Orion.

[44]"International Crime Control Strategy," Trends in Organized Crime, Vol. 4, No. 1, p. 9.

[45]Ibid, p. 11.

[46]Rensselaer Lee (1991). The White Labyrinth. New Brunswick, NJ: Transaction.

180

[47]Moldea, 1978.

[48]Alfred W. McCoy, (1992). "Heroin as a Global Commodity: A History of Southeast Asia's Opium Trade," in War on Drugs, Alan Block and Alfred McCoy (ed.) Boulder: Westview Press; Alfred W. McCoy (1991). "The CIA Connection," The Progressive, July, 1991.

[49]Lee, 1991.

[50]Bruce Bullington (1992). "A Smuggler's Paradise: Cocaine Trafficking through the Bahamas," in War on Drugs, ed. Alan Block and Alfred McCoy. Boulder: Westview Press; McCoy, 1992; Lee, 1991.

[51]Lee, 1991.

[52]Alfred W. McCoy (1972). The Politics of Heroin in Southeast Asia. New York: Harper and Row; McCoy, 1992.

[53]Ibid.

[54]Ibid.

[55]McCoy, 92:266.

[56]Alan A. Block (1992). "Failures at Home and Abroad: Studies in the Implementation of U.S. Drug Policy," in War on Drugs, Alan A. Block and Alfred W. McCoy, (eds.). Boulder, CO: Westview Press. p. 43

[57]The Mollen Commission Report on Police Corruption (1993). City of New York.

[58]Although as of May 1998, the American media was reporting that increased law enforcement pressure along the Mexican border was shifting shipment routes back to the Caribbean basin.

[59]Chris Eskridge and Brandon Paeper (1998). "The Mexican Cartels: A Challenge for the 21st Century," Criminal Organizations, Vol. 12, No.1&2, pp. 5-15.

[60]Jeff Builta (1997). "Corruption, Crime, Drug Trafficking, and Political Intrigue," Crime and Justice International: Worldwide News and Trends, Vol. 13, No. 1, Feb. 1997, pp. 7-12.

[61]Ibid.

[62]Ibid.

[63]Ibid.

[64]Lyman and Potter, 1997.

[65]"Colombia's air force said infiltrated by drug dealers," The Pittsburgh Tribune Review, November 16, 1998, p. A2.

[66]Alan A. Block (1993). Personal communication.

[67]Michael D. Maltz, Herbert Edelhertz, and Harvey H. Chamberlain (1976). Combating Cigarette Smuggling, Organized Crime Desk, Enforcement Division, Office of Regional Operations, Law Enforcement Assistance Administration, U.S. Department of Justice.

[68]Ibid.

[69]Ibid.

[70]Ibid.

[71]The Pennsylvania Crime Commission (1970). Report on Organized Crime. Office of the Attorney General: Commonwealth of Pennsylvania. p. 54.

[72]Ibid.

[73]Ibid.

[74]Pennsylvania Crime Commission, 80:157.

[75]Ibid.

[76]The Pennsylvania Crime Commission, 1980.

[77]Alan A. Block and Frank R. Scarpitti (1985). Poisoning for Profit: the Mafia and Toxic Waste Disposal in America. New York: William Morrow.

[78]Block, 1991a.

[79]Ibid.

[80]Alan A. Block (1996). "On the Origins of Fuel Racketeering: The Americans and the 'Russians' in New York," in Russian Organized Crime, Phil Williams, ed. London: Frank Cass.

[81]Organized Crime Links to the Waste Disposal Industry (1981). Hearing before the Subcommittee on Oversight and Investigations of the Committee on Energy and Commerce, 97th Congress, 1st Session. Washington D. C.: U.S. Government Printing Office; Profile of Organized Crime: Great Lakes Region (1984). Hearings before the Permanent Subcommittee on Investigations of the Committee on Governmental Affairs, United States Senate, 98th Congress, 2nd session. Washington D.C.: U.S. Government Printing Office; Block, 1991; Block and Scarpitti, 1985; Profile of Organized Crime: Mid-Atlantic Region, 1983.

[82]Trends in Organized Crime, Vol. 4, No. 1, p. 15.

[83]The Pennsylvania Crime Commission, 80:244.

[84]Ibid.

[85]Ibid.

[86]Ibid.

[87]Block, 1996.

[88]Block, 1996.

[89]PA Crime Commission, 1980.

[90]"The Changing Faces of Organized Crime," Crime and Justice International: Worldwide News and Trends, Vol. 13, No. 10., Nov. 1997, p. 21-22.

[91]Pizzo, M. Fricker, and P. Muolo (1989). Inside Job. New York: McGraw Hill; Potter and Lyman, 97:397-403.

[92]Pizzo, et. al., 1989.

[93]Crime and Justice International: Worldwide News and Trends, 1997.

[94]Trends in Organized Crime, Vol. 4, No. 1, p. 8.

[95]Louis J. Freeh (1997). "Impact of Encryption on Law Enforcement and Public Safety." Statement before the U.S. Senate Committee on Commerce, Science, and Transportation, Washington D.C., March 19, 1997– excerpted in Trends in Organized Crime, Vol. 3, No. 1, p. 93.

[96]Dorothy E. Denning and William E. Baugh (1998). "Encryption and Evolving Technologies: Tools of Organized Crime and Terrorism." U.S. Working Group on Organized Crime, National Strategy Information Center, Washington D.C., July 1997– excerpted in Trends in Organized Crime, Vol. 3, No. 3, pp. 44-75.

[97]Moldea, 1978.

[98]Francis A.J. Ianni (1974). Black Mafia: Ethnic Succession in Organized Crime. New York: Simon and Schuster; Nelli, 1976.

[99]Nelli, 1976.

[100]Moldea, 1978.

[101]Nelli, 1976.

[102]James B. Jacobs, Christopher Panarella, and Jay Worthington (1994). Busting the Mob: U.S. v. Cosa Nostra. New York: New York University Press.

[103]Ibid.

[104]Ibid.

[105]Ibid.

[106]Patrick J. Ryan (1995). Organized Crime: A Reference Handbook. Santa Barbara, CA: ABC-CLIO, Inc.

[107]Ibid.

[108]G. Robert Blakey (1985). "Asset Forfeiture Under the Federal Criminal Law," in The Politics and Economics of Organized Crime, Herbert E. Alexander and Gerald E. Caiden (eds.). Toronto: D.C. Heath and Company; Ryan, 1995; Jacobs et. al., 1994.

[109]An Introduction to Organized Crime in the United States (1993). Organized Crime/Drug Branch, Criminal Investigative Division. Washington D.C.: U.S. Government Printing Office.

184

[110]Jacobs et. al., 1994.

[111]Ibid.

[112]Ibid.

[113]Ibid.

[114]The Pennsylvania Crime Commission (1989). 1989 Report. Conshohocken, PA: Commonwealth of Pennsylvania; Jacobs et. al., 1994.

[115]Jacobs et. al., 1994.

[116]The Pennsylvania Crime Commission (1990). Organized Crime in Pennsylvania: A Decade of Change, Conshohocken, PA: Commonwealth of Pennsylvania.

[117]The President's Commission on Organized Crime (1985). Organized Crime of Asian Origin. Washington D.C.: U.S. Government Printing Office; President's Commission on Organized Crime, 1986.

[118]Organized Crime of Asian Origin, 1985.

[119]PA Crime Commission, 1980, 1990; President's Commission on Organized Crime, 1986; Profile of Organized Crime: Mid-Atlantic Region, 1983.

[120]Claire Sterling (1994). Thieves' World: the Threat of the New Global Network of Organized Crime. New York: Simon and Schuster; Freemantle, 1995.

[121]Alan A. Block (1986). "A Modern Marriage of Convenience: A Collaboration Between Organized Crime and U.S. Intelligence," in Organized Crime: A Global Perspective, Robert J. Kelly (ed.). Totowa, NJ: Rowman and Littlefield; Moldea, 1978.

[122]Moldea, 1978.

[123]Stephen Fox (1989). Blood and Power. New York: William Morrow; Moldea, 1978.

[124]Moldea, 1978.

[125]Ibid.

[126]Alan A. Block (1991b). Masters of Paradise. New Brunswick, NJ: Transaction.

[127]Block, 1991b; Potter and Lyman, 1997.

[128]Lyman and Potter, 1997.

[129]Ibid.

[130]"Report: CIA Worked with Contra Traffickers." The Pittsburgh Tribune Review, July 18, 1998, p. A4.

[131]Stephen M. Rosoff, Henry N. Pontell, and Robert Tillman (1998). Profit Without Honor: White-Collar Crime and the Looting of America. Upper Saddle River, NJ: Prentice Hall.

[132]Ibid.

[133]Judicial Watch Interim Report on Crimes and Other Offenses Committed by President Bill Clinton Warranting His Impeachment and Removal from Elected Office, Judicial Watch, Inc. (The Judicial Watch report was submitted to the House Judiciary Committee on September 28, 1998, and can be accessed at www.judicialwatch.org).

[134]Jeff Gerth first broke the Whitewater story in The New York Times in 1992. See the following government hearings: Investigation of Whitewater Development Corporation and Related Matters (hearings held June 1995 to June 1996). The Committee on Banking, Housing, and Urban Affairs, United States Senate, 104th Congress, 1st session. Washington D.C.: U.S. Government Printing Office; Investigation of Whitewater Development Corporation and Related Matters: Final Report (1996). United States Senate, 104th Congress, 2nd session. Washington D.C.: U.S. Government Printing Office; Also see James Ring Adams (1994). "April and Webb and Jean and Jack," The American Spectator, October 1994. (additional articles by Adams like "Beyond Whitewater" and "The Obstructionists" are quite in depth and can be accessed at www.spectator.org).

[135]"Once Upon a Time in Arkansas" (visual). Frontline transcript. Air date: October 7, 1997. (Transcript and video may be accessed at www.pbs.org). The author perceives that some readers are screaming by now: "if Bill and Hillary Clinton were undoubtedly involved in the S&L ripoff as the author contends, then why didn't Ken Starr indict them after four years of investigation?" The answer is quite simple. The American criminal justice system works quite differently when targets for prosecution are rich and powerful– the quantum of proof required to indict is, in practical terms, well above "beyond a reasonable doubt." To put it more succinctly, Presidents of the United States (and their wives) are above the law.

186

[136]Micah Morrison (1996). "The lonely crusade of Linda Ives," The Wall Street Journal, April 18, 1996; Micah Morrision (1997). "Mysterious Mena: CIA disclosures, Leach disposes," The Wall Street Journal, January 29, 1997, p. A.10.

[137]The Mena Connection (1995– visual). Citizens for an Honest Government, Integrity Films; Morrison, 1997.

[138]The Clinton Chronicles (1995– visual). Citizens for an Honest Government, Integrity Films.

[139]The Clinton Chronicles, 1995.

[140]"Tyson Executive Indicted by Feds in Espy Scandal," The Pittsburgh Tribune Review, January 16, 1998, p. A4.

[141]The Clinton Chronicles, 1995.

[142]Byron York (1997). "Mob Rules: Bill and Arthur's Beautiful Friendship," The American Spectator, April 1997.

[143]Investigation of Illegal or Improper Activity in Connection with 1996 Federal Election Campaigns (1997– hereafter Senate report 105-167). Senate Governmental Affairs Committee, Permanent Subcommittee on Investigations. Washington D.C.: U.S. Government Printing Office; "Tamraz admits he bought top access," The Pittsburgh Tribune Review, September 19, 1997, p. A1.

[144]Ibid.

[145]Edward Timperlake and William C. Triplett II (1998). The Year of the Rat. Washington D.C.: Regnery.

[146]Timothy W. Maier and Keith Russell (1998). "Rockets' Red Scare," Insight on the News, Vol. 14, No. 22, June 15, 1998 (also available at www.insightmag.com).

[147]Ibid.

[148]Conduit Payments to the Democratic National Committee. Hearing Before the Committee on Government Reform and Oversight, House of Representatives, 105th Congress, 1st Session, October 9, 1997; Campaign Finance Improprieties and Possible Violations of Law. Hearing before the Committee on Government Reform and Oversight, House of Representatives, 105th Congress, 1st session, October 8, 1997; Federal Election Commission Enforcement Actions: Foreign Campaign Contributions and Other FECA Violations. Hearing before the Committee on

Government Reform and Oversight, House of Representatives, 105th Congress, 2nd session, March 31, 1998; <u>Venezuelan Money and the Presidential Election</u>. Hearing before the Committee on Government Reform and Oversight, House of Representatives, 105th Congress, 2nd session, April 30, 1998; Senate Report 105-167, 1997; Timperlake and Triplett, 1998.

[149]James Ring Adams (1995). "What's Up in Jakarta?" <u>The American Spectator</u>, September 1995 (available at www.spectator.org); Senate Report 105-167, 1997; Timperlake and Triplett, 98:21.

[150]Timperlake and Triplett, 98:27.

[151]James Ring Adams (1996). "John Huang's Bamboo Network," <u>The American Spectator</u>, December 1996 (available at www.spectator.org); Timperlake and Triplett, 1998.

[152]Timperlake and Triplett, 98:39.

[153]Timperlake and Triplett, 98:41.

[154]Fred Thompson (R-Tenn.) chaired the committee to investigate campaign finance abuses. While the facts revealed throughout the dozens of hearings were a scathing indictment of the American political process, no one seemed to care. White House lawyer and "spin-doctor" Lanny Davis suggested gleefully as the hearings were being conducted that the issues involved were "too complex" for the average American. But the attention deficiency problem of most Americans doesn't explain why both Democrats and Republicans on the Thompson Committee were not all that interested in getting at the truth. The complicity of President Clinton and officials at the DNC explain why Democrats like John Glenn, Robert Toricelli, and Carl Levin behaved like defense lawyers for the President throughout the hearings. What could have been the most dramatic series of governmental hearings in American history ended with a whimper. The non-cooperation of the White House in turning over documents and video tapes in a timely matter and the flight of dozens of witnesses did not help, but why would Republicans steer away from campaign finance illegalities in the midst of some of the most damning testimony? (For example, the Committee did not even subpoena Vernon Weaver or other members of the Stephens Inc. crowd). The answer no doubt involves documented illegalities on the part of the Republican National Committee (RNC) as well as some Republican Senators on the Thompson Committee. For example, the RNC funneled money through tax-exempt shells and purposefully concealed the identity of donors in the 1996 elections cycle, while the RNC chairperson, Haley Barbour, laundered foreign money to the RNC in a complex scheme that made the Democratic money laundering efforts look amateurish. While Chairman of the National Republican Senatorial Committee, Oklahoma Republican

188

Don Nickles held meetings at the White House for $10,000 donors. Pennsylvania Republican Arlen Specter promised a $1,000 a head "White House Briefing and Reception" for donors in 1992, could not identify 25% of his donors' professions as required by law, and has been fined by the FEC for illegal use of corporate jets during his campaigns. The Chairman of the Senate Committee, Fred Thompson, accepted money from Iran-Contra figure Farad Azima and is one of the top ten Senators for receiving donations from children (a method of circumventing donation limits). Still, the Democratic cries of "Republicans do it too" is hardly exculpatory. See "Wanted for halting an investigation" at www.judicialwatch.org, and the PBS Frontline documentary "Washington's Other Scandal" (air date October 6, 1998). The Frontline transcript is available at www.pbs.org.

[155]Senate Report 105-167, 1997; Timperlake and Triplett, 98:56.

[156]Timperlake and Triplett, 1998.

[157]Senate Report 105-167, 1997; Timperlake and Triplett, 1998.

[158]Timperlake and Triplett, 98:75.

[159]Timperlake and Triplett, 98:81.

[160]Senate Report 105-167, 1997; Timperlake and Triplett, 1998.

[161]Timperlake and Triplett, 1998.

[162]"Memo links Clinton, foreign money," The Pittsburgh Tribune Review, June 9, 1998, p. A1; "Chung: DNC knowingly accepted improper campaign contributions," The Pittsburgh Tribune Review, June 20, 1998, p. A9; "What did the President know when?" The Wall Street Journal, July 7, 1997, p. A18.

[163]Timperlake and Triplett, 1998.

[164]Kenneth R. Timmerman (1997). "While America Sleeps," The American Spectator, June 1997 (also available at www.spectator.org); Timothy W. Maier (1997a). "Why Red China Targeted the Clinton White House," Insight on the News, Vol. 13, No. 19, May 26, 1997 (also available at www.insightmag.com); Timothy Maier (1997b). "PLA Espionage Means Business," Insight on the News, Vol. 13, No. 11, March 24, 1997 (also available at www.insightmag.com); Timperlake and Triplett, 1998.

[165]"Lott: China used U.S. technology to beef up military," The Pittsburgh Tribune Review, July 15, 1998, p. A1; "CIA says U.S., China launchers identical," The Pittsburgh Tribune Review, May 22, 1998, p. A1.

[166]"Probe cites uncooperative witnesses," The Pittsburgh Tribune Review, December 23, 1997, p. A1; Timperlake and Triplett, 1998.

[167]"Justice won't give up memos," The Pittsburgh Tribune Review, July 28, 1998, p. A5.

[168]Timperlake and Triplett, 1998.

[169]"Chung to cooperate in fund-raising probe," The Pittsburgh Tribune Review, March 6, 1998, p. A1.

Chapter 6

Organized Crime Theories

Since organized crime is a social phenomenon that involves a group or groups of people, it is not surprising and is in fact appropriate that the foundations for organized crime theory lie within the realm of sociology. However, it is also appropriate that today the study of organized crime has become a multi-disciplinary endeavor, with scholars and theorists drawing upon a variety of methods and perspectives. In addition to its sociological under-pinnings, the study of organized crime has become a field of interest for historians, economists, political scientists, and legal scholars. Although there exist numerous and diverse viewpoints, theories of organized crime have developed along the lines of and may be grouped into three major theoretical paradigms: the alien-conspiracy/bureaucracy paradigm, the enterprise approach, and the patron-client relations perspective. While these three perspectives are the focus of Part III, a full appreciation of theories meant to account for the existence and prevalence of organized crime is dependent on an understanding of the sociological and criminological thinkers who paved the way for future scholars.

The Sociological Foundation of Organized Crime Theory

A good place to begin a discussion of organized crime theory is with the Chicago Crime Commission and the Chicago School of Sociology. Scholars including Charles Merriam, V.O. Key, Virgil Peterson, John Landesco, and Harold Lasswell studied organized crime in 1920's Chicago[1] and found that the phenomenon was very much like legal business activity, the only obvious difference being that criminal businesses provide *illegal* goods and services.[2] While the work of the "Chicago School" was not widely recognized at that time, Landesco's work for the Chicago

Crime Commission in 1929 as well as the Chicago Vice Commission report of 1910 are two of the more significant early works on organized crime in the United States.[3] Other early Chicago School theorists were Ernest Burgess and Robert Parks, who saw the city as "a living, growing, organic whole, and the various areas of the city as organs that served different functions."[4] Criminological theorist Gregg Barak summarizes the position of the Chicago School:

> According to the Chicago School of the 1920's, also known as the Ecological School or the School of Human Ecology, because it applied the principles of plant and animal ecology to the task of explaining social deviance, the sources of crime were to be found in the physical, social, and cultural context of human activity. The social ecologists, for the most part, argued that crime was the result of *social disorganization* that characterized the inner-city areas. They argued further that social disorganization was caused by rapid social change whereby dominant legitimate values and norms compete with each other as well as with the illegitimate norms and values. In turn, various subcultures engage in conflict, young generations clash, and social cohesion dissolves as otherwise normally operating social systems or communities experience social deviance and disruption.[5]

With the Chicago/Ecological School, one can see the framework for what has been described as the most influential theoretical orientation in American sociology– the structural-functional approach. Structural-functional sociologists envision society as a "system of interrelated parts," with an emphasis on "social balance."[6] This approach to explaining different societal phenomena is very much concerned with the *structure* of society, and seeks to answer the question of how each part or structure within society "contributes to the functioning of the society as a whole."[7]

Another prominent sociological perspective that falls within the realm of the structural-functional tradition is called "anomie" or "strain" theory. Like ecological and social disorganization theorists of the Chicago School, anomie/strain theorists rely on a "systems model and an organic metaphor to describe society."[8] However, unlike ecological theorists who see crime as a problem of adapting to environmental change, strain/anomie thinkers conceptualize crime as *normal* responses to "structural contradictions" that a society organizes itself around.[9] In 1893 the French sociologist Emile Durkheim first integrated the concept of anomie (a Greek word which means literally, "without norms") into sociological and criminological thought. Durkheim observed that as societies change and become more complex, societal norms naturally break down over time, and it is this breaking down of norms which leads to crime.[10] In the middle part of the twentieth century, the American sociologist Robert Merton developed the concept of anomie to a greater extent, introducing into the mix the notion of "blocked opportunity." Gregg Barak summarizes Merton's position:

> In short, Merton argues that crime or deviant adaptations emerge especially in those societies where material wealth is idealized and where the available or legitimate means for obtaining the valued ends are systematically denied to groups of people. In response to the social problem of anomie/strain, people adapt in one or more of several ways, including acceptance of innovation or the pursuing of the cultural goals of success through illegitimate or criminal means.[11]

Essentially, Merton believed that social structures exert pressure on some people (marginal/disadvantaged groups) to behave in nonconforming ways.[12] According to Merton, criminals accept the legitimate goals of society (material wealth/status/power) but reject the approved means for achieving those goals because legitimate channels are blocked.[13]

The concept of anomie as developed by Durkheim and Merton established the framework for the development of another important branch of sociological thought, subculture theories. Subculture theorists like Albert Cohen, Walter Miller, Marvin Wolfgang, Franco Ferracuti, Richard Cloward, and Lloyd Ohlin stress the importance of the social values of informal groups or collectives within the wider society.[14] The subculture perspective is relevant to an understanding of organized crime because it provides a basis for the study of juvenile street gangs, a "kissing cousin" to more sophisticated types of organized criminality. Modern subculture theories and the study of gangs were preceded by the work of Frederic Thrasher, who studied over 1300 gangs in the slums of Chicago. Thrasher observed that gangs developed from innocent play groups who came into conflict over space within the crowded inner city, and concluded that gang activity was a result of social disorganization. In the "sociological classic" *Street Corner Society*, William F. Whyte challenged Thrasher's position, and posited that the inner city was actually characterized by social *organization*. Whyte theorized that gangs developed because of conflict between the different social status systems that exist in inner cities and the rest of society.[15] Today, with the proliferation of urban and suburban street gangs in cities throughout the U.S., the study of gangs has become an increasingly popular pursuit, even spawning a specialized criminological journal. The importance of gang research to the study of organized crime concerns the very real potential (and in some cases the empirical reality) that some of today's juvenile street gangs may evolve into more sophisticated criminal enterprises.

One of the more influential social-structural perspectives in recent years, and an orientation which lends itself well to an explanation of *organized crime*, is called critical criminology, which is itself rooted in the broader "conflict perspective." Embodied in the thinking of Karl Marx and Friedrich Engels, the conflict perspective is one that sees crime as an unavoidable by-product of capitalism, where the stratified class structure inherent to capitalist economic systems breeds conflict. According to conflict theorists, law is a tool used by the elites in society to maintain the status-quo, while the underclasses often turn to crime because of their poverty. In sum, Marxists and neo-Marxists would say that capitalism creates a "climate of motivation" for criminal behavior.[16]

While conflict-oriented theories are not a unified group, there is one branch of Marxist thinking that has been applied directly to the problem of organized crime. "Structural Marxism," embodied most prominently in the works of David Greenberg, Steven Spitzer, and William Chambliss, posits that the state in tandem with certain economic interests do play the most significant role in societal power structures, but also adds that government and law are best viewed as "attempts to resolve societal crises aroused by the inherent contradictions of capitalism."[17] For example, Alan Block and William Chambliss have suggested that organized criminality may be seen as developing from state formation and competitive capitalism. Their position states:

> ... as capitalism develops and conflicts between social classes continue, more and more acts will be defined as criminal and the amount of crime will increase. From this perspective, criminal law and criminal behavior are best understood not in terms of customs, norms, or value-conflict and interest-group activity, but as directly linked to efforts by the state to create laws as a resolution to dilemmas created by conflicts that develop out of basic contradictions in the political economy.[18]

In a capitalist economic system a basic contradiction inevitably emerges between capital and labor because the logic of capitalism dictates that both employers and workers pursue their own interests. The state generally responds to dilemmas created by contradictions in the political economy by focusing on the conflicts as opposed to the underlying contradictions, creating a dynamic and cyclical process in which the search for resolutions sews the seeds of future conflict. That is, the state defines more and more behaviors as illegal in defense of those controlling the means of production. Another fundamental dilemma built into a capitalist economy is the desire to consume goods, but for large numbers of workers, the inability to earn the money necessary to purchase those goods. In addition to public entities starving for funds, such an innate contradiction leads inexorably to the development of illegal enterprises.[19]

Block and Chambliss's theory suggests that it is the highly competitive nature of capitalism and the ever-present desire to restrain trade which leads to the development of organized crime. A good example are those economic sectors characterized by a high degree of competition, local product markets, and markets inhabited by many small unintegrated firms, where illegal trade associations often form for the purpose of driving up prices and forcing non-member firms to join. The nature of competitive capitalism, then, has led unavoidably to the formation of organized crime in such industries as the garment trade. Entrepreneurs in such industries, striving for profit, seek to create illegal monopolies and neutralize trade unions, in the process creating criminal syndicates which mediate conflicts through the use of extortion and private violence.[20] Significantly, a theory of organized crime driven by class conflict and capitalism and structured along the lines of unequal power relationships among patrons and clients suggests that the phenomenon be conceptualized not as organized crime, but as a function of vice, corruption, bureaucracy, and power. Denoted by William Chambliss as "crime cabals," criminal syndicates may be viewed in terms of the collusive arrangements among politicians, upper-world clients, and under-world power brokers. A Structural-Marxist perspective suggests that examining just those criminal elements traditionally viewed as organized criminals would contribute little to what is known about organized crime, since two-thirds of those involved would not be considered.[21]

Up to this point in the discussion the theories that have been examined are best described as "social-structural," where attempts at explaining criminality are oriented around societal structures and the functional or dysfunctional role of those structures. Another broad group of sociological theories that also have some bearing on organized crime thinking are called "social-process" theories, which attempt to account for the *process* by which people become criminals. One of the most influential social-process theorists was Edwin Sutherland, who formulated the theory of differential association. According to Sutherland, criminal behavior is best understood "in the context of how individuals construct their social reality through communication with one another."[22] "Differential association" refers to the process of social interaction which lends meaning to a given behavior. Put another way, people *learn* to be criminals because they are isolated from non-criminal situational "meanings" but associate with attitudes, motivations, and techniques of crime. Sutherland's theory is most significant because it addresses issues left unanswered by anomie/strain theorists, such as why the vast majority of people who do live in socially disorganized communities and experience blocked opportunity do *not* become criminals.[23] Finally, Sutherland's theory of differential association is important because it was the first attempt to account for so-called "street crimes" *as well as* the crimes committed by powerful persons and institutions.[24]

A recent development in criminological theory is an *approach* to understanding crime, called the "routine activity approach." Developed by Lawrence Cohen and Marcus Felson, this viewpoint suggests that the incidence of crime may be explained by the convergence of three elements: likely offenders, suitable targets, and a lack of capable guardians. When these three elements appear together, Cohen and Felson posit that crime is more likely to occur.[25] This approach seems especially relevant because it pivots on what may be the most important concept in predicting the likelihood of organized crime: opportunity.

The Development of Organized Crime Theory

Scholarly theories of organized crime have been slow to develop. Aside from the Chicago School criminologists (whose work was given scant attention for many years), conceptualizations of organized crime in the earlier part of the 20th century were shaped largely by law enforcement officials, who invariably characterized organized crime in terms of ethnicity. The Kefauver Committee hearings in 1951, the notorious Appalachin conference in 1957, and the McClellan Committee hearings in the late 1950's and early 1960's all fueled the notion that organized crime in America was synonymous with the "Mafia." In 1965 the Oyster Bay Conferences marked a turning point in the study of organized crime as law enforcement officials and academics came together for the first time in an attempt to define organized crime and construct a strategy for its demise. Two years later many of the same people came together again as members of President Johnson's Task Force on Organized Crime.[26] That task force and its report formed the basis for what has come to be called the alien conspiracy theory of organized crime, a viewpoint that has been embraced by the U.S. Government, the law enforcement community, and the general public.

No organized crime perspective has received more attention, scholarly and otherwise, than that paradigm called the alien conspiracy/bureaucracy[27] model. As the dual name implies, this viewpoint is based on two distinct notions: 1) organized crime in America is comprised of a vast conspiracy on the part of Italian-Americans; and 2) organized crime is very much like a formal, bureaucratic, hierarchically structured corporation.[28] According to this perspective, organized crime throughout the United States is subject to monopoly control by a powerful monolithic organization called the "Mafia," or "Cosa Nostra" (although recently conspiracy theorists have acknowledged that other ethnic crime groups are "emerging"). Although factually incorrect in many areas, the alien conspiracy/bureaucracy framework has shaped the law enforcement response to the problem of criminal entrepreneurship over the last thirty years, and it has come to embody the popular perception of what organized crime is (the reader will recall that the basis for this framework and criticisms of it were provided in chapter 1).

While heavily criticized, it should be noted that not all of Donald Cressey's (the chief expositor of alien conspiracy propositions) observations and ideas are without merit. Some researchers have noted that certain elements of Cressey's model have "stood the test of time,"[29] and others have even suggested that the bureaucratic framework is not entirely inconsistent with other organized crime perspectives.[30] Unfortunately, the elements of Cressey's theory that have been embraced by the public and public officials are those ones that have proven to be incorrect.[31]

Beginning in the 1970's, organized crime scholars, recognizing the limitations in the alien conspiracy orientation, began to search for alternative explanations of organized crime. Perhaps the most important development was the re-introduction of a notion suggested by John Landesco in the 1920's: namely, that organized crime is a "mirror of the legitimate business world."[32] Now commonly referred to as the enterprise model, this viewpoint pivots on the idea that because of the similarity between legal and illegal business, organized crime can be assessed using the same theories and principles that have been used to analyze enterprises in the legal market sector.[33] The enterprise paradigm has in fact provided the theoretical foundation for some of the most important work on organized crime to date,[34] while its premise that the phenomenon is best understood in terms of legal and economic realities is obviously superior to the sensational and romanticized conceptions previously relied upon. However, a critical examination of the assumptions upon which the enterprise paradigm is founded indicate that this perception of organized crime may also be flawed in fundamental ways (a full discussion of limitations in the enterprise approach is undertaken in chapter 7). In fact, critical thinking and empirical evidence suggest that criminal entrepreneurship of the organized sort is perhaps best understood from a patron-client relations perspective, the third and least explored of the major organized crime paradigms.[35] In any event, nearly all academics agree that both the enterprise and patron-client models are superior to the alien-conspiracy/bureaucracy orientation.

The discussion will now turn to the two most prominent organized crime paradigms.

The Patron-Client Relations Paradigm

The study of patron-client relationships is reported in a truly vast body of literature which has emerged in opposition to the classical functionalist approach in anthropology and the structural-functional school of sociology. Rather than focusing on primarily groups and their needs and "boundary maintaining mechanisms," an examination of patronage systems stresses the importance of "personal and interpersonal relations, quasi-groups, networks, and power relations."[36] As opposed to the alien conspiracy/bureaucracy or enterprise perspectives, where organized crime is seen as a criminal *organization* or *organizations*, patron-client relationships are just that: countless informal and fluid *relationships*. Instead of groups of criminals responding to problems presented from within and external to an organization with rigid boundaries, the patron-client viewpoint sees the shape of illegal markets and the manner in which illegal goods and services are provided as being determined by groups or "quasi-groups" of individuals who channel the flow of societal resources/illicit revenue based upon an unequal holding of power. Rather than a collective of people organized rationally to achieve a common goal, the study of patron-client relations stresses the importance of individuals who relate together with the primary purpose of furthering their own *personal* goals– this does not preclude the possibility of coordination in illegal markets, only the possibility that important societal players are excluded from the analysis.

In its simplest form a patron-client relationship may be defined as a "vertical dyadic alliance, i.e., an alliance between two persons, of unequal status, power or resources each of whom finds it useful to have as an ally someone superior or inferior to himself." The superior member of such an alliance is called the patron, and the person with less power the client.[37] Verena Burkolter found that a survey of the literature on patronage yields the following definition:

> Two parties unequal in status, wealth and influence form a dyadic, particularistic, self-regulating (no formal normative regulations are needed) relationship of asymmetrical commitment and face-to-face contact, and legitimated by certain values. The relationship depends on the formation and maintenance of reciprocity in the exchange of resources (goods and services) in totalistic terms (package deal), meaning that none of these resources can be exchanged separately.[38]

Schmidt adds:

> In these relationships patrons and clients are in many ways dependent on each other. Each party at any time can supply the other with something that they cannot normally obtain on their own. In most circumstances, the favors that patrons do for their clients are material, while clients usually provide to their patron the expenditure of labor or effort.[39]

Asymmetry in patron-client relationships is seen as resulting from the unequal distribution of chances (potential of power, prestige, and wealth) among societal participants. Other theorists have suggested that the differences in power arise out of the "transactional process" itself, not just from the prior status of the given actors. All agree that "power is dependent on the degree to which the patron monopolizes the flow of information, goods, and services to and between his clients."[40] The degree of asymmetry in patron-client relationships varies. In some relationships the patron and client have nearly equal status, while in others the power of the client is so little that the exchange of resources is coercive.[41] If the extremes in equality or inequality are reached, then that particular patron-client relationship would cease.[42] Burkolter suggests that the durability of patron-client ties is maintained under the following circumstances:

> * the status differences of patrons and clients remains high.
> * the tie is reinforced by modeling it after kin-relations.
> * a balance in the exchange transactions of patron and client is never permitted.
> * the extent of a patron-client network is large or at least in the process of growing, because a patron with a large clientele is more powerful than one with only a few clients.[43]

Naturally, the strength of the patron-client tie is compromised with the absence of these elements.

The actual shapes of patron-client relationships exist in many forms, including instrumental friendships, ritual kinships, and patron-client clusters. Instrumental friendships are characterized by a balanced reciprocity and a minimization of affect or emotion. Ritual kinships, for example god-parenthood, are not concerned with political or economic obligations but are merely symbolic. Their purpose is to create "areas of trust in situations where other solidarities clash or do not exist."[44] In the majority of patron-client relationships the patron has a number of patron-client ties that can be described as a patron-client "cluster" or "clientele." The patron naturally seeks to expand his clientele, as this makes him/her more powerful. A simple patron-client cluster would resemble a "set of vertical dyads extending upwards from various shared clients to a single shared patron who is the central individual of a vertical primary star."[45] However, sometimes clienteles become "pyramided" upon one another. "A patron-client pyramid or hierarchy develops when a client acts in his own right as a patron to sub-clients or when a patron is himself a client of a patron above him."[46]

Clients often act in a way so as to bring more clients into their patron's cluster. Theoretically, such horizontal ties among clients will lead to new vertical or horizontal ties which would tend to undermine the patron's power. In practice, the horizontal ties of the clients to friends and kin tend to complement the already established ties between patron and clients. Generally, client-client ties occur only as a latent structure, as clients' decisions are made only via the patron.[47] Patron-patron ties have been observed, but are generally seen as not likely to occur. M. Kenny observes: "Circling the peaks of patronage-pyramids are groups composed of patrons of more or less equal power who communicate with each other on behalf of their respective clients."[48] Some studies have found that two or more patrons may establish a "trust" or "cartel" in order to exclude other patrons from access to vital resources. Still, cooperation between more than two patrons rarely exists, and they often compete for clients. The predominant pattern is one of "shifting alliances" among patrons.[49]

In modern patron-client relations, "intermediaries or brokers act as a link between national and local systems, and bridge the difference between differing value systems."[50] Jeremy Bossevain distinguishes between patronage and brokerage by noting that patronage creates limited credit and brokerage unlimited credit. Patrons must dispense their "first-order" resources, whereas brokers have access to persons who have a monopoly over "first-order" resources.[51] Traditionally seen in underdeveloped countries, brokerage is also prevalent in modern industrialized societies where the "multiplicity of powerful interlocking institutions" leads many would-be clients into a corner of helplessness and powerlessness. The broker steps in to bridge what would otherwise be an insurmountable gap– he brings people together who otherwise would not develop a relationship. The broker, as patron to his clients, enables these relatively powerless individuals to become clients of a powerful patron who can grant them the favors they seek.[52]

Systems of patronage and clientelism have been examined in a wide variety of cultures and social settings. Further, the interest in patronage has been connected to questions specifically asked in the different fields of inquiry it addresses– anthropology, sociology, and political science. Anthropologists have been most concerned with kinship structures, sociologists with primary groups and their functions within formalized settings, and political scientists with corruption in developing societies and machine politics. Fortunately, some researchers, most notably Joseph Albini,[53] Anton Blok,[54] Henner Hess,[55] and Pino Arlachi[56] have found the patron-client relations perspective specifically well suited to an analysis of organized crime (Blok, Hess, and Arlachi applied the notion of patronage and clientelism to the appearance of the *mafiosi* in post-feudal Sicily– described in chapter 1).

In organizing and regulating the exchange or flow of resources among societal participants, one can see that the unequal power relationships characteristic of patron-client networks is especially relevant to an examination of organized crime. Joseph Albini has refuted the idea that organized crime is a rigid, formally structured organization, but has instead embraced and developed the notion of patronage systems.[57] Albini observed that powerful individuals in syndicate crime do not exercise equal power, and therefore patron-client relationships develop between syndicate functionaries and "legitimate society," and among syndicate members themselves. In organized crime networks, patron-client relationships appear to operate at several levels (patron-client clusters in the form of pyramids), so that a patron in one relationship may be a client in another. Kinship, friendship, and contractual business relationships complicate the system of interaction even further, so that variations in patron-client relations are numerous.[58] Albini argues further that a rigidly structured, bureaucratic organization is not conducive to effective syndicate activity. As such, syndicate enterprises are characterized as being very fluid and changeable. Basically, the structure of a criminal organization is determined by the type of activity in which it is involved at a particular time.[59] Rather than complex formal organizations, then, patron-client relations theorists view criminal syndicates as networks of loosely structured and informal relationships which function because each participant is interested in furthering his/her own welfare. Albini concludes that since patron-client, friendship, and business relationships are constantly changing, attempts at charting or assigning boundaries to the number and specific types of relationships is impossible.[60]

Alan Block also subscribes to the patron-client perspective, and in fact describes organized crime as being "formulated through patron-client cliques and coalitions," and defines it as "a system composed of under- and upper-world individuals in complicated relations of reciprocity."[61] Through the examination of historical documents, Block has observed that organized crime is at once comprised of a social *system* and a social *world*– the system is the sum of the reciprocal exchange relationships between professional criminals, politicians, law-enforcers, and various entrepreneurs, marked by continuity. The social world, on the other hand, is marked by chaos and the manifestation of personal and uneven power.[62] Block feels that criminal syndicates are of two types: Illegal enterprises such as prostitution, bootlegging, and gambling, which provide illicit goods and services to demanding consumers, and power syndicates, which use extortion to exact profits from illegal entrepreneurs and to take advantage of opportunities in the industrial world of labor/management relations.[63] Economist Paul Rubin conceptualizes organized crime in much the same way: criminal firms (power syndicates) sell goods and services to secondary firms (enterprise syndicates) which actually deal with the public. The services which power syndicates provide to illegal entrepreneurs are capital, bribery, and violence.[64] Historically, Block observed that whatever role power syndicates assumed in relation to enterprise syndicates, whether it be the repression of competition, the nullification of law enforcement, or the provision of capital, the payment for services ultimately evolved into the extortion of payments as the price for staying in business.[65] In fact, both economists and historians agree that the ultimate manifestation of patron-client relations in organized crime and the engine which drives organized crime operations is extortion.[66]

Those patrons with the greatest power may not involve themselves in illegal entrepreneurship, political office, or union positions. Instead they focus solely on the distribution and brokerage of *informal power*, completely independent of institutional or formal authority. Among organized criminals it is power and the occasional use of private violence and coercion which characterizes exchange relationships in patron-client networks, through which organized crime mediators channel the distribution of resources.[67] Perhaps the full significance of patron-client relations as complex social arrangements is expressed best by S.N. Eisenstadt and Louis Roniger: "patron-client relations denote, in their fullest expression, a distinct mode of regulating crucial aspects of institutional order: the structure of the flow of resources, exchange and power relations, and their legitimation in society."[68]

A major strength of the patron-client relations perspective is how it explains the role of public officials and otherwise "legitimate" businessmen. From other organized crime viewpoints, these important players are seen as being peripheral to actual criminal organizations. Politicians are "corrupted," and businesses are "infiltrated." Their participation is characterized as passive. From a patron-client viewpoint, no distinction is made between criminals on the street selling illegal goods and services and criminals in city hall pocketing their share and deciding generally how resources will be distributed. Public officials and other concerned parties are not perceived as being somehow peripheral to criminal *organizations*, but are recognized as active participants in the *processes* that organize crime.[69]

The Enterprise Paradigm

As with the patron-client relations perspective, the enterprise perspective is really an *approach* to studying the problem of organized crime, an approach grounded in the structural-functional school of sociology, general systems theory, and the theories of formal legal organizations. However, the enterprise paradigm does not attempt to explain organized crime in just sociological terms– it also recognizes the importance of legal and economic realities. As opposed to a great ethnic conspiracy, a behavioral system bounded by cultural values, or complex networks of unequal power relationships, the enterprise school conceptualizes organized crime as being governed by the same economic principles which apply to legitimate businesses and legal markets. As such, the study of organized crime utilizing this perspective has been guided principally by frameworks describing the dynamics of the legitimate marketplace and theories of formal legal organizations. Under the enterprise model, rather than studying specific groups or even individual personalities, the unit of analysis becomes the illegal marketplace.[70]

Perceiving organized crime as the extension of legitimate market activities into illegal spheres is not new. John Landesco in a sense founded the enterprise school of thought with his study of organized crime in Chicago in the 1920's, when he said organized crime was like a "mirror of the legitimate business world."[71] However, Landesco's theory was not developed in any systematic way until the 1970's, when Dwight Smith introduced his "spectrum-based theory of enterprise." Based on the idea that organized crime is a manifestation of wider economic and social problems where the organization of crime and the relationships which govern the behavior of illegal entrepreneurs are but segments on a continuum of economic activity, Smith's theory asserts that "entrepreneurial transactions can be ranked on a scale that reflects levels of legitimacy within a specific marketplace."[72]

Defined by Dwight Smith as "the extension of legitimate market activities into areas normally proscribed– i.e., beyond existing limits of the law– for the pursuit of profit and in response to latent illicit demand,"[73] the examination of illegal enterprises is the mission of enterprise theorists. An examination of illegal enterprises pivots on two notions: 1) the marketplace does not end at the edge of legitimacy– in fact, legal boundaries often change, and 2) so long as demand exists, a marketplace exists, and entrepreneurs will seek to meet that demand regardless of legality. In order to apply a standard for the analysis of illegal enterprises, then, Smith suggests an examination of the markets in a given industry. If this is done, a series of markets may be observed, ranging from very legal to very illegal. For example, an entrepreneur involved in the distribution of cocaine provides drugs in a particular market in the same manner as pharmaceutical companies, the difference being that one enterprise is perceived as legitimate while the other is not– they operate at opposite ends of the "spectrum of legitimacy."[74] The banking industry may serve as another example of a market spectrum, where institutions engaged in the investment or loaning of funds, from very legitimate to illegal, may be visualized as existing on a continuum from trust companies at the legitimate end of the banking spectrum and loansharks at the illegal pole. In the banking example, legitimacy is a function of the interest rates charged on loans. Moreover, if one views the loaning of money by businesses as existing on a continuum, then the demarcation between legal and illegal business behaviors is not well-defined. For example, many consumers probably see little difference between loansharks and consumer finance companies which charge 25% interest on loans.

W. Allen Martin expanded on Smith's framework by suggesting that a continuum of business propriety may be described by examining the legality of the product or service offered and the method in which the product or service is distributed. For example, a legitimate business which purchases legal products in a legal manner and sells those products in a legal manner represents one extreme of the legitimacy spectrum. At the other end of the continuum are firms which buy illegal goods in order to sell illegal goods in an illegal manner. The possible variations which comprise the middle of the spectrum are numerous: legal products may be sold legally, but the firm's supplies may be obtained illegally; normally legal products may be supplied and distributed illegally; or legal products could be supplied from illegal sources and sold legally.[75] In truth, many organizations are not entirely illicit, and very few are entirely legitimate.

At any rate, the enterprise conceptualization of organized crime has become very popular in academic circles, and has laid the foundation for further theoretical development and research. The general purpose of utilizing a spectrum-based analysis of markets is to stress the *similarity* between legal and illegal enterprises, which allows for the application of theories meant to explain the structure and functioning of formal legal organizations and markets to the problem of illegal enterprises. Under the enterprise framework, instead of an "alien conspiracy" preying upon a helpless public, organized crime is seen as meeting a demand for goods and services which just happen to be illegal.

In sum, Smith's "spectrum-based theory of enterprise" pivots on the following assumptions: 1) legal and illegal businesses exist on a continuum of economic activity; 2) because they exist on a continuum, legal and illegal businesses are similar and respond to the same economic and organizational principles; 3) because legal and illegal businesses are similar, it is possible to apply theories developed for the study of formal legal organizations to the study of illegal enterprises. Based on these suppositions, Smith further assumed that the "systems perspective" in the sociological study of organizations is well suited to an analysis of illegal enterprises. The "systems perspective" is itself the foundation for contingency theory, which states that there exists an interdependent relationship between organizations (legal and illegal) and the environments in which they exist. Smith concludes that because of this interdependent relationship with what is usually a hostile environment (other illegal firms can threaten to take over an enterprise/ the police can extort money or arrest), there are structural and behavioral consequences for enterprises which operate under a proscribed status.[76]

Because Smith based much of his thinking on the systems perspective and the enterprise approach is itself related to contingency theory, a discussion of those frameworks is in order.

The Systems Perspective and Contingency Theory

A major assumption of "open systems" theory, an approach that has dominated the analysis of formal legal organizations, is that organizations function as they do because of their interdependent relationship with the external environment.[77] As such, developing an understanding of how illegal enterprises are structured and how they operate depends on an explanation of how the organizations deal with the technical problems which confront them. Smith used the following quote by organizational theorist James Thompson to explain open and closed system perspectives and the principle of interdependence:

> Most of our beliefs about... organizations follow from one or the other of two distinct strategies. The closed-system strategy seeks certainty by incorporating only those variables positively associated with goal achievement and subjecting them to a monolithic control network. The open-system strategy shifts attention from goal achievement to survival, and incorporates uncertainty by recognizing organizational interdependence with environment. A newer tradition enables us to conceive of the organization as an open system, but subject to criteria of rationality, and hence needing uncertainty.[78]

A systems perspective of formal organizations accounts for how enterprises interact with their environment to ultimately provide their goods and services. At the heart of every enterprise is its core technology, defined as "the technical functions by which it is able to create and dispose of its end products or services." The core technology responds to closed system strategies, which are rational and goal-oriented, and seeks to protect the inner technology from the outside world.[79] A set of conditions external to the organization, called the "task environment," is comprised of four primary forces— suppliers, customers, competitors, and regulators. The task environment responds to open-system strategies "aimed at survival in an arena of uncertainty." Formal organizations, then, must balance these open and closed system requirements. This enables businesses to function while simultaneously presenting difficulties for their survival.[80]

Formal organizations seek to protect their technological cores by utilizing a variety of buffering devices, including but not limited to marketing forecasts, inventory controls, and legal representation. Efforts to protect the core technology result in the formation of "domain," defined as "a set of claims staked out in terms of a range of products, populations served, or services rendered."[81] The enterprise naturally seeks to protect or extend its domain, which exists in the task environment of the enterprise. Because the establishment, maintenance, and expansion of domain must occur in an environment where numerous external variables act upon the enterprise, an exchange relationship characterized by interdependence shapes the activities and structure of the given organization. Smith again quoted James Thompson:

> Only if the organization's claims to domain are recognized by those who can provide the necessary support, by the task environment, can a domain be operational. The relationship between an organization and its task environment is essentially one of exchange, and unless the organization is judged by those in contact with it as offering something desirable, it will not receive the inputs necessary for survival... The specific categories of exchange vary from one type of organization to another, but in each case... exchange agreements rest upon prior consensus regarding domain.[82]

If businesses are viewed as existing on a "spectrum of legitimacy," then interdependence with the environment and consensus regarding domain must also apply to illegal enterprises. This leads to the primary conclusion of enterprise theorists: because of this interdependence with environment there are specific organizational and behavioral consequences for enterprises which provide goods and services in an illegal marketplace.[83]

In his theory, Smith stressed the importance of technology in describing what illegal enterprises look like. In the sense used here, technology refers to more than scientific or mechanical operation. The wider process which governs the activities through which goods and services are produced and marketed is the "technology" of the enterprise.[84] Work in the sociology of industrial organization (which details the internal structure of industrial firms in terms of production technology) and in the economics of industrial structure (which explains the division of labor in terms of market conditions and technology) provides the theoretical framework utilized by enterprise theorists to describe what an illegal enterprise *should look like* if it is to be successful. The approach is explained by Mary McIntosh:

> (a) At a given stage of social and technological development a given criminal act presents certain technical (including social) problems which must be solved for its successful completion; (b) we can specify the most efficient kind of organization for dealing with those technical problems; (c) the existence of that kind of organization is explained in terms of its technical efficiency in the situation.[85]

With this approach, the focus is on survival, and survival for an illegal enterprise is *contingent* on how efficiently it deals with the technical constraints imposed upon it by its task environment (this is the central assumption of contingency theory). Like contingency theory and the "open systems" perspective, the enterprise framework holds that the demands of the external environment and subsequent adaptations determine the structure of organizations, whether legal or illegal.

To sum up once again, Smith's "spectrum-based theory of enterprise" and the enterprise paradigm in general pivots on the following assumptions: 1) legal and illegal businesses exist on a continuum of economic activity; 2) because they exist on a continuum, legal and illegal businesses are similar and respond to the same economic and organizational principles; 3) because legal and illegal businesses are similar, it is possible to apply theories developed for the study of formal legal organizations to the study of illegal enterprises 4) Smith assumed that the "systems perspective" in the sociological study of organizations is well suited to an analysis of illegal enterprises; 5) based on the "systems perspective" (itself linked to the broad perspective in sociology called structural-functionalism and more specifically to the contingency theory of organizations), there exists an interdependent relationship between illegal entrepreneurs and their environment; and 6) because of this interdependent relationship with what is usually a hostile task environment, there are structural and behavioral consequences for enterprises which operate under a proscribed status. Economist Peter Reuter took Smith's argument one step further and predicted and observed exactly what the consequences of product illegality are for illegal enterprises: 1) they tend to be relatively small; 2) they are generally short-lived; 3) they are limited in scope geographically; and 4) illegal markets are competitive and fragmented as opposed to being monopolized by one or a few firms (recall the more detailed discussion of Reuter's work in chapter 1).[86]

Economics and Crime

Although the enterprise paradigm of organized crime is largely grounded in sociological theory, particularly as it pertains to the study of formal organizations, most of the research using the enterprise approach as a foundation is based on economics and the notion that legal and illegal businesses respond to the same economic forces and principles. In fact, crime and economics has become somewhat of an "autonomous" area of research.[87] Most of the work in this area (including that of Peter Reuter) has "targeted on individual agents' allocative choice between legal and illegal activities in the face of different deterrence systems and different opportunity costs."[88] In an economic sense, then, individual entrepreneurs make "rational choices" about what is best for them and their business enterprises. In this light, economists like Peter Reuter, Gianluca Fiorentini, Diego Gambetta, Herschel I. Grossman, and Vito Tanzi (to name a few) have applied various economic approaches to the problem. Essentially, their work flows from two distinct conceptualizations of organized crime, one developed by Peter Reuter, the other by Thomas Schelling.

According to Schelling, the difference between unorganized criminal activity and organized crime is that the "latter seek to govern and control the whole economic structure of the underworld."[89] Schelling believes that organized crime involves at its most fundamental level a monopoly of violence which allows it to attain and maintain a rule-making role. As such, organized criminals control, regulate, and tax the criminal firms *actively* involved in the production and distribution of illegal goods and services. So it is this monopoly of violence and threats which allow organized crime to "reap most of the rents" generated in illegal market sectors without running the risks associated with the direct management of illegal enterprises.[90] The actual enterprises producing and distributing in illicit markets are vulnerable to law enforcement pressure and competition from other illegal entrepreneurs, and it is this reality, according to Schelling, which gives rise to organized crime and its coordinating influence. On the other hand, Peter Reuter would say that vulnerability in illegal markets does not lead to centralized control but results in fragmented markets. Reuter's position, then, explicitly downplays the importance of violence and corruption as organizing influences.[91]

Economists Gianluca Fiorentini and Sam Peltzman have observed that both Schelling's and Reuter's conceptualizations have been supported in part by the available evidence. In fact, the degree of organization in organized crime seems to vary from one type of illegal activity to the next depending on several factors, including idiosyncratic features of the various distribution systems and prevailing attitudes and public policies concerning the given illegal commodity. As Schelling observed, the centralization of illegal markets occurs in those industries which readily lend themselves to monopolization.[92]

The economic analysis of organized crime is a promising and growing field of inquiry. A recent conference at the University of Bologna assimilated the thinking of international economists, which was manifested in a 1995 volume called *The Economics of Organized Crime*. The economic approach seems to be especially helpful in "emphasizing the potential effects of economic variables such as disposable incomes, education levels, and other policy variables more directly under governmental control, such as the level of sanctions and the likelihood of their enforcement."[93] In fact, economists agree that the role played by government in defining what is criminal and in adopting a regulatory approach is the most important variable in determining the shape and scope of organized crime as well as the "allocation decisions" of criminal entrepreneurs. Some of the more fruitful economic theories explore the collusive relationships between criminal organizations and government officials. Others view the origin of criminal organizations in the context of government and organized crime as competitors in the levying of taxes and the provision of public goods and services.[94]

Having reviewed the major theoretical frameworks used to conceptualize organized crime, the final chapter will critically examine the utility of the two leading paradigms– enterprise and patron-client relations.

Endnotes

[1]Peter Lupsha (1986). "Organized Crime in the United States," in Robert J. Kelly (ed.) Organized Crime: A Global Perspective. Totowa, N.J.: Rowman and Littlefield.

[2]John Landesco (1976). Organized Crime in Chicago, Part III of the Illinois Crime Survey, in The Crime Society, Francis Ianni (ed.) New York: New American Library.

[3]Lupsha, 1986.

[4]Sue Titus Reid (1994). Crime and Criminology, 7th edition. Fort Worth: Harcourt Brace.

[5]Gregg Barak (1998). Integrating Criminologies. Needham Heights, MA: Allyn and Bacon.

[6]Donald Light Jr. and Suzanne Keller (1975). Sociology. New York: Alfred A. Knopf, Inc.

[7]Ibid.

[8]Barak, 98:152.

[9]Ibid.

[10]Reid, 1994.

[11]Barak, 98:153.

[12]Reid, 1994.

[13]See Emile Durkheim (1893;1947). The Division of Labor in Society. Translation by George Simpson, Glencoe, IL: Free Press; Emile Durkheim (1938). The Rules of Sociological Method. Chicago: University of Chicago Press; Robert Merton (1957). Social Theory and Social Structure. New York: Free Press.

[14]Barak, 1998.

[15]Reid, 1994.

216

[16]Ibid.

[17]Barak, 98:161.

[18]Alan A. Block and William Chambliss (1981). Organizing Crime. Amsterdam, The Netherlands: Elsevier.

[19]Block and Chambliss, 1981.

[20]Alan A. Block (1983). East Side-West Side: Organizing Crime in New York, 1930-1950. New Brunswick, NJ: Transaction.

[21]William Chambliss (1988). "Vice, Corruption, Bureaucracy, and Power," in Criminal Justice: Law and Politics, ed. George F. Cole. Pacific Grove, CA: Brooks/Cole.

[22]Barak, 98:155

[23]Barak, 1998.

[24]Edwin Sutherland (1961). White Collar Crime. Yale.

[25]Ibid.

[26]Lupsha, 1986.

[27]The author attaches "bureaucracy" to this theory because elements of the alien conspiracy position are universally intertwined with notions of hierarchy and formal corporate-like structures.

[28] The classification scheme used here is subject to debate. Some scholars feel that the bureaucratic/hierarchically structured component of what the present author calls the alien conspiracy/bureaucracy paradigm deserves its own theoretical niche. However, because these two ideas almost universally appear in tandem within the organized crime literature, it seems logical to place them within the same theoretical paradigm.

[29]Robert J. Kelly (1992). "Trapped in the Folds of Discourse: Theorizing About the Underworld," Journal of Contemporary Criminal Justice, Vol. 8, No. 1, Feb., pp. 11-35.

[30]Kelly, 1992.

[31]Lupsha, 1986.

[32]Landesco, 1976.

[33]Mark H. Haller (1990). "Illegal Enterprise: A Theoretical and Historical Interpretation." Criminology, 28:207-235; Dwight C. Smith (1975). The Mafia Mystique. New York: Basic books.

[34]See the following works of Peter Reuter: Peter Reuter and John Haaga (1989). The Organization of High-Level Drug Markets: an Exploratory Study. Santa Monica, CA: The Rand Corporation; Peter Reuter (1989). Quantity Illusions and Paradoxes of Drug Interdiction: Federal Intervention into Vice Policy. Santa Monica, CA: The Rand Corporation; Peter Reuter, Jonathan Rubinstein, and Simon Wynne (1983). Racketeering in Legitimate Industries: Two Case Studies. U.S. Department of Justice; Michael Kennedy, Peter Reuter, and Kevin Jack Riley (1994). A Simple Economic Model of Cocaine Production. Santa Monica, CA: The Rand Corporation; Jonathan Cave and Peter Reuter (1988). The Interdictor's Lot: a Dynamic Model of the Market for Drug Smuggling Services. Santa Monica,CA: The Rand Corporation; Peter Reuter (1983). Disorganized Crime: The Economics of the Visible Hand. Cambridge, Mass.: MIT Press; Reuter, Peter (1985). The Organization of Illegal Markets: An Economic Analysis. Washington D.C.: U.S. Government Printing Office.

[35]The three paradigms used here– alien-conspiracy/bureaucracy, enterprise, and patron-client relations– is the author's way of making sense of the organized crime literature. Not everyone will agree with the way organized crime thought has been classified here; indeed, other scholars have divided organized crime theories into other paradigms. For example, Jay Albanese (1985) has suggested that organized crime theories can be divided into three paradigms: conspiracy, local ethnic groups, and enterprise. A close look at Albanese's local ethnic group paradigm reveals that it encompasses the patron-client perspective. However, because patron-client relations transcend questions of ethnicity and are the subject of a vast body of literature in anthropology, sociology, and political science, they are deserving of a separate designation and should stand alone as an organized crime paradigm. The component of ethnicity, on the other hand, is quite often a separate issue from patronage systems and clientelism. Perhaps we should divide organized crime thinking into four paradigms, with Albanese's "local ethnic groups" being the fourth.

[36]Louis Roniger and S.N. Eisenstadt (1980). "Patron-Client Relations as a Model of Structuring Social Exchange," Society for Comparative Study of Society and History. The Truman Research Institute.

[37]Steffen W. Schmidt (1977). Friends, Followers, and Factions: A Reader in

218

Political Clientelism. Berkeley: University of California Press. pp. xx.

[38]Verena Burkolter (1976). The Patronage System: Theoretical Remarks. Basel: Social Strategies Publishers.

[39]Schmidt, 77:xx.

[40]Burkolter, 76:10.

[41]Burkolter, 76:11.

[42]Burkolter, 76:12.

[43]Ibid.

[44]Burkolter, 76:13-14.

[45]Schmidt et al, 77:xx.

[46]Ibid.

[47]Burkolter, 76:20.

[48]Ibid.

[49]Burlkolter, 76:21.

[50]Burkolter, 76:22.

[51]Jeremy Boissevain (1974). Friends of Friends: Networks, Manipulators, and Coalitions. St. Martin's Press: New York.

[52]Burkolter, 76:23.

[53]Joseph Albini (1971). The American Mafia: Genesis of a Legend. New York: Appleton-Century Crofts.

[54]Anton Blok (1974). The Mafia of a Sicilian Village, 1860-1960. New York: Harper and Row.

[55]Henner Hess (1973). Mafia and Mafioso: The Structure of Power. Lexington, MA: D.C. Heath.

[56]Pino Arlachi (1987). <u>Mafia Business: The Mafia Ethic and the Spirit of Capitalism</u>. New York: Verso.

[57]Albini, 1971.

[58]Ibid.

[59]Ibid.

[60]Ibid.

[61]Alan A. Block (1994). <u>Space, Time, and Organized Crime</u>. New Brunswick, NJ: Transaction.

[62]Block, 1983.

[63]Ibid.

[64]Paul Rubin (1973). "The Economic Theory of the Criminal Firm," in Simon Rottenberg (ed.), <u>The Economics of Crime and Punishment</u>. Washington D.C.: American Enterprise Institute.

[65]Block, 1983.

[66]Thomas C. Schelling (1967). "Economic Analysis of Organized Crime," appendix D in <u>Task Force Report: Organized Crime</u>. President's Commission on Law Enforcement and the Administration of Justice. Washington D.C.: U.S. Government Printing Office; Block, 1983.

[67]Block, 1983.

[68]Roniger and Eisenstadt, 80:49.

[69]Chambliss, 1971.

[70]The enterprise perspective, then, is grounded in sociological theory (particularly the structural-functional perspective and organization theory) but manifests itself in the academic literature most prominently in the realm of economics.

[71]Landesco,1976.

[72]Smith, 75:336.

220

[73]Ibid.

[74]Ibid.

[75]W. Allen Martin (1981). "Toward Specifying a Spectrum-based Theory of Enterprise," Crime and Delinquency, 6:54-57.

[76]Smith, 1975.

[77]Dwight Smith (1980). "Paragons, Pariahs, and Pirates: A Spectrum-based Theory of Enterprise," Crime and Delinquency, 26:358-386.

[78]James D. Thompson (1967). Organizations in Action. New York: McGraw-Hill. p. 13.

[79]Smith, 1980.

[80]Ibid.

[81]Ibid.

[82]Thompson, 67:13.

[83]Smith, 1975; Peter Reuter, 1983.

[84]Ibid.

[85]Mary McIntosh (1975). The Organisation of Crime. New York: MacMillan.

[86]Peter Reuter and Jonathan Rubinstein (1982). Illegal Gambling in New York: A Case Study in the Operation, Structure, and Regulation of an Illegal Market. Washington D.C.: U.S. Government Printing Office; Peter Reuter (1985). The Organization of Illegal Markets: An Economic Analysis. Washington D.C.: U.S. Government Printing Office; Reuter, 1983.

[87]Gianluca Fiorentini and Sam Peltzman (1995). The Economics of Organized Crime. Cambridge: Cambridge University Press.

[88]Fiorentini and Peltzman, 95:1.

[89]Fiorentini and Peltzman, 95:4.

[90]Fiorentini and Peltzman, 1995.

[91]Ibid.

[92]Schelling, 1967.

[93]Fiorentini and Peltzman, 95:2.

[94]Fiorentini and Peltzman, 1995.

Chapter 7

Organized Crime and Patron-Client Relations

The limitations of the alien conspiracy/bureaucracy paradigm have been widely cited– nearly all scholars of organized crime now agree that the orthodox view adopted by the Government is flawed in significant ways. The most popular perspective of organized crime in recent years has been the enterprise paradigm, which attempts to explain the phenomenon in legal and economic realities (a major improvement over previous conceptualizations). Peter Reuter's application of economic theories (which certainly falls within the realm of the enterprise perspective) is arguably the most important research on organized crime to date. Nevertheless, there may be a better way to view organized crime: as complex networks of patron-client relationships.

In order to demonstrate the superiority of the patron-client relations viewpoint, it is first important to analyze the inappropriateness of framing the problem of organized crime in terms of the broader theoretical positions upon which the enterprise paradigm is based. It is no accident that the fundamental assumptions of the patron-client relations school are a direct challenge to structural-functionalism, that broad perspective in sociology upon which the enterprise paradigm of organized crime is ultimately founded. An analysis of the structural-functional school (and its progeny) and its limitations will naturally lead down the road to an argument in favor of a patron-client relations approach.

Structural-Functionalism, Open Systems, and
Contingency Theory

Structural-functionalism is a broad perspective in sociology (and anthropology) that has been dominant in sociological thought this century. It views society as "a system of enduring groups composed of statuses and roles supported by a set of values and related sanctions which maintain the system in equilibrium."[1] Sociological functionalism also shares common characteristics with "open system" models. In fact, its fusion with "general systems" theory provides the "equilibrium model" for the analysis of formal organizations, and it is the "systems perspective" in sociology that is the basis for the human relations, socio-technical, and contingency approaches to organizational analysis.[2]

John Hassard has observed that "the social systems approach draws inspiration from writings which suggest conceptual parallels between societies and organisms."[3] For example, the sociologist Herbert Spencer saw society as a "self-regulating system" that could be explained by analyzing its different "organs" and how they function. The renowned French sociologist Emile Durkheim drew upon biological thinking to analyze industrial society, which he saw emerging from a "mechanical" to an "organic" solidarity based on a "normative belief system" and the "interdependence of parts."[4] Here one can already see how early attempts to explain social order as a "holistic interdependence of living parts" laid the foundation for the systems orthodoxy in the sociological study of organizations. The "systems" perspective sees formal organizations, and in a broader sense society, as living organisms in that the individual parts function in ways that contribute to the whole.

Although thinkers like Spencer and Durkheim provide much of the basis for the structural-functional school of thought, an "explicitly functional approach to social science" originated with the anthropologists Bronislaw Malinowski and A.R. Radcliffe Brown, and the first definitive statement of sociological functionalism is found with the American sociologist Talcott Parsons. Parsons is renowned for his attempt to develop a "general systems theory of society," while many of the principles he enumerated form the basis for the "orthodoxy of functionalist sociology."[5] Parsons saw society as a "system of functionally interdependent variables," with the chief concern of the component parts being "boundary maintenance."[6] Again, one can see that Parsons attempted to explain the organization of society with a biological model in mind. Organizations, like organisms, constantly adapt to their environment so as to be in equilibrium with it.

As stated previously, the structural-functional approach is closely linked to that perspective which sees organizations as "open systems." The following quote illuminates what is meant by the "open systems" approach:

> ...in the open systems perspective the organization is in a dynamic relationship with its environment: it receives various inputs, transforms these inputs in some way and exports outputs. The organization is "open" not only in relation to its environment, but also in relation to itself; it is open internally in that interactions between components affect the system as a whole. The open system adapts to its environment by adjusting the structures and processes of its internal components.[7]

John Hassard asserts that "contingency theory represents the most influential of modern open systems perspectives on organizational analysis."[8] Embodied in the work of Paul Lawrence and Jay Lorsch, contingency theory pivots on two related notions: "The first is the principle that as systems become larger we find demands for the greater differentiation and integration of parts; the second is the view that a central function of any system is its adaptation to the demands of the wider environment."[9] In other words, the way that organizations are structured and the way that they function is contingent on the demands of the physical environment (the principle underlying assumption of the enterprise approach).

Enterprise theorists Dwight Smith and Peter Reuter would almost certainly agree that because criminal organizations are part of a social system, the shape of illegal enterprises is determined by their relationships with and the demands of the surrounding environment. Reuter went one step further and predicted what illegal

226

firms and markets should look like based on the need to implement appropriate structural adaptations given the constraints of the wider social system. So, we find that the enterprise model as it has been developed by organized crime theorists Dwight Smith and Peter Reuter is ultimately based on central tenets of the structural-functional approach in sociology and anthropology, "general systems theory" in sociology (especially the "open systems" perspective), and the contingency theory of organizations. Observing the limitations of those perspectives will reveal potential flaws in the enterprise paradigm and simultaneously bolster the patron-client relations position.

Criticisms of Structural-Functionalism

Although it has been described as the dominant paradigm of sociological thought this century, the structural-functional school has been the object of much criticism in both sociology and anthropology. An early critic of structural-functional theory was C. Wright Mills, who felt that among other things such thinking disregarded social change and conflict and removed historical considerations from sociological analysis. Mills said that by "stressing the centrality of values in attaining social consensus," social order and its legitimation had become unproblematic.[10] Although sociological theory has gone off in several directions as a reaction against structural-functionalism, advocates of a patron-client relations perspective are especially critical of that approach. The limitations of sociological functionalism and the advantages of a patron-client perspective are expressed well by Jeremy Boissevain:

> ...the failure of existing theory to take into account the range of social forms usually dismissed as informal organization. Instead of looking at man as a member of groups and institutional complexes passively obedient to their norms and pressures, it is important to try to see him as an entrepreneur who tries to manipulate norms and relationships for his own social and psychological benefit.

and

> ...it is clear that the view that man is also a self-interested operator opens up important lines of investigation. Instead of trying to answer the question, "why did he do that?" with only the structural-functional questions "what are the rules of behavior in such a case (or, as so often happens, "why did he say that he did it?" which usually amounts to the same thing) I suggest it is equally important to ask "what is he getting out of it?"[11]

Boissevain and theorists of like mind are attempting to reintroduce people into sociological analysis, "from where they have been banished since Durkheim."[12] Instead of the organization or social system emphasis of structural-functionalism, a patron-client relations orientation stresses the importance of individual interaction in coalitions and networks.

S.N. Eisenstadt and Miriam Curelaru have also enumerated limitations of the structural-functional school. First, it does nothing to explain social conflict and the processes of social change, a problem that can be traced to the assumption that there exists a basic social consensus regarding societal goals and values. Arguments against this assumption have been advanced by scholars like Ralf Dahrendorf, John Rex, and C. Wright Mills, and are synthesized in the following quotation:

> First, in any society, the dominant social goals and values are never accepted by all its members. In fact, they reflect and serve the interests of groups which are powerful enough to make their will dominant. Thus, it is the control of resources and power, not the presumed consensus on common values, that constitutes the core of the institutional setting of any society and the major mechanism of its continuity. Moreover, they (critics of structural-functionalism) claimed that it was wrong to postulate the existence of general universal needs of any social system. Whatever concrete needs developed in any concrete social system were determined by the specific goals of the system. And these, in turn, were set up largely through coercion and manipulation by ruling elites.[13]

Structural-functionalism implicitly minimizes the role of power and coercion in

228

directing social integration and change. Another shortcoming is that it does nothing to explain the historical variability in social systems, and is in fact "necessarily ahistorical." Instead of seeing any concrete historical situation as being shaped by past influences or processes, structural-functional theorists tend to conceive of social order as a "static" phenomenon where "equilibrating mechanisms" counteract any "functional maladjustments or inconsistencies."[14] Based on the underlying assumptions of structural-functional thinking, one can see how some theoretical reactions against it are categorized as "individual-rational" models (emphasizing exchange among individuals as opposed to systemic or functional qualities of societies– the patron-client relations paradigm falls within this range) or historical models molded along the lines of conflict or neo-Marxist perspectives.[15]

Limitations of Contingency Theory

The direction that Dwight Smith has taken the enterprise paradigm of organized crime is closely aligned with contingency theory. Mittie Southerland and Gary Potter directly addressed the issue of whether it is appropriate to apply theories established for the study of formal legal organizations to the study of organized crime. The researchers made the following observation:

> The basic assumption of contingency theory is that market organizations compete on the basis of the effectiveness and efficiency of their operations, and that effectiveness and efficiency in part results from appropriate structural adaptation. But in illicit markets, economic efficiency and effectiveness may never become a determining factor in survival. If this is the case, the applicability of the efficiency driven hypothesis established from research on legal businesses is questionable for studies of criminal enterprise.[16]

The central assumption of contingency theory does not agree with what is known about real life illegal enterprises. The best adapted, most efficient, and most profitable illegal businesses are not always the ones that last. Survival may simply be a result of which entrepreneurs are most favored by the police, whether or not someone is related to someone else through real or fictive kinship or instrumental friendships, and perhaps something as simple and personal as whether someone *likes* someone else. The technical aspects of work processes, the demands of the environment, and how efficiently the illegal "firm" deals with certain problems may never come into play. For example, whether the form of law enforcement be legitimate or otherwise, its presence tends to naturally eliminate smaller and less established illegal enterprises. In situations like these, appropriate structural adaptations to the physical environment (or in purely economic terms, the "rational" allocation decisions made by involved parties) have nothing to do with the size and scope of firms and the shape of the illegal market. Another example of how *little* appropriate structural adaptation and efficiency may have to do with survival in the illegal market sector is what Southerland and Potter call the "crime tariff." With the crime tariff, profits are increased as a function of inflated prices through *non-market* restrictions of supply. In these situations where prices are artificially inflated, competition is effectively reduced, and illegal entrepreneurs can make a good return on investments without increasing the supply of goods and services to the market. Because of the "crime tariff," the efficiency of organizations in illegal markets may never become a factor in determining profitability or survival.[17]

In addition to natural differences between legal and illegal market forces, it is the symbiotic relationships among political patrons, criminal justice system functionaries, and illegal entrepreneurs, and the manner in which power is exerted, often through violence, which shape illegal enterprises and illegal markets (as opposed to "appropriate structural adaptations" related to efficiency concerns). Of course, underlying the premises of contingency theorists are tenets of the structural-functional approach, which assume that social systems function as they do based on a consensus among societal functionaries. Countless historical examples depicting extremely violent conflict among organized criminals suggest that "consensus" does not always characterize relationships in the illegal market sector.

The Nature of Illegal Enterprises

Explaining illegal enterprises in the language used by organizational theorists like James Thompson is not difficult. Dwight Smith did so effectively, first in his book *The Mafia Mystique* (1975), and later in a widely cited article.[18] At first glance, historical research seems to validate the accuracy of describing illegal enterprises in the language of formal organization theory. For example, Block has observed that illegal enterprise syndicates "appear to be rather precariously situated between two zones of power."[19] Illegal enterprises are quite often subject to pressure from other illegal entrepreneurs, who may become employees of the organization as "protectors," or who may simply take control of the enterprise themselves. A second zone of power which influences the operation of illegal enterprises is the criminal justice system. Because of this pressure from the surrounding environment, enterprise syndicates must structure themselves and adapt so that the risk of arrest is low, and buffer their business operations by employing bondsmen, attorneys, and public officials. Illegal entrepreneurs, then, appear to be especially vulnerable to principles of interdependence, where elements in their "task environment" seek to limit their "domain." Competitors (underworld power brokers/other syndicate operations) and regulators (police/courts) necessitate that illegal enterprises shield their "technological cores" with "buffering devices" (bribes, employment of bondsmen and lawyers, etc.) and structure their activities in certain ways. Historically, many of the relationships which govern the principle actors in such arrangements are indeed based on "prior consensus regarding domain." These observations coincide with the assertions made by Smith and the language employed to explain organized crime from an organization theory and "open systems" perspective.

While this all seems to fit quite nicely, the reason that Smith's analysis is flawed can be traced to a central facet of what makes an organization an organization. Talcott Parsons observed that "primacy of orientation to the attainment of a specific goal is the defining characteristic of an organization."[20] Empirical evidence indicates that attainment of a common goal is not always a prominent feature of the phenomenon called organized crime. One good in-depth example of this can be found in a recent study of the numbers gambling industry where it was observed that the most important players ("important" here refers to those persons who were most responsible for the shape and scope of illegal enterprises and the distribution of resources) were not part of an organization in any sense of the word because they had no common goal. In that study, accounting center clerks and controllers and collectors (numbers workers responsible for taking bets and tabulating wagers) had a common goal of processing wagers and there was a rational division of labor, but at the level where decisions affecting the structure of firms and of the market were made, the principal actors were concerned primarily with furthering their individual agendas– without a glimpse of a complex formal organization in sight.[21]

A major pitfall in the enterprise approach is that it sees illegal enterprises as formal organizations with definite boundaries, organizations that seek to maintain those boundaries by reacting appropriately to internal and external demands. A complete picture of organized crime demonstrates that the provision of illicit goods and services is not accomplished merely by an illegal organization or organizations, but by a wide variety of societal players embroiled in countless informal relationships, most of these based on uneven distributions of power. If one is concerned with what forces structure illegal markets and what processes channel the flow of societal resources, then focusing on the level where fundamental work tasks are performed and how those "organizations" seek to resolve technical constraints is not very useful. Such an orientation blinds the researcher to the vital roles played by the most important illegal functionaries (unfortunately, in many cases, public officials/police). Obviously, then, adopting that perspective most amenable to explaining the symbiotic relationships among underworld and upperworld crooks is crucial to developing a responsible criminology of organized crime. With the patron-client relations paradigm, mayors, drug dealers, bookmakers, pimps, district attorneys, "Cosa Nostra" bosses, madams, police officers, lawyers, numbers bankers, and city councilmen are all viewed as members of the various cliques, networks, factions, coalitions, and informal groups which comprise organized crime.

Conclusion

Perhaps the most significant problem with the enterprise paradigm is that it implicitly (or perhaps explicitly) minimizes the roles played by public officials and informal power brokers in the organization of crime. By insisting on viewing organized crime in terms of *organizations* with definite boundaries, enterprise theorists unequivocally place the activities of street-level entrepreneurs who physically perpetrate organized crimes at the epicenter of their analysis, while the affairs of the most important players ("legitimate" businessmen/public officials/power brokers) are relegated to the periphery. Most people, including many organized crime theorists, tend to see organized crime as something that involves violent criminals who *infiltrate* legitimate industries and *corrupt* public officials. Over the last three decades, many scholars have advanced the idea that organized crime involves primarily the distribution of illegal goods and services to willing and demanding consumers. The problem lies in concentrating blame on just the illegal entrepreneurs, particularly as organized crime is a social network that includes not only vice entrepreneurs and labor racketeers, but also politicians, law enforcement officials, court officials, "legitimate" business persons, and consumers. All of these actors engage in complex and changeable networks of patron-client relationships that may be viewed as the "social world" of organized crime. From this perspective, legitimate businesses are not infiltrated and public officials are not corrupted. Instead, they are viewed as existing in a state of symbiosis with those law breakers that traditionally have been perceived as organized criminals.[22]

Developing a criminology of organized crime is dependent on recognizing that public officials, power brokers, illegal entrepreneurs, and otherwise "legitimate" business people are all part of countless exchange relationships where there are no organizational boundaries. To suggest that all of these different people are members of the same *organizations* pursuing common goals is not realistic. On the other hand, the patron-client relations paradigm allows for analyses that take into account the *active* role played by those persons who have traditionally been perceived as being mere "associates" of organized criminals. Unlike other organized crime perspectives, a patron-client relations view of the world accounts for the entire *process* through which crime is organized.

While quite popular among organized crime scholars, the enterprise paradigm may be seriously flawed because the central assumptions upon which the framework is founded are inconsistent with empirical reality. The conclusions of enterprise theorists pivot on the notion that legal and illegal businesses are *similar*, and that they respond to the same economic forces and principles. However, many observations of organized crime reveal important structural and behavioral differences between licit and illicit business activities. What is commonly referred to as organized crime often fails to resemble formal organizations with precise boundaries. Likewise, the engine which drives entrepreneurial activity in illegal market sectors commonly defies legal market-place dynamics. Instead of stressing the similarity between legal and illegal businesses, as attractive as that approach may be, it may be more appropriate to recognize that fundamental *differences* exist between legal and illegal businesses. When John Landesco described organized crime in Chicago as "a mirror of the legitimate business world," perhaps he should have said a *carnival* mirror of the legitimate business world, where illegal enterprises and illegal markets are distorted as a function of their proscribed status under the law. And that is exactly the point– *there are differences between legal and illegal organizations.* Because illegal enterprises are not the formal, complex, and rational entities found on the legal side of the market spectrum, it may be inappropriate to apply theories of formal legal organizations to the study of organized crime. The danger lies in the predilection for theorists to interpret and shape events in terms that are familiar, a practice which leads inevitably to "sterile theorizing."[23] The conceptualization of social situations based on theory established to explain phenomena peripheral to a given research problem is misguided, while conclusions are subject to preconceived notions of what is real.[24]

The study of patronage and patron-client relations intrinsically rejects the basic tenets of the structural-functional school of sociology and anthropology (upon which the enterprise model is founded), where society is likened to a biological organism: organizations, like organs, operate interdependently based on a consensus of the way things ought to be run; organisms, like society, could not function without this consensus and interdependence of components which maintains the system in equilibrium. The patron-client relations paradigm views society as nothing so neat or well-defined as an organism. Instead, society is perceived in terms of countless exchanges among individuals based on an uneven holding of power that takes into account the complex vagaries of interpersonal relationships. Unlike the enterprise model, which attempts to explain organized crime based on an analysis of criminal *organizations* and how those organizations interact with their environments, the patron-client relations perspective is specifically oriented towards explaining phenomena such as the complex relationships observed among public officials and the purveyors of illegal goods and services.

A Final Thought

Much of the previous discussion was centered on arguing for the superiority of the patron-client relations paradigm of organized crime. However, readers should recognize that the enterprise and patron-client positions are not mutually exclusive, and may even possess the potential for being integrated into a holistic approach. Despite the observed limitations, the enterprise paradigm, especially the economic-based direction it has taken, is an intriguing and promising step in the study of organized crime. Obviously, organized crime is a phenomenon that should be conceptualized from a variety of perspectives, integrating thinking in sociology, economics, and political science. Of course, such a multi-disciplinary understanding would be void of meaning without empirical reality to make sense of theoretical propositions. In short, for there to be any chance of developing a common approach to building our knowledge of organized crime, countless case studies must be undertaken, searching for answers in a broad array of criminal settings. Like many social phenomena, the future of organized crime research lies in documenting what is and what has already happened.

Endnotes

[1]Jeremy Boissevain (1974). <u>Friends of Friends: Networks, Manipulators, and Coalitions</u>. St. Martin's Press: New York.

[2]John Hassard (1993). <u>Sociology and Organization Theory: Positivism, Paradigms, and Postmodernism</u>. Cambridge, England: Cambridge University Press.

[3]Hassard, 93:4.

[4]Hassard, 93:17.

[5]Hassard, 93:21.

[6]Ibid.

[7]Hassard, 93:32.

[8]Hassard, 93:45.

[9]Ibid.

[10]S. N. Eisenstadt and M. Curelaru (1976). <u>The Forms of Sociology: Paradigms and Crises</u>. Wiley and Sons: New York. pp. 194-195.

[11]Boissevain, 74:4-7.

[12]Ibid.

[13]Eisenstadt and Curelaru, 76:197.

[14]Eisenstadt and Curelaru, 76:196-97.

[15]Eisenstadt and Curelaru, 76:194-97.

[16]Mittie Southerland and Gary Potter (1993). "Applying Organization Theory to Organized Crime," <u>Journal of Contemporary Criminal Justice</u>, vol. 9, No. 3, 262-263.

[17]Potter and Southerland, 1993.

[18]Dwight Smith (1980). "Paragons, Pariahs, and Pirates: A Spectrum-based Theory of Enterprise," <u>Crime and Delinquency</u>, 26:358-386.

[19]Alan A. Block (1983). East Side-West Side: Organizing Crime in New York, 1930-1950. New Brunswick, NJ: Transaction. p. 159.

[20]Hassard, 93:24.

[21]Don Liddick (1995). Numbers Gambling in New York City, 1960-1969. Unpublished PhD dissertation. The Pennsylvania State University.

[22]See William Chambliss (1988). "Vice, Corruption, Bureaucracy, and Power," in Criminal Justice: Law and Politics, 5th edition, George Cole (ed.). Belmont, CA: Wadsworth.

[23]Alan A. Block and William J. Chambliss (1981). Organizing Crime. Amsterdam, The Netherlands: Elsevier.

[24]In this sense, the enterprise paradigm is little improvement over the alien conspiracy/bureaucracy paradigm. Both are similar in that they are founded on basic tenets of the structural-functional school in sociology, which characterizes society in terms of enduring groups that operate interdependently to maintain the equilibrium of systems. From this perspective, organized crime is seen as being comprised of criminal organizations with precise boundaries that are shaped by a generally hostile "task environment." Although the enterprise model is to be admired for emphasizing the overlap between legitimate society and the so-called underworld, it mistakenly suggests that legal and illegal businesses can be analyzed using the same theoretical assumptions. Current trends in organized crime research favor the enterprise paradigm, which insists on seeing organized crime in terms of organizations. While I believe this is not the best way to perceive the organized crime phenomenon, the enterprise approach is nevertheless a far superior conceptualization as compared to that which has been embraced by the Government and the law enforcement community. Also, it should be noted that there are numerous theories of formal organizations and markets which have not been utilized to examine organized crime. Until other applications of the enterprise framework are explored, let us not "throw out the baby with the bathwater." Perceiving organized crime as being on a continuum of economic activity at least finally banishes the black and white notion of "good guys" and "bad guys," where there is legality on one hand, illegality on the other, and nothing in between.

Bibliography

Abadinsky, Howard (1985). Organized Crime, 2nd ed. Chicago: Nelson-Hall.

---- (1990). Organized Crime, 3rd ed. Chicago: Nelson-Hall.

Adams, James Ring (1994). "April and Webb and Jean and Jack," The American Spectator, October 1994 (www.spectator.org).

---- (1995). "What's Up in Jakarta?" The American Spectator, September 1995 (www.spectator.org).

---- (1996). "John Huang's Bamboo Network," The American Spectator, December 1996 (www.spectator.org).

Albanese, Jay (1985). Organized Crime in America. Cincinatti: Anderson Publishing Company.

---- (1996). Organized Crime in America 3rd ed. Cincinnati: Anderson Publishing Company.

Albini, Joseph (1971). The American Mafia: Genesis of a Legend. New York: Appleton-Century Crofts.

Albini, Joseph, R.E. Rogers, Victor Shabalin, Valery Kutushev, Vladimir Moiseev, and Julie Anderson (1995). "Russian Organized Crime: Its History, Structure and Function," Journal of Contemporary Criminal Justice, Vol. 11, No. 4, pp. 213-243.

Alexander, Herbert E., and Gerald E. Caiden (1985). The Politics and Economics of Organized Crime. Toronto: D.C. Heath and Company.

Anderson, Annelise (1979). The Business of Organized Crime: A Cosa Nostra Family. Stanford, CA: Hoover Institution Press.

An Introduction to Organized Crime in the United States (1993). Organized Crime/Drug Branch, Criminal Investigative Division. Washington D.C.: U.S. Government Printing Office.

Arlachi, Pino (1987). Mafia Business: The Mafia Ethic and the Spirit of Capitalism. New York: Verso.

Asbury, Herbert (1962). Excerpt from The Gangs of New York (1928), in Organized Crime in America: A Book of Readings, Gus Tyler (ed.). Ann Arbor, Michigan: University of Michigan Press.

Barak, Gregg (1998). Integrating Criminologies. Needham Heights, MA: Allyn and Bacon.

Bell, Daniel (1976). "Crime as an American Way of Life," in The Crime Society, ed. Francis A.J. Ianni and Elizabeth Reuss-Ianni. New York: New American Library.

Blakey, G. Robert (1985). "Asset Forfeiture Under the Federal Criminal Law," in The Politics and Economics of Organized Crime, Herbert E. Alexander and Gerald E. Caiden (eds.), Toronto: D.C. Heath and Company.

Block, Alan A. (1979). "The Snowman Cometh: Coke in Progressive New York," Criminology, 17:75-99.

---- (1983). East Side-West Side: Organizing Crime in New York, 1930-1950. New Brunswick, NJ: Transaction.

---- (1986). A Modern Marriage of Convenience: A Collaboration Between Organized Crime and U.S. Intelligence," in Organized Crime: A Global Perspective, Robert J. Kelly (ed.). Totowa, NJ: Rowman and Littlefield.

---- (1991). The Business of Crime. Boulder: Westview Press.

---- (1991). Masters of Paradise. New Brunswick, NJ: Transaction.

---- (1992). "Failures at Home and Abroad: Studies in the Implementation of U.S. Drug Policy," in War on Drugs, Alan A. Block and Alfred W. McCoy, (eds.). Boulder, CO: Westview Press.

---- (1991). "Organized Crime and Toxic Waste: An Overview," in Space, Time, and Organized Crime, New Brunswick, NJ: Transaction, pp. 203-230.

---- (1993). Personal communication with the author.

---- (1994). Personal communication with the author.

---- (1994). Space, Time, and Organized Crime. New Brunswick, NJ: Transaction.

---- (1996). "On the Origins of Fuel Racketeering: The Americans and the Russians in New York," in Russian Organized Crime, Phil Williams, ed. London: Frank Cass.

Block, Alan A., and Alfred W. McCoy (1992). War on Drugs. Boulder: Westview Press.

Block, Alan A., and Frank R. Scarpitti (1985). Poisoning for Profit: the Mafia and Toxic Waste Disposal in America. New York: William Morrow.

Block, Alan A., and William Chambliss (1981). Organizing Crime. New York: Elsevier.

Blok, Anton (1974). The Mafia of a Sicilian Village, 1860-1960. New York: Harper and Row.

Boissevain, Jeremy (1974). Friends of Friends: Networks, Manipulators, and Coalitions. St. Martin's Press: New York.

Builta, Jeff (1997). "Corruption, Crime, Drug Trafficking, and Political Intrigue," Crime and Justice International, Vol. 13, No. 1, Feb. 1997, pp. 7-12.

Bullington, Bruce (1992). "A Smuggler's Paradise: Cocaine Trafficking through the Bahamas," in War on Drugs, ed. Alan Block and Alfred McCoy. Boulder: Westview Press.

Burkolter, Verena (1976). The Patronage System: Theoretical Remarks. Basel: Social Strategies Publishers.

Burlingame, Timothy M. (1997). "Criminal Activity in the Russian Banking System," Transnational Organized Crime, Vol. 3, No. 3, pp. 46-72.

Campaign Finance Improprieties and Possible Violations of Law. Hearing before the Committee on Government Reform and Oversight, House of Representatives, 105th Congress, 1st session, October 8, 1997. Washington, D.C.: U.S. Government Printing Office.

"Carey disqualified from Teamsters' rerun election," Pittsburgh Tribune Review, November 18, 1997, p. A1.

Cave, Jonathan, and Peter Reuter (1988). The Interdictor's Lot: a Dynamic Model of the Market for Drug Smuggling Services. Santa Monica, CA: The Rand Corporation.

Chambliss, William J. (1978). On the Take: From Petty Crooks to Presidents. Bloomington: Indiana University Press.

---- (1988). "Vice, Corruption, Bureaucracy, and Power," in Criminal Justice: Law and Politics, ed. George F. Cole. Pacific Grove, CA: Brooks/Cole.

"Chung: DNC knowingly accepted improper campaign contributions," The Pittsburgh Tribune Review, June 20, 1998, p. A9.

"Chung to cooperate in fund-raising probe," The Pittsburgh Tribune Review, March 6, 1998, p. A1.

242

"CIA says U.S., China launchers identical," <u>The Pittsburgh Tribune Review</u>, May 22, 1998, p. A1.

Clapp, Jennifer (1997). "The Illicit Trade in Hazardous Wastes and CFCs: International Responses to Environmental 'Bads.'" Paper prepared for SSRC-MacArthur Workshop on "Liberal Internationalism, the State, and the Illicit World Economy," Cornell University, Ithaca, New York, November 8-10, 1996: 1-42– excerpted in <u>Trends in Organized Crime</u>, Vol. 3, No. 2, pp. 14-18.

"Colombia's air force said infiltrated by drug dealers," <u>The Pittsburgh Tribune Review</u>, November 16, 1998, p. A2.

<u>Conduit Payments to the Democratic National Committee</u>. Hearing Before the Committee on Government Reform and Oversight, House of Representatives, 105th Congress, 1st Session, October 9, 1997. Washington, D.C.: U.S. Government Printing Office.

Conklin, John E. (1998). <u>Criminology</u>, 6th ed. Needham Heights, MA: Allyn and Bacon.

Cressey, Donald R. (1969). <u>Theft of the Nation: The Structure and Operations of Organized Crime in America</u>. New York: Harper and Row.

---- (1972). <u>Criminal Organization: Its Elementary Forms</u>. New York: Harper and Row.

Denning, Dorothy E., and William E. Baugh (1998). "Encryption and Evolving Technologies: Tools of Organized Crime and Terrorism." U.S. Working Group on Organized Crime, National Strategy Information Center, Washington D.C., July 1997– excerpted in <u>Trends in Organized Crime</u>, Vol. 3, No. 3, pp. 44-75.

Dunn, Guy (1997). "Major Mafia Gangs in Russia," in <u>Russian Organized Crime</u>, Phil Williams (ed.). London: Frank Cass.

Durkheim, Emile (1938). <u>The Rules of Sociological Method</u>. Chicago: University of Chicago Press.

---- (1893;1947). <u>The Division of Labor in Society</u>. Translation by George Simpson, Glencoe, IL: Free Press.

Eisenstadt, S.N., and M. Curelaru (1976). <u>The Forms of Sociology: Paradigms and Crises</u>. Wiley and Sons: New York.

Eskridge, Chris, and Brandon Paeper (1998). "The Mexican Cartels: A Challenge for the 21st Century," <u>Criminal Organizations</u>, Vol. 12, No.1&2, pp. 5-15.

Federal Election Commission Enforcement Actions: Foreign Campaign
Contributions and Other FECA Violations. Hearing before the Committee on
Government Reform and Oversight, House of Representatives, 105th Congress,
2nd session, March 31, 1998. Washington, D.C.: U.S. Government Printing
Office.

"Financial Crimes and Money Laundering," the International Control Strategy
Report, 1996, released by the Bureau for International Narcotics and Law
Enforcement Affairs, U.S. Department of State in March 1997– excerpted in
Transnational Organized Crime, Vol. 3, No. 1, pp. 87-113.

Fiorentini, Gianluca, and Sam Peltzman (1995). The Economics of Organized
Crime. Cambridge: Cambridge University Press.

Fox, Stephen (1989). Blood and Power. New York: William Morrow.

Freeh, Louis J. (1997). "Impact of Encryption on Law Enforcement and Public
Safety." Statement before the U.S. Senate Committee on Commerce, Science, and
Transportation, Washington D.C., March 19, 1997– excerpted in Trends in
Organized Crime, Vol. 3, No. 1, p. 93.

Freemantle, Brian (1995). The Octopus: Europe in the Grip of Organized Crime.
London: Orion.

"Fund-raising scheme uncovered," The Pittsburgh Tribune Review, January 25,
1998, A11.

Gardiner, John A. (1970). The Politics of Corruption: Organized Crime in an
American City. Beverly Hill, CA: Russell Sage Foundation.

Gardiner, John A., and David J. Olson (1967). Task Force Report: Organized
Crime. (Annotations and Consultants' Papers). "Appendix B: Wincanton– The
Politics of Corruption." Washingtion D.C.: U.S. Government Printing Office.

Gilbert, James N. (1996). "Organized Crime on the Western Frontier," Criminal
Organizations, Vol. 10, No. 2, pp. 7-13.

Hagan, Frank (1983). "The Organized Crime Continuum: A Further Specification
of a New Conceptual Model," Criminal Justice Review, 8 [Spring], 52-57.

Haller, Mark H. (1976). "Gambling in Perspective," in Gambling in America, The
Commission on the Review of the National Policy Towards Gambling.
Washington D.C.: U.S. Government Printing Office.

---- (1979). "The Changing Structure of American gambling in the Twentieth
Century," Journalof Social Issues, Volume 35, No. 3, pp. 87-111.

244

---- (1990). "Illegal Enterprise: A Theoretical and Historical Interpretation." Criminology, 28:222.

Handelman, Stephen (1995). Comrade Criminal: Russia's New Mafiya. New Haven: Yale University Press.

Hassard, John (1993). Sociology and Organization Theory: Positivism, Paradigms, and Postmodernism. Cambridge, England: Cambridge University Press.

Hess, Henner (1973). Mafia and Mafioso: The Structure of Power. Lexington, MA: D.C. Heath.

Hinchey, Maurice D. (1991). "Criminal Infiltration of the Toxic and Solid Waste Disposal Industries in New York State," a preliminary report to the New York State Assembly Standing Committee on Environmental Conservation and the New York State Legislature, September 13, 1984, in The Business of Crime, Alan A. Block (ed.). Boulder, CO: Westview. pp. 175-196.

Ianni, Francis A. J. (1972). A Family Business: Kinship and Social Control in Organized Crime. New York: Russell Sage Foundation.

---- (1974). Black Mafia: Ethnic Succession in Organized Crime. New York: Simon and Schuster.

Ianni, Francis A. J., and Elizabeth Reuss-Ianni (1976). The Crime Society. New York: New American Library.

Illegal Trade by the People's Republic of China and Taiwan in Rhinoceros and Tiger Parts and Products (1994). Communication from the President of the United States. Washington, D.C.: U.S. Government Printing Office.

"International Crime Control Strategy," Trends in Organized Crime, Vol. 4, No. 1. Investigation of Illegal or Improper Activity in Connection with 1996 Federal Election Campaigns (1997). Senate Governmental Affairs Committee, Permanent Subcommittee on Investigations. Washington D.C.: U.S. Government Printing Office.

Investigation of Whitewater Development Corporation and Related Matters (hearings held June 1995 to June 1996). The Committee on Banking, Housing, and Urban Affairs, United States Senate, 104th Congress, 1st session. Washington D.C.: U.S. Government Printing Office.

Investigation of Whitewater Development Corporation and Related Matters: Final Report (1996). United States Senate, 104th Congress, 2nd session. Washington D.C.: U.S. Government Printing Office.

Jacobs, James B., Christopher Panarella, and Jay Worthington (1994). Busting the Mob: U.S. v. Cosa Nostra. New York: New York University Press.

Johnson, David R. (1977). "A Sinful Business: The Origins of Gambling Syndicates in the United States, 1840-1887," in Police and Society, ed. David H. Bayley. Beverly Hills: Sage.

---- (1981). American Law Enforcement: A History. St Louis: Forum Press.

Jones, Mark, and Patrick J. Ryan (1996). "Identifying Core Writings on Organized Crime," Criminal Organizations, Vol. 10, No. 2, pp. 6-7.

Judicial Watch Interim Report on Crimes and Other Offenses Committed by President Bill Clinton Warranting His Impeachment and Removal from Elected Office (1998). Judicial Watch, Inc.

"Justice won't give up memos," The Pittsburgh Tribune Review, July 28, 1998, p. A5.

Keh, Douglas, and Graham Farrell (1997). "Trafficking Drugs in the Global Village," Transnational Organized Crime, Vol. 3, No.2, pp. 90-110.

Kelly, Robert J. (1986). Organized Crime: A Global Perspective. Totowa, NJ: Rowman and Littlefield.

---- (1992). "Trapped in the Folds of Discourse: Theorizing About the Underworld," Journal of Contemporary Criminal Justice, Vol. 8, No. 1, Feb., pp. 11-35.

Kennedy, Michael, Peter Reuter, and Kevin Jack Riley (1994). A Simple Economic Model of Cocaine Production. Santa Monica, CA: The Rand Corporation.

Knapp Commission Report on Police Corruption (1972). George Braziller: New York.

Kuzio, Taras (1997). "Crime Still Ukraine's Greatest Enemy," Jane's Intelligence Review, Vol. 9, No. 1, January 1997: 10-13– excerpted in Trends in Organized Crime, Vol. 3, No. 1, pp. 27-30.

Landesco, John (1929). Organized Crime in Chicago. Chicago: University of Chicago Press.

---- (1976). Organized Crime in Chicago, Part III of the Illinois Crime Survey, in The Crime Society, Francis Ianni (ed.) New York: New American Library.

---- (1976). "The Funerals of Gangsters," in The Crime Society, Francis and Elizabeth Reuss-Ianni, ed. New York: New American Library.

Lasswell, Harold, and Jeremiah McKenna (1972). The Impact of Organized Crime on an Inner City Community. New York: The Policy Sciences Center.

246

Lee III, Rensselaer W. (1989). The White Labyrinth. New Brunswick, NJ: Transaction.

---- (1996). "Recent Trends in Nuclear Smuggling," Transnational Organized Crime, Vol. 2, No. 4, pp. 109-121.

Liddick, Don (1995). Numbers Gambling in New York City, 1960-1969: A Social and Political History. Unpublished PhD dissertation. The Pennsylvania State University.

---- (1997). "Race, Ethnic-Succession, and Organized Crime: The Ethnic Composition of the Numbers Gambling Industry in New York City," Criminal Organizations. Vol. 10, No. 4, pp. 13-18.

---- (1999). The Mob's Daily Number: Organized Crime and the Numbers Gambling Industry. Lanham, MD: University Press of America.

Lifschultz, Lawrence (1992). "Pakistan: The Empire of Heroin," in War on Drugs, Alan A. Block and Alfred W. McCoy (eds.). Bouder, CO: Westview Press.

Light, Ivan (1977). "Numbers Gambling Among Blacks: A Financial Institution," American Sociological Review, Vol. 42, December: 892-904.

---- (1977). "The Ethnic Vice Industry," American Sociological Review, Vol. 42, June: 464-479.

Light Jr., Donald, and Suzanne Keller (1975). Sociology. New York: Alfred A. Knopf, Inc.

"Lott: China used U.S. technology to beef up military," The Pittsburgh Tribune Review, July 15, 1998, p. A1.

Lupsha, Peter (1981). "Individual Choice, Material Culture, and Organized Crime," Criminology, 19:3-24.

---- (1986). "Organized Crime in the United States," in Organized Crime: A Global Perspective, Robert J. Kelly (ed.). Totowa, N.J.: Rowman and Littlefield.

---- (1996). "Transnational Organized Crime versus the Nation-State," Transnational Organized Crime, Vol. 2, No. 1, pp. 21-48.

Lyman, Michael D., and Gary W. Potter (1997). Organized Crime. Upper Saddle River, NJ: Prentice Hall, Inc.

Maier, Timothy W. (1997). "PLA Espionage Means Business," Insight on the News, Vol. 13, No. 11, March 24, 1997.

---- (1997). "Why Red China Targeted the Clinton White House," Insight on the News, Vol. 13, No. 19, May 26, 1997.

Maier, Timothy W., and Keith Russell (1998). "Rockets' Red Scare," Insight on the News, Vol. 14, No. 22, June 15, 1998.

Maltz, Michael D., Herbert Edelhertz, and Harvey H. Chamberlain (1976). Combatting Cigarette Smuggling, Organized Crime Desk, Enforcement Division, Office of Regional Operations, Law Enforcement Assistance Administration, U.S. Department of Justice.

"Maritime Crime," Trends in Organized Crime, Vol. 3, No. 4, Summer 1998, pp. 68-71.

Martin, W. Allen (1981). "Toward Specifying a Spectrum-based Theory of Enterprise," Crime and Delinquency, 6:54-57.

McCoy, Alfred W. (1972). The Politics of Heroin in Southeast Asia. New York: Harper and Row.

---- (1991). "The CIA Connection," The Progressive, July, 1991.

---- (1992). "Heroin as a Global Commodity: A History of Southeast Asia's Opium Trade," in War on Drugs, Alan Block and Alfred McCoy (ed.) Boulder: Westview Press.

McIntosh, Mary (1975). The Organization of Crime. New York: MacMillan.

"Memo links Clinton, foreign money," Pittsburgh Tribune Review, June 9, 1998, p. A1.

Merton, Robert (1957). Social Theory and Social Structure. New York: Free Press.

Moldea, Dan E. (1978). The Hoffa Wars. New York: Shapolsky.

Mollen Commission Report on Police Corruption (1993). City of New York.

Moore, William Howard (1974). The Kefauver Committee and the Politics of Crime. Columbia: Universtiy of Missouri Press.

Morrison, Micah (1996). "The lonely crusade of Linda Ives," The Wall Street Journal, April 18, 1996.

---- (1997). "Mysterious Mena: CIA disclosures, Leach disposes," The Wall Street Journal, January 29, 1997, p. A10.

Neff, James (1989). Mobbed Up. New York: Dell.

248

Nelli, Humbert (1976). The Business of Crime: Italians and Syndicate Crime in the United States. New York: Oxford University Press.

New York State Organized Crime Task Force (1990). Corruption and Racketeering in the New York City Construction Industry. New York: New York University Press.

"Once Upon a Time in Arkansas" (visual). Frontline transcript. Air date: October 7, 1997.

"Organized Crime and the Environment," Trends in Organized Crime, Vol. 3, No. 2, pp. 4-5.

Organized Crime in Boxing: Final Report (1986). Trenton, NJ: New Jersey Committee on Investigation.

Organized Crime Links to the Waste Disposal Industry (1981). Subcommittee on Oversight and Investigations of the Committee on Energy and Commerce, House of Representatives, 97th Congress, First Session. Washington D.C.: U.S. Government Printing Office.

Owen, H. C. (1962). Excerpt from King Crime (1932), in Organized Crime in America: A Book of Readings, Gus Tyler (ed.) Ann Arbor, Michigan: University of Michigan Press.

Palmer, Richard L. (1997). "The New Russian Oligarchy: the Nomenclature, the KGB and the Mafiya." Paper presented to the Working Group on Organized Crime, National Strategy Information Center, Washington D.C., May 1997– excerpted in Trends in Organized Crime, Vol. 3, No. 1, pp. 8-14.

The Pennsylvania Crime Commission (1970). Report on Organized Crime. Office of the Attorney General: Commonwealth of Pennsylvania.

---- (1980). A Decade of Organized Crime. St. David's, PA: Commonwealth of Pennsylvania.

---- (1989). 1989 Report. Conshohocken, PA: Commonwealth of Pennsylvania.

---- (1990). Organized Crime in Pennsylvania: A Decade of Change, Conshohocken, PA: Commonwealth of Pennsylvania.

---- (1992). 1992 Report. Conshohocken: PA.: Commonwealth of Pennsylvania.

Peterson, Virgil (1962). Excerpt from The Barbarians in Our Midst (1952), in Organized Crime in America: A Book of Readings, Gus Tyler (ed.). Ann Arbor, Michigan: University of Michigan Press.

Pizzo, Stephen, Mary Fricker, and Paul Muolo (1989). Inside Job. New York: McGraw-Hill.

"Political Criminal Nexus," Trends in Organized Crime," Vol. 3, No. 1.

Potter, Gary W. (1994). Criminal Organizations: Vice Racketeering, and Politics in an American City. Prospect Heights, IL.: Waveland Press, Inc.

---- (1997). The Antecedents of Southern Organized Crime." Paper presented at the 1997 ACJS conference, March 1997, Louisville, Kentucky.

Potter, Gary W., and Larry K. Gaines (1992). "Country Comfort: Vice and Corruption in Rural Settings," Journal of Contemporary Criminal Justice, Vol. 8, No. 1. pp. 36-61.

Potter, Gary W., and Philip Jenkins (1985). The City and the Syndicate: Organizing Crime in Philadelphia. Lexington, MA: Ginn Press.

President's Commission on Law Enforcement and the Administration of Justice (1967). Task Force Report: Organized Crime. Washington D.C.: U.S. Government Printing Office.

President's Commission on Organized Crime (1985). Organized Crime and Gambling. Washington D.C.: U.S. Government Printing Office.

---- (1985). Organized Crime of Asian Origin. Washington D.C.: U.S. Government Printing Office.

---- (1986). The Impact: Organized Crime Today. Washington D.C.: U.S. Government Printing Office.

"Probe cites uncooperative witnesses," The Pittsburgh Tribune Review, December 23, 1997, p. A3.

Profile of Organized Crime: Great Lakes Region (1984). Hearings before the Permanent Subcommittee on Investigations of the Committee on Governmental Affairs, United States Senate, 98th Congress, 2nd session. Washington D.C.: U.S. Government Printing Office.

Profile of Organized Crime: Mid-Atlantic Region (1983). Permanent Subcommittee on Investigations of the Committee on Governmental Affairs, the United States Senate, 98th Congress, First Session. Washington D.C.: U.S. Government Printing Office.

Pryce-Jones, David (1997). "Corruption Rules the World." The American Spectator December, pp. 22-25 (www.spectator.org).

Reid, Harry (Statement made by the U.S. Senator from Nevada– 1994). U.S. Senate Committee on Indian Affairs Oversight Hearing on the Need for Amendments to the Indian Gaming Regulatory Act, April 20, 1994– excerpted in Trends in Organized Crime, Vol. 3, No. 2, pp. 39-42.

Reid, Sue Titus (1994). Crime and Criminology, 7th edition. Fort Worth: Harcourt Brace.

"Report: CIA Worked with Contra Traffickers." The Pittsburgh Tribune Review, July18, 1998, p. A4.

Resendiz, Roslava (1998). "International Auto Theft: An Exploratory Research of Organization and Organized Crime on the U.S./Mexico Border," Criminal Organizations, Vol. 12, No. 1&2, pp. 25-30.

Reuter, Peter (1983). Disorganized Crime: The Economics of the Visible Hand. Cambridge, Mass.: MIT Press.

---- (1985). The Organization of Illegal Markets: An Economic Analysis. Washington D.C.: U.S. Government Printing Office.

---- (1989). Quantity Illusions and Paradoxes of Drug Interdiction: Federal Intervention into Vice Policy. Santa Monica, CA: The Rand Corporation.

Reuter, Peter, and John Haaga (1989). The Organization of High-Level Drug Markets: an Exploratory Study. Santa Monica, CA: The Rand Corporation.

Reuter, Peter, and Jonathan Rubinstein (1982). Illegal Gambling in New York: A Case Study in the Operation, Structure, and Regulation of an Illegal Market. Washington D.C.: U.S. Government Printing Office.

Reuter, Peter, Jonathan Rubinstein, and Simon Wynn (1982). Racketeering in Legitimate Industries: Two Case Studies. Washington, D.C.: National Institute of Justice.

Roniger, Louis, and S.N. Eisenstadt (1980). "Patron-Client Relations as a Model of Structuring Social Exchange," Society for Comparative Study of Society and History. The Truman Research Institute.

Rosoff, Stephen M, Henry N. Pontell, and Robert Tillman (1998). Profit Without Honor: White-Collar Crime and the Looting of America. Upper Saddle River, NJ: Prentice Hall.

Roth, William V. (1997). Statement before U.S. Senate Permanent Subcommittee on Investigations, Committee on Governmental Affairs hearing on "The Asset Forfeiture Program– A Case Study of the Bicycle Club Casino," March 19, 1996– excerpted in Trends in Organized Crime, Vol. 3, No.2, pp. 36-38.

Rubin, Paul (1973). "The Economic Theory of the Criminal Firm," in Simon Rottenberg (ed.), The Economics of Crime and Punishment. Washington D.C.: American Enterprise Institute.

Ryan, Patrick J. (1995). Organized Crime: A Reference Handbook. Santa Barbara, CA: ABC-CLIO, Inc.

Salzano, Julie, and Stephen W. Hartman (1998). "Cargo Crime," Transnational Organized Crime, Vol. 3, No. 1, p. 20.

Savona, Ernesto (1996). "European Money Trails," Transnational Organized Crime, Vol. 2, No. 4, pp. 1-20.

Schelling, Thomas C. (1967). "Economic Analysis of Organized Crime," appendix D in Task Force Report: Organized Crime. President's Commission on Law Enforcement and the Administration of Justice. Washington D.C.: U.S. Government Printing Office.

Schmid, Alex P. (1996). "Links Between Transnational Organized Crime and Terrorist Crimes," Transnational Organized Crime, Vol. 2, No. 4, pp. 41-81.

Schmidt, Steffen W. (1977). Friends, Followers, and Factions: A Reader in Political Clientelism. Berkeley: University of California Press.

Scott, Peter Dale (1992). "Honduras, the Contra Support Network, and Cocaine: How the U.S. Government Has Augmented America's Drug Crisis," in War on Drugs, Alan A. Block and Alfred W. McCoy (eds.). Boulder, CO: Westview Press.

"Senate Targets Internet Gambling," The Pittsburgh Tribune Review, July 24, 1998, p. A10.

Shelley, Louise I. (1997). "The Price Tag of Russia's Organized Crime," Transition, Vol. 8, No. 1. Feb. 1997: 7-8 – excerpted in Trends in Organized Crime, Vol. 3, No. 1, pp. 24-26.

Simon, David R. (1996). Elite Deviance, 5th edition. Needham Heights, Mass.: Allyn and Bacon.

Smith, Dwight C. (1975). The Mafia Mystique. New York: Basic books.

---- (1980). "Paragons, Pariahs, and Pirates: A Spectrum-based Theory of Enterprise," Crime and Delinquency, 26:358-386.

Southerland, Mittie, and Gary W. Potter (1993). "Applying Organization Theory to Organized Crime," Journal of Contemporary Criminal Justice, vol. 9, No. 3, 262-263.

Sterling, Claire (1994). Thieves' World: the Threat of the New Global Network of Organized Crime. New York: Simon and Schuster.

"Sting targets child porn on "Net," The Pittsburgh Tribune Review, September 3, 1998, p. A4.

"Suicides follow raid on child porno ring," The Pittsburgh Tribune Review, October 24, 1998, p. A10.

Sullivan, Brian (1996). "International Organized Crime: A Growing National Security Threat." Institute for National Strategic Studies, No. 74, May.

Sullivan, Edward D. (1930). Excerpt from Chicago Surrenders, in Organized Crime in America: A Book of Readings, Gus Tyler (ed.). Ann Arbor, Michigan: University of Michigan Press.

Sutherland, Edwin H. (1961). White Collar Crime. New York: Holt, Rinehart, and Winston.

"Tamraz admits he bought top access," The Pittsburgh Tribune Review, September 19, 1997, p. A1.

"The Changing Faces of Organized Crime," Crime and Justice International: Worldwide News and Trends, Vol. 13, No. 10., Nov. 1997, pp. 21-22.

The Clinton Chronicles (1995– visual). Citizens for an Honest Government, Integrity Films.

The Growing Threat of International Organized Crime (1996). House of Representatives Subcommittee on Crime, Committee on the Judiciary. Washington, D.C.: U.S. Government Printing Office.

The Mena Connection (1995– visual). Citizens for an Honest Government, Integrity Films.

The Threat from Russian Organized Crime (1996). Hearing before the Committee on International Relations, House of Representatives, 104th Congress, 2nd session. Washington D.C.: U.S. Government Printing Office.

Thompson, James D. (1967). Organizations in Action. New York: McGraw-Hill.

Timmerman, Kenneth R. (1997). "While America Sleeps," The American Spectator, June 1997 (www.spectator.org).

Timperlake, Edward, and William C. Triplett II (1998). The Year of the Rat. Washington D.C.: Regnery.

"Trafficking in Women and Children," Trends in Organized Crime, Vol. 3, No. 4, pp. 3-68.

Turbiville, Graham H. (1997). "Weapons Proliferation and Organized Crime: The Russian Military and Security Force Dimension," *Occasional Paper*, U.S. Air Force Institute for National Security Studies (INSS), Colorado Springs, Colorado, 1996: 1-29– excerpted in Trends in Organized Crime, Vol. 3, No. 3, pp. 18-22.

Tyler, Gus (1962). Organized Crime in America: A Book of Readings. Ann Arbor, Michigan: University of Michigan Press.

---- (1976). "Socio-dynamics of Organized Crime," in The Crime Society, Francis Ianni (ed.) New York: New American Library.

"Tyson Executive Indicted by Feds in Espy Scandal," Pittsburgh Tribune Review, January 16, 1998, p. A4.

United Nations International Drug Control Programme, World Drug Report, New York: Oxford Unviversity Press, 1997: 1-332– excerpted in Trends in Organized Crime, Vol. 3, No. 2, pp. 12-13.

Venezuelan Money and the Presidential Election. Hearing before the Committee on Government Reform and Oversight, House of Representatives, 105th Congress, 2nd session, April 30, 1998. Washington, D.C.: U.S. Government Printing Office.

Voronin, Yuriy A. (1997). "The Emerging Criminal State: Economic and Political Aspects of Organized Crime," in Russian Organized Crime, Phil Williams (ed.). London: Frank Cass.

Wang, Zheng (1996). "Ocean-Going Smuggling of Illegal Chinese Immigrants: Operations, Causation and Policy Implications," Transnational Organized Crime, Vol. 2, No. 1, pp. 49-65.

"Washington's Other Scandal" (visual). Frontline transcript. Air date: October 6, 1998.

Waterfront Corruption (1981). Hearings before the Permanent Subcommittee on Investigations the Committee on Governmental Affairs, U.S. Senate, 97th Congress, 1st session. Washington D.C.: U.S. Government Printing Office.

Webster, Donovan (1997). "The Looting and Smuggling and Fencing and Hoarding of Impossibly Precious, Feathered, and Scaly Wild Things," The New York Times Magazine, Section 6, Feb. 16, 1997: 26-33– excerpted in Trends in Organized Crime, Vol. 3, No. 2, pp. 9-10.

"What did the President know when?" The Wall Street Journal, July 7, 1997, p. A18.

254

Williams, Phil (1996). "Problems and Dangers Posed by Organized Transnational Crime in the Various Regions of the World," in The United Nations and Transnational Organized Crime, Phil Williams and Ernesto U. Savona (eds.). London: Frank Cass.

---- (1997). "Money Laundering," Criminal Organizations, Vol. 10, No. 4, pp. 18-27.

---- (1997). Russian Organized Crime. London: Frank Cass.

Williams, Phil, and Ernesto U. Savona (1996). The United Nations and Transnational Organized Crime. London: Frank Cass.

Winer, Jonathan M. (1997). "Alien Smuggling: Elements of the Problem and the U.S. Response," Transnational Organized Crime, Vol. 3, No. 1, pp. 50-58.

Yeager, Matthew G.(1973). "The Gangster as White Collar Criminal: Organized Crime and Stolen Securities," in The Crime Society, Francis Ianni (ed.) New York: New American Library.

York, Byron (1997). "Mob Rules: Bill and Arthur's Beautiful Friendship," The American Spectator, April 1997 (www.spectator.org).

Index

CRIMINOLOGY STUDIES